THE ROMANTICS AND THE BRITISH LANDSCAPE

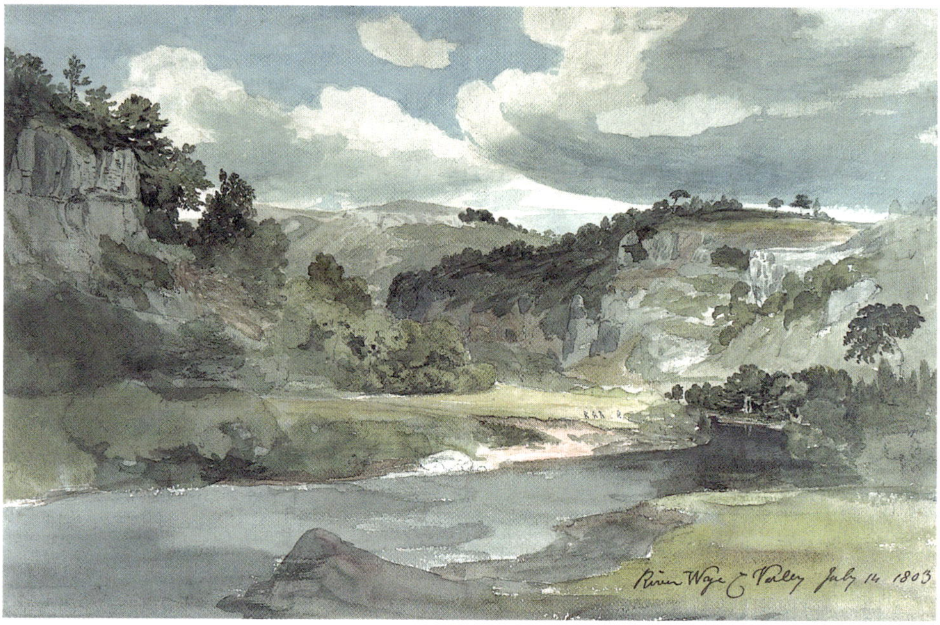

'River Wye & Valley', by Cornelius Varley, 13 July 1803.

STEPHEN HEBRON

The Romantics and the British Landscape

THE BRITISH LIBRARY

First published in 2006 by The British Library,
96 Euston Road, London NW1 2DB

British Library Cataloguing in Publication Data
A catalogue for this title is available from The British Library

ISBN 0 7123 0676 5

Designed and typeset by Stephen Hebron
Printed in Hong Kong by South Sea International Press

CONTENTS

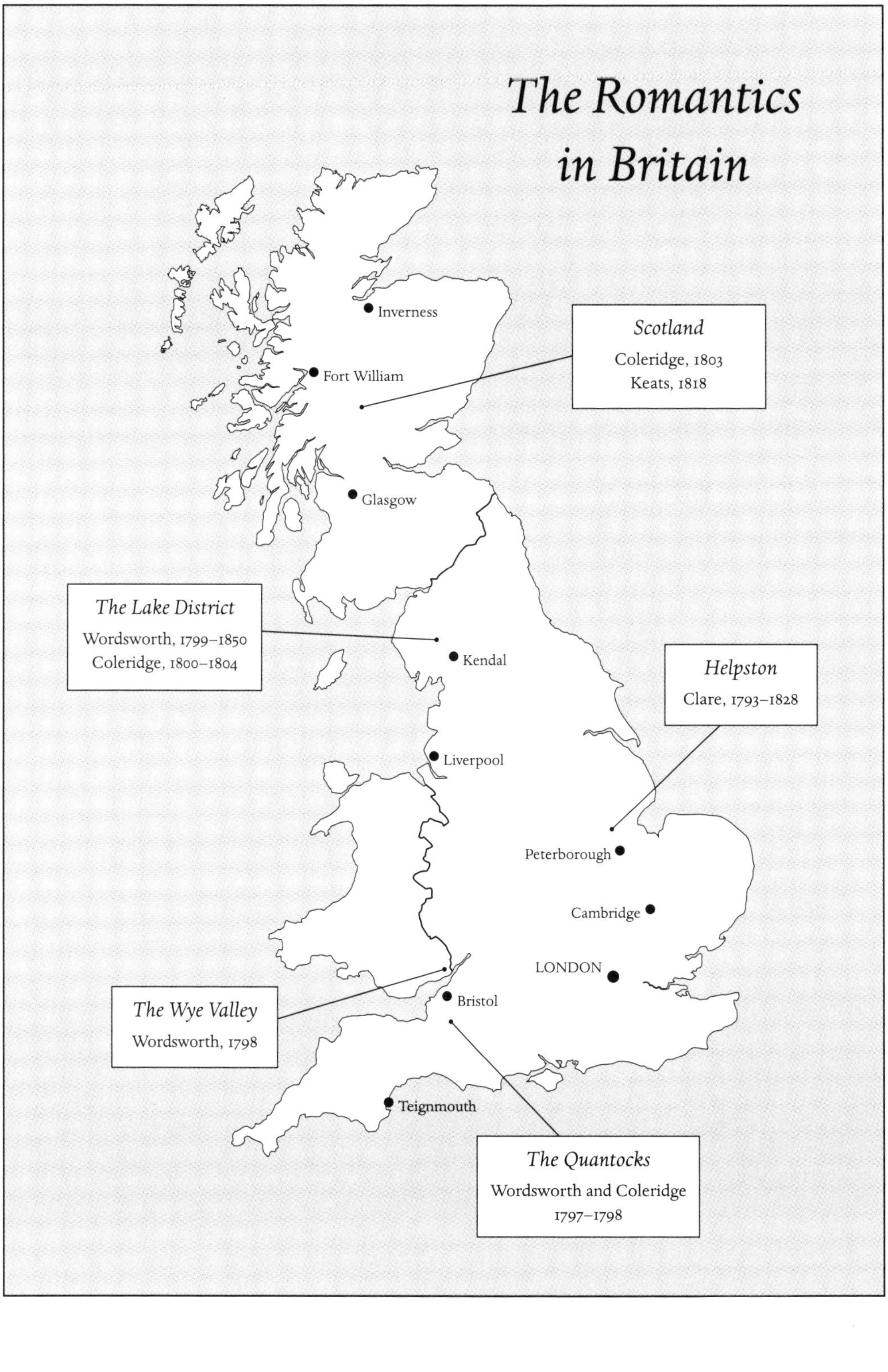

The Romantics in Britain
Inverness
Fort William
Glasgow
Scotland
Coleridge, 1803
Keats, 1818
The Lake District
Wordsworth, 1799–1850
Coleridge, 1800–1804
Kendal
Helpston
Clare, 1793–1828
Liverpool
Peterborough
Cambridge
LONDON
The Wye Valley
Wordsworth, 1798
Bristol
Teignmouth
The Quantocks
Wordsworth and Coleridge
1797–1798

INTRODUCTION

In 1798 Samuel Taylor Coleridge came across a worn-out copy of James Thomson's poem *The Seasons* lying on a window seat in a country inn. 'That is fame!' he remarked to his companions. At that time, *The Seasons* was the most popular evocation of the British landscape in literature. First published in the 1720s, it depicts the routines of rural life and the changing face of the natural world through the seasons. It is a very pictorial poem, rich in precise, closely observed descriptions, from the play of light upon summer leaves to the intricate shapes of snow crystals.

Coleridge and his fellow Romantic poets approached the landscape differently. For them, the external forms of nature were less important than the internal effects they had upon the mind. They explored the way the landscape played upon the observer's memories and emotions, and showed how it could be transformed by the imagination. As the painter Samuel Palmer put it, 'landscape is of little value, but as it hints or expresses the thoughts and doings of man.' Romantic appreciation of landscape was highly subjective; it changed according to the writer's purpose, mood and state of mind. This makes it difficult to talk about in general terms, so, instead, I have focused on particular periods of time when the relationship between a poet and a landscape, between the observer and the observed, was especially close. They were periods not only of poetic confidence and inspiration, but also of anxiety and emotional turmoil. And, more often than not, they ran contrary to the prevailing fashions and opinions of the literary world. In presenting these moments, I have drawn extensively on both the published works (the poems, guidebooks and reviews), and the unpublished poetic drafts, letters and journals which, in their rushed, unpunctuated immediacy, show how close the poet's relationship with the landscape could be.

William Wordsworth composed his great poem, 'Lines written a few miles above Tintern Abbey', while touring the lower Wye Valley in July 1798. This was one of the most fashionable landscapes in Britain. It was a favourite destination of lovers of the Picturesque, an eighteenth-century pursuit that viewed the landscape according to the aesthetic rules of art, and had been frequently described in poems, guidebooks and travel literature of all kinds. But Wordsworth's poem offered something completely new: despite its title, it was not a description of the celebrated scenery around Tintern Abbey, but a passionate meditation upon the memories, feelings and hopes that the landscape provoked.

Wordsworth's profound identification with the landscape was shared, briefly but intensely, by his close friend Coleridge. For most of the eight years between 1797 and 1804 the two poets were neighbours, first in the Quantock hills of Somerset, and then in the Lake District. At first Coleridge delighted in the retired rural life. The twelve months that he spent in Wordsworth's company in the Quantocks resulted in exquisite poems such as 'This Limetree Bower my Prison' and 'Frost at Midnight'. He saw himself as the passive instrument of nature, which played over his mind like a breeze over harp strings. And when, in 1799, Wordsworth returned to his native Lake District, Coleridge followed him there. With extraordinary energy he explored the fells, bringing them to life in a series of scintillating notebook entries. But, after a while, his rural existence became a claustrophobic world of isolation, ill health, opium addiction and domestic unhappiness. As his imagination failed, so his perception of the landscape darkened, a process he articulated in his poem 'Dejection, An Ode'. Friends such as Charles Lamb and William Godwin tried to persuade him to return to London, where he always thrived, while the Wordsworths, flourishing in Grasmere, watched their friend's decline with growing dismay. Others, more critically, saw Coleridge's living in the remote countryside as the waste of a great literary talent.

John Keats came to the Lake District in the summer of 1818, as part of a walking tour through the north of England and Scotland. Landscape enthusiasts were making such tours in increasing numbers, and would often publish accounts of their journey. But for Keats, the tour was as much a mental journey as a physical one. After several false starts in his poetic career, he hoped that his tour would bring him the knowledge and experience he needed, that the mountainous scenery would inspire him to write the epic poem that was his greatest ambition. The long letters he wrote to family and friends, while ostensibly a travel journal, read more like an exploration of his own self, and show a growing impatience with the conventions of travel writing. Not content with merely describing the physical journey, its famous landscapes and views, Keats explored instead the corresponding effects of the mountains on his mind.

For a brief period, Keats's contemporary, John Clare, enjoyed considerable popularity. The high sales of his first volume, *Poems Descriptive of Rural Life*, 1820, owed much to the contemporary taste for so-called 'peasant poetry'.

Clare's background was extremely humble, and, like Robert Burns before him, he was welcomed as an untutored child of nature who brought the landscape, in all its natural simplicity, into the drawing room. But these celebrated early poems were, in fact, derivative of earlier poets such as Thomson and Oliver Goldsmith. It was in Clare's later, mostly unpublished work that he was to find his unique voice as a poet. These later poems speak not only of his deep attachment to his native landscape, but also of his growing sense of alienation from it. A rising tension between the hidden, intimate world of his birthplace, the small Northamptonshire village of Helpston, and the public world of literary London (its readers, critics and patrons), pervades these apparently simple poems. It was a tension that would, ultimately, contribute towards Clare's later madness.

After writing 'Lines written a few miles above Tintern Abbey', Wordsworth had retired to the Lakes for seclusion, there to compose a great philosophical poem, 'The Recluse'. But before long he witnessed the growing popularity of the area, as tourists came in ever-increasing numbers. In response, he wrote his greatest prose work, *A Guide through the District of the Lakes*. In contrast to earlier guidebooks to the area, which had catered largely for the tourist, this was a deep-felt description of the Lake District by someone who had known it since childhood. Formerly a place of privacy and solitude, the landscape was, Wordsworth recognised, becoming public property. His hope was that, by sharing his love and knowledge of the Lake District, he would educate the visitor, and so help towards the preservation of its essential character.

Wordsworth's *Guide through the District of the Lakes* would become the most popular guidebook to the area, but it would take time for the Romantic approach to the landscape to become widely known. In the early nineteenth century few people read Wordsworth's and Coleridge's *Lyrical Ballads* or Keats's odes, and no one, of course, knew of the notebooks and letters, or the unpublished poems, which included Clare's later work and Wordsworth's greatest meditation on his relationship with the landscape, *The Prelude*. Instead people continued to read Thomson's *The Seasons* in huge numbers, and follow William Gilpin on his picturesque tours around Britain. But in time the Romantic poets' reverence for nature would leave a lasting impression on the British landscape and, today, after two centuries, there are parts of Britain that now seem inseparable from their lives and work.

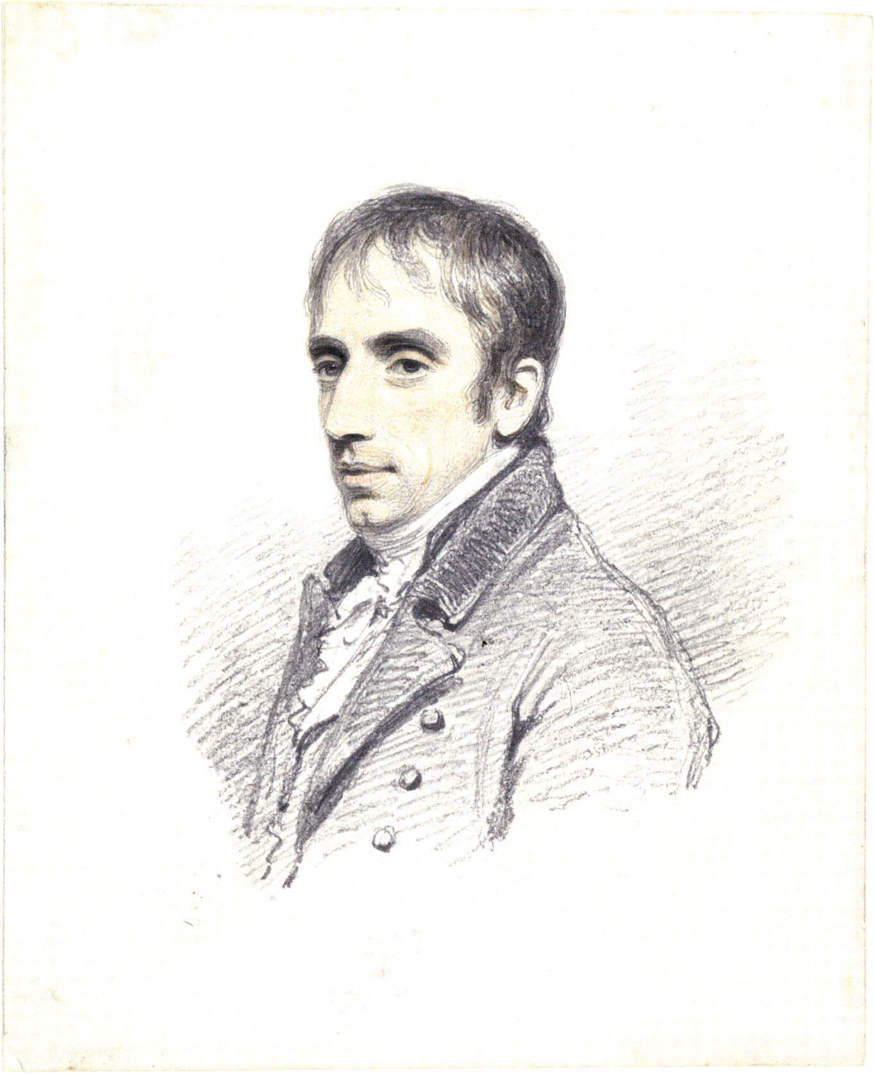

William Wordsworth by Henry Edridge, 1805.

'INTO THE LIFE OF THINGS'

Wordsworth and the Wye, 1798

On 8 July 1798 William and Dorothy Wordsworth went to Shirehampton, a village near Bristol, to see their friend James Losh. There they met a local curate, Richard Warner, who had just published an account of a pedestrian tour of Wales he had made the previous summer. This had concluded, most successfully, with a walk along the River Wye as it wound its way from Ross down to Chepstow and the Bristol Channel. 'Nothing, indeed, can exceed the beauty of the banks of this romantic river,' Warner told his readers. 'The scenery, though not stupendous is often grand, sometimes sublime, and never uninteresting.' Encouraged, no doubt, by Warner, Wordsworth and his sister made their own tour of the Wye Valley just two days later. Starting from Chepstow, they walked up to Tintern, crossed the river, and spent the next four days rambling along its banks. As he left Tintern, Wordsworth began to compose a poem in his head, and he finished it just as they arrived back in Bristol on the evening of 13 July. 'No poem of mine was composed under circumstances more pleasant for me to remember than this,' he recalled more than forty years later. 'Not a line of it was altered, and not any part of it written down till I reached Bristol.' 'Lines, written a few miles above Tintern Abbey, on revisiting the banks of the Wye during a tour, July 13 1798' was published a few weeks later as the conclusion to *Lyrical Ballads*, a collection of poems he and his friend Samuel Taylor Coleridge had recently assembled. It has since become the best-known literary response to the scenery of the Wye. At the time, however, it was but one among many. For, at the end of the eighteenth century, the forty-mile stretch of river between Ross and Chepstow was one of the most popular landscapes in Britain, and, as such, had already been described, as Warner admitted in *A Walk through Wales*, 'by Tourists out of number'.

The first visitors were the antiquaries of the early eighteenth century, who sought to retrieve Britain's native past by studying and preserving its architectural relics. In 1732, Samuel and Nathaniel Buck published the earliest view of the Wye Valley's finest relic, Tintern Abbey, as part of their *Antiquities of Great Britain*. This ambitious series of engravings was conceived, as the

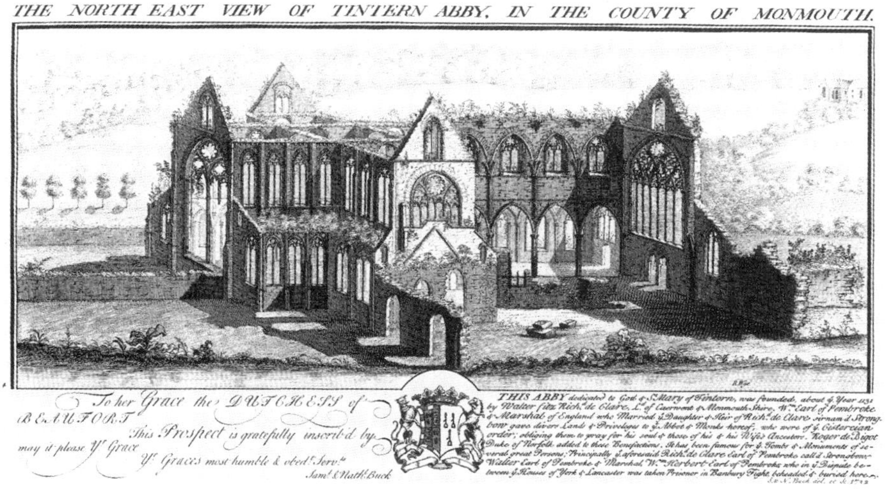

The earliest view of Tintern Abbey, published by Samuel and Nathaniel Buck in 1732 as part of their *Antiquities of Great Britain*.

Bucks had colourfully put it in their 1724 prospectus, 'to rescue the mangled remains of these aged and venerable edifices from the inexorable jaws of time'. The antiquaries saw Britain's decaying remains as a source of national pride and argued that they had been neglected for far too long in favour of the classical delights of the Grand Tour through Europe. 'Temples and palaces of the polite nations of antiquity engross our attention, while the works and memorials of our own priests and heroes have no effect on our curiosity,' complained Richard Gough, and by the end of the eighteenth century, thanks to the energies of patriotic antiquaries like him, antiquarianism was no longer just the pursuit of the scholarly few and had become a fashionable activity; 'without a competent fund of Antiquarian learning', commented the amateur antiquary Francis Grose in 1775, the year of his own visit to the Wye, 'no one will ever make a respectable figure'.

The antiquaries were followed by well-to-do travellers who came simply to enjoy the landscape. John Egerton, appointed Rector of Ross in 1745, and 'the Father of the Voyage down the Wye', liked to take his friends on excursions down the river in his private boat, and it was this river journey that became the celebrated 'Wye Tour'. A few eccentrics, like Richard Warner, chose to walk, and some, like John Byng, 5th Viscount Torrington, in 1791, covered the route on horseback. But walking for pleasure was still a new pastime, and riding, though cheap, was hard, sometimes dangerous, work. Arthur Young, in his *Six Weeks Tour through the Southern Counties of England and Wales* (1768), described the roads from Chepstow as 'mere rocky lanes, full of hugeous stones as big as one's horse, and abominable holes'; 'much is employ'd in mending the roads', wrote Byng, 'but I rode over them in fear'. The preferred way to enjoy the scenery was, therefore, to take a boat; 'the water passage ought in every respect to be preferred', wrote Henry Penruddocke Wyndham. 'The views from the Wye are exceedingly magnificent; the rocks on each side seem to be from 300 to 600 feet high; they are sometimes perpendicular and wholly naked, and sometimes the very precipices are covered with woods, from the river's brink to their summits, for continued miles.'

By the end of the eighteenth century, at least eight pleasure boats were taking tourists down the river. Usually hired from local inns, these varied in size. The smaller vessels could be rowed by two men and carried six passengers; the largest could carry up to twenty passengers and were well fitted out with cushioned seats, a curtained awning, carpets, and a table from which wine and cold collations were served. Prices were high: in 1797 Richard Colt Hoare paid £1 11s 6d for the passage to Monmouth, plus ten shillings 'for watermen's victuals', and the same again for the journey from Monmouth to Chepstow. Several years after his journey on horseback, Byng returned and took the boat. He admitted that it was comfortable, but found it 'shamefully expensive ... the boatmen pretend the great difficulty and tediousness of returning against the stream'.

The Wye Tour generally took two days, and few begrudged the price, for the journey was, as the poet Thomas Gray told his friend Joseph Wharton in 1771, 'a succession of nameless wonders'. Tourists embarked at Ross, often at dawn, and after three miles were treated to their first great sight, Goodrich Castle. Built in red sandstone in the eleventh and twelfth centuries, it held a commanding position among the trees on the high right bank of the river. Four miles further downstream was Symond's Yat, or gate, a natural amphitheatre created by the steep banks of the Coldwell Rocks and the 470-foot Yat Rock. Here, wrote Warner, 'the scene becomes truly majestic', and in 1800 an astonished Archdeacon Coxe wildly reckoned Yat Rock to be 2,000 feet high. Travellers would lunch in the shadow of the Coldwell Rocks, then disembark and follow the path to the summit of Yat Rock, which offered stunning views. Next came the most spectacular stretch of the river: the gorge narrowed and deepened, the limestone cliffs grew higher, and the rapids at the Seven Sisters Rocks and the iron forge at New Weir impressed the tourists' minds with a feeling of awe. Then, towards evening, came Monmouth, and the end of the first day's travelling.

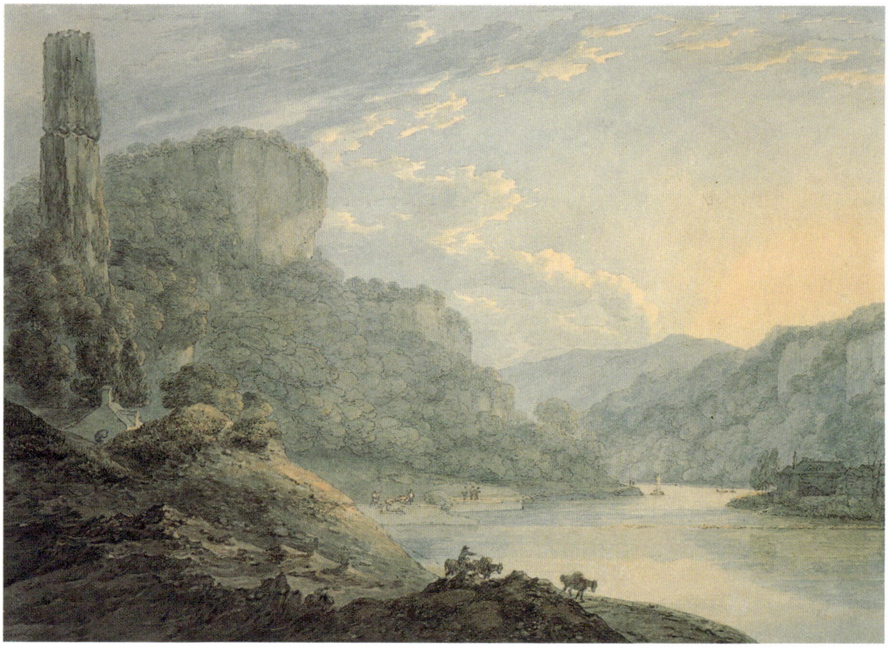

A view of the Wye by Thomas Hearne, *c.*1794, showing Symond's Yat on the left.

The second day, from Monmouth to Chepstow, took the tourist through open meadows, past more industrial iron and tin works at Redbrook and Brockweir, and on to the village of Tintern. Then, a little below the village, round a bend in the river, came the highlight of the tour, Tintern Abbey itself. Following the dissolution of the monasteries in the sixteenth century, the abbey had quickly been abandoned and by the eighteenth century local villagers were using the ruins for games like fives and quoits. The poor raised makeshift homes against the walls. Matters improved in 1745 when the 4th Duke of Beaufort inherited the abbey. Taking a new pride in the ruins, he employed over one hundred workmen to clear the interior of the church, level and turf the ground, and heap the fragments of fallen masonry into ornamental piles. Rubbish was thrown into the river, and the church was protected from vandalism by locking doors, hung at the west front, and iron gates at other principal entry points. Tourists could procure a key from the nearby Beaufort Arms, and so enjoy the restored abbey in its splendid setting. 'The ruins of Tintern abbey,' wrote David Williams in his *History of Monmouthshire*, 'to an enthusiast in landscape, are among the most interesting objects in Great Britain. … The ruin is in a profound, narrow, and woody valley, on the banks of the Wye; the perspective of it is uncommonly beautiful:

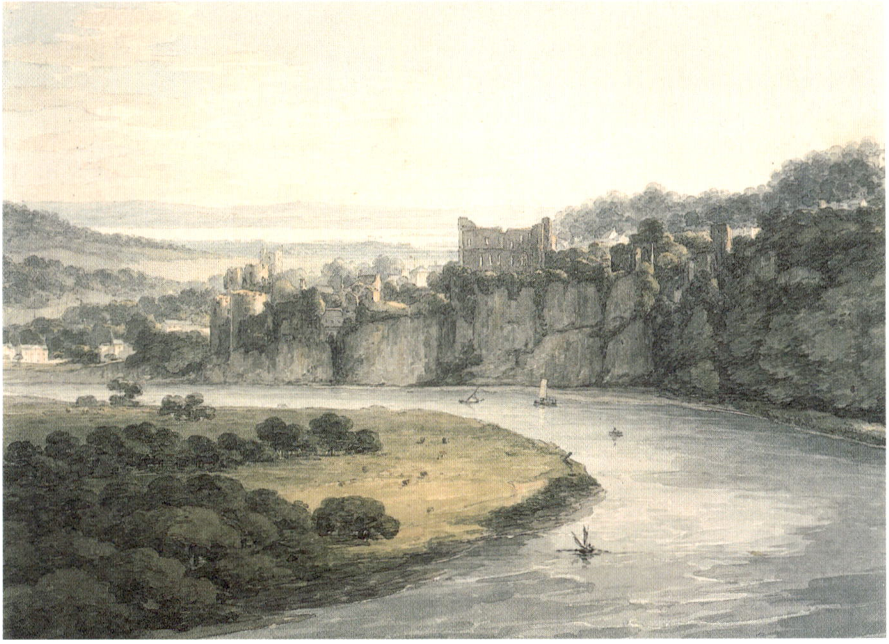

The view of Chepstow from Piercefield, by Thomas Hearne, *c.*1794.

arches obscured by foliage, or edged by the tendrils of ivy; walls, clustered columns, and divisions of ayles, shaded by tufts and wreaths: every thing impressing the mind with the idea of decay; but offering shattered memorials of former grandeur, which entrance the fancy, and occupy it in obviating the depredations of time, and restoring all the parts of the crumbling structure.'

There was one further highlight before journey's end at Chepstow: a few miles downstream from the abbey was the 300-acre Piercefield estate. In the 1750s its owner, Valentine Morris (employing the same Chepstow builder who had worked on Tintern Abbey for the Duke of Beaufort), had laid out a park in the style of those landscaped by Capability Brown, creating a system of walks that exploited the park's stunning position on a tight bend in the river. These walks were open to the public on Tuesdays and Fridays and had ten stations giving different views over the Wye valley, Chepstow Castle, and, beyond, the Severn estuary. They included stone-built platforms, an alcove-shaped grotto lined with minerals and rock crystals, and the Giant's Cave, a tunnel and chamber cut into the cliff, complete with a stone giant about to hurl a boulder above his head. Swivel guns were kept nearby and visitors could, if they wished, leave some gunpowder with a gardener and have the guns fired to appreciate the echo.

The Wye Tour was a popular one, a fine mix of beauty, grandeur and antiquity that provided a little education and a great deal of pleasure, and its popularity was both sustained and shaped by a vast amount of literature and art, from fine exhibited watercolours to mass-produced engravings, from deluxe illustrated volumes to amateur poems and cheap, Grub Street guidebooks. The better known the Wye became, the more its appreciation was influenced by contemporary moods and fashions, and the primary influence was undoubtedly William Gilpin.

Born in Carlisle in 1724, Gilpin was a Church of England clergyman who had, incidentally, given Richard Warner his early curacy at Lymington. From 1753 to 1777 he managed Cheam School for Boys, in Surrey, where he was known as a fine teacher and an enlightened disciplinarian. Later, in 1791, he endowed two further schools at Boldre in the New Forest. But it is for what he called his 'amusements' that Gilpin was celebrated. In 1768 he published, anonymously, an *Essay on Prints* in which he explored 'the Principles of picturesque Beauty'. 'Picturesque' he defined as 'that peculiar kind of beauty, which is agreeable in a picture'. In the summer vacations he travelled around different parts of the country, including Cumberland and Westmoreland, the Scottish Highlands, south-west England and the Isle of Wight, north Wales and the Wye Valley, in search of this 'peculiar kind of beauty'. Every evening he would make notes and sketches based on the day's travelling, and from these working notebooks would put together more finished manuscripts. These manuscripts circulated widely, and often became very elaborate; by 1774 the manuscript of his Lake District tour, for instance, consisted of 830 pages, with 249 sketches, bound together in eight volumes. Friends and admirers urged Gilpin to publish, and though at first reluctant – 'I have not the most distant idea of printing them,' he told William Mason, who had praised the Lakes tour – he finally agreed. His various *Observations* of picturesque beauty were published between 1783 and 1789.

Gilpin toured the Wye in 1770, and in 1783 his account of the trip became the first of the *Observations* to be published. It included fifteen prints (after Gilpin's original drawings) by his nephew William Sawrey Gilpin, and was the first, and remained the most famous, of the many guidebooks to the area. In it Gilpin did more than map out a suggested route; he introduced the public to his theory of the Picturesque. 'The following little work,' he wrote, 'proposes a new object of pursuit; that of not barely examining the face of a country; but of examining it by the rules of picturesque beauty; that of not merely describing; but of adapting the description of natural scenery to the principles of artificial landscape; and of opening the sources of those pleasures, which are derived from the comparison.' The tourist was thus invited to become not just an observer, but a critic of scenery, viewing nature according to the principles of its presentation in art. The particular value of the Wye, as it wound through the landscape, was to offer 'amidst some general sameness, infinite peculiarities'.

As they viewed the Wye scenery with 'the picturesque eye ... in search of beauty', Gilpin and his followers usually found that it was in need of improvement. As Gilpin wrote to William Mason, when the latter criticised his Wye drawings for being unrealistic, 'I did all I could to make people believe they were general ideas, or illustrations, or any thing, but what they would have them to be, exact portraits ... I am so attached to my picturesque rules, that if nature gets it wrong, I cannot help putting her right.' Tintern Abbey presented particular challenges. Gilpin allowed that the abbey was 'esteemed, with its appendages, the most beautiful and picturesque on the river', but could not give it unqualified praise as a distant object, for 'a number of gabel-ends hurt the eye with their regularity and disgust it by the vulgarity of their shape'. Worse, the ruins were surrounded by 'shabby houses' which spoiled its appearance from the river; 'At some trifling expense,' wrote John Byng briskly, 'the surrounding cottages and orchards might be removed; and then the abbey would stand nobly back'd by woods, and open to the water: at present it is shamefully blocked up.'

These buildings were a reminder of another difficulty faced by the genteel tourist: the extreme poverty of the local inhabitants, who lived in wretched conditions around the ruins and who sought to make a living off the tourists. Where the antiquarians saw ruins as places of historical investigation and instruction, later tourists saw the decaying, ivy-clad stones as expressive of delicate, finely wrought emotion. The Reverend Sneyd Davis wrote in 1742:

> At length our pilgramage's home appears,
> Her venerable fabric *Tintern* rears;
> While the sun, glancing in its calm decline,
> With his last gilding beautifies her shrine; ...
> Here my lov'd friend, along the mossy dome
> In pleasurable sadness let me roam,
> Look back upon the world, in haven safe;
> Weep o'er its ruins, at its follies laugh.

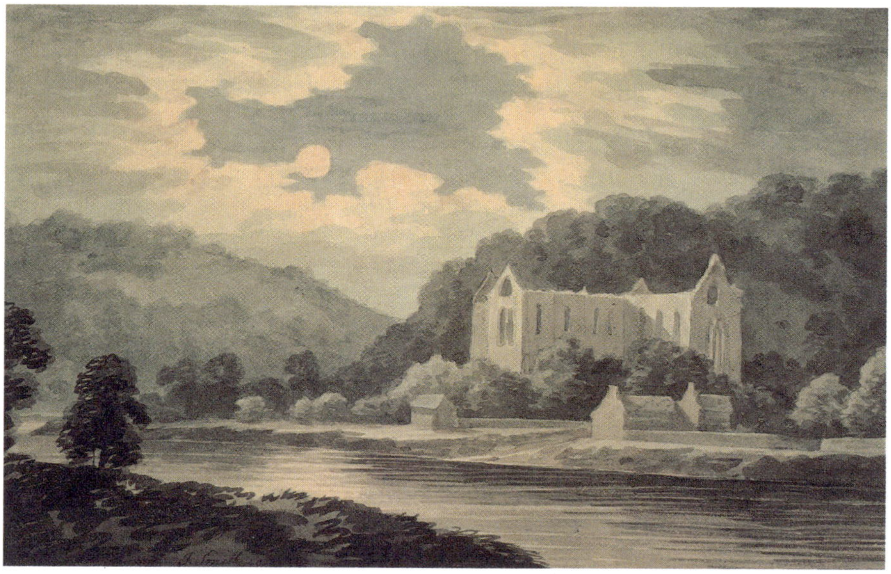

Tintern Abbey in moonlight, by John 'Warwick' Smith, 1779.

Ruins were places of solitude, places where one could meditate on what Richard Warner described as 'the impossibility of resisting the silent, but uninterrupted attacks of Time, who sooner or later levels with the dust all the monuments of human vanity, and all the efforts of human labour'. The stark proximity of real deprivation did little to encourage such reveries. 'One poor woman we followed, who had engaged to shew us the monk's library,' wrote William Gilpin, '... could scarce crawl; shuffling along her palsied limbs, and meagre, contracted body, by the help of two sticks. She led us, through an old gate, into a place overspread with nettles and briars; and pointing to the remnant of a shattered cloister, told us, that was the place. It was her own mansion. ... When we stood in the midst of this cell of misery; and felt the chilling damps, which struck us in every direction, we were rather surprised, that the wretched inhabitant was still alive; than that she had only lost the use of her limbs.'

William Coxe's solution was to walk half a mile downstream where he could look back on the abbey 'without the intervention of a single cottage to obstruct the view'. There he sampled its 'pleasing intermixture of wildness and culture', and enjoyed 'impressions of pleasing melancholy inspired by the awful ruins and tempered by the beauties of nature'. Ingeniously, John Byng retained the services of his guide ('a very old man who had forgotten everything'), because 'his venerable grey beard, and locks, added dignity to my thoughts; and I fancied him the hermit of the place'. The proper way to enjoy Tintern, he said, 'is to bring wines, cold meat, with corn for the horses; (bread, beer, cyder, and commonly salmon, may be had from the Beaufort Arms;) spread your table in the ruins; and possibly a Welsh harper may be procured from Chepstow'.

The presence nearby of heavy industry was another distraction. This had been at Tintern, and indeed in most of the lower Wye Valley, since the sixteenth century, when the first iron foundries were built. By the 1790s the ironworks at Tintern had grown to such a size that they operated ceaselessly, both day and night, and employed upwards of 1,500 people. Gilpin complained that the works introduced 'noise and bustle into these regions of tranquillity', and the sketch he made of them is noticeably absent from the published *Observations*. Warner incorporated them into the scene more successfully. Watching the 'scene of bustle amidst smoke and fire' from the Beaufort Arms at night, he wrote, 'produced a most impressive effect on the mind. We saw Virgil's description realised, and the interior of Etna, the forges of the Cyclops, and their fearful employment, immediately occurred to us.' Just as ruins inspired 'pleasurable sadness', so industry, awesome and infernal, provoked an 'agreeable terror' that could express itself in quotations from Virgil or Milton.

Images of the Wye valley in general, and Tintern Abbey in particular, proliferated. Responding to demand, many of the country's leading landscape artists came to the Wye, including Paul Sandby, Edward Dayes and Philippe de Loutherbourg. Thomas Hearne toured the Wye twice, first in 1787, and then in 1794, in the company of Sir George Beaumont. He exhibited views of the abbey and Chepstow Castle at the Royal Academy in 1788 and 1789 respectively, and his view of the west front of Tintern Abbey was published in the *Antiquities of Great Britain* in 1804, the most extensive survey of British ruins since that published by the Bucks in 1732. The young J.M.W. Turner made three tours between 1792 and 1798, exhibiting a view of Tintern Abbey at the Royal Academy in 1794. Self-taught artists were also not without ambition. Encouraged by Gilpin, tourists added drawing to their journal writing, and the table found in the middle of the larger pleasure boats served as a useful sketching surface. In 1797, a year before Wordsworth's tour, Samuel Ireland published his *Picturesque Views on the River Wye*, an expensive volume containing thirty-one sepia aquatints. In a direct reference to Gilpin, he writes that his intention is to provide the reader with descriptions and images 'which, if he visits the spot, he trusts he will find, and, if the spot is known to him already, he assures himself he will recognise'.

Images of the Wye were, therefore, everywhere. Engravings (whether issued singly, or contained in travel books or expensive antiquarian volumes) ensured that its landscape was immediately recognisable, whether one had been there or not. Fanny Price, heroine of Jane Austen's *Mansfield Park*, had a transparency of Tintern Abbey in the window of her attic room, where it 'held its station between a cave in Italy, and a moonlight lake in Cumberland'. The abbey was a popular subject for exhibition works, and paintings found their way into private collections. One such painting was seen by the printer Charles Heath, as he walked around the picture gallery at Hagley, the Worcestershire seat of Lord Lyttleton. Heath found his attention 'particularly arrested by a fine painting of Tintern Abbey; which, from being executed on a large scale, afforded the artist full scope for the delineation of this admirable (and to me *novel*) pile of ruins'. On a subsequent excursion to Tintern (which he entered 'with a mingled portion of awe and admiration'), Heath found that he 'wanted some intelligent guide to impart innumerable circumstances, which the contemplation of such a scene naturally excited in the mind of every curious and observant traveller'. The following spring, after he had set himself up as a printer in Monmouth and had presently become well acquainted with the area, he found that travellers through the town looked to him for any information, be they only fragments, which he could supply.

Heath had recognised a gap in the market. In 1793 he published *Descriptive Account of Tintern Abbey ... selected from Grose, Gilpin, Shaw ... and other esteemed writers*, an inexpensive octavo volume that drew together some of the best-known, but often difficult-to-find writings on Tintern. It was a success, and in 1803 he produced a much larger second edition 'sold also by Mr. Gethen, who has the care of the abbey; and at all the inns in the county'. Around extracts from Gilpin, Wheatley, Shaw and Francis Grose he assembled a wealth of informative material: a guided walk along the river from Monmouth to Tintern; poetical descriptions; historical information drawn from both written sources and local anecdote; the history of the local ironworks; maps and dimensions of the abbey ruins. To this he added practical information for tourists: the Beaufort Arms is recommended, 'should FATIGUE take precedence of the reader's curiosity'; travellers by boat should allow no more than *two hours* at Tintern Abbey so as not to miss the tide, 'They therefore would do right to avoid detaining the Boatmen at Monmouth'; from Tintern, 'I would recommend [the traveller] to engage some little boy of the village for A GUIDE ... Mr. Gethen will soon provide a little rustic ready to attend.'

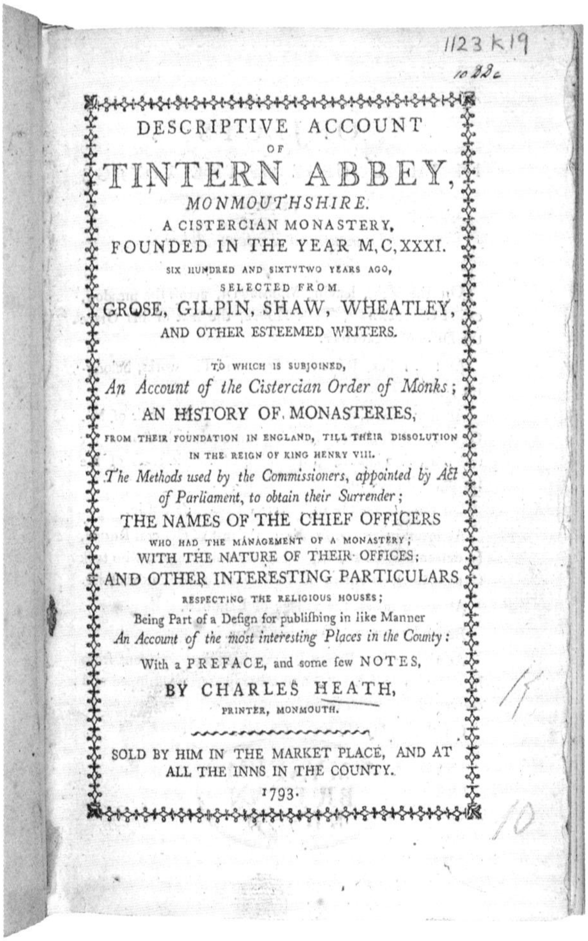

DESCRIPTIVE ACCOUNT
OF
TINTERN ABBEY,
MONMOUTHSHIRE.
A CISTERCIAN MONASTERY,
FOUNDED IN THE YEAR M,C,XXXI.
SIX HUNDRED AND SIXTYTWO YEARS AGO,
SELECTED FROM
GROSE, GILPIN, SHAW, WHEATLEY,
AND OTHER ESTEEMED WRITERS.

TO WHICH IS SUBJOINED,
An Account of the Cistercian Order of Monks;
AN HISTORY OF MONASTERIES,
FROM THEIR FOUNDATION IN ENGLAND, TILL THEIR DISSOLUTION
IN THE REIGN OF KING HENRY VIII.
The Methods used by the Commissioners, appointed by Act of Parliament, to obtain their Surrender;
THE NAMES OF THE CHIEF OFFICERS
WHO HAD THE MANAGEMENT OF A MONASTERY;
WITH THE NATURE OF THEIR OFFICES;
AND OTHER INTERESTING PARTICULARS
RESPECTING THE RELIGIOUS HOUSES;
Being Part of a Defign for publifhing in like Manner
An Account of the most interesting Places in the County:
With a PREFACE, and some few NOTES,
BY CHARLES HEATH,
PRINTER, MONMOUTH.

SOLD BY HIM IN THE MARKET PLACE, AND AT
ALL THE INNS IN THE COUNTY.
1793.

The first edition of Charles Heath's *Descriptive Account of Tintern Abbey*, a handy compendium for tourists.

And Heath kept the price low. It would have been easy, he wrote in a preface, 'to have swelled out the materials into a respectable volume, by printing it in a large character, with extensive margins, and afterwards to have extended the sale price by expensive engravings, but I must here repeat my opinion, *that all information, if useful, should come recommended in the cheapest form possible*, an axiom I have never swerved from'. Tourists were thus furnished with a single volume that condensed all previous writings, and brought together all they needed for a visit: where to go, how to get there, what to see, what they were seeing, and even how to see it.

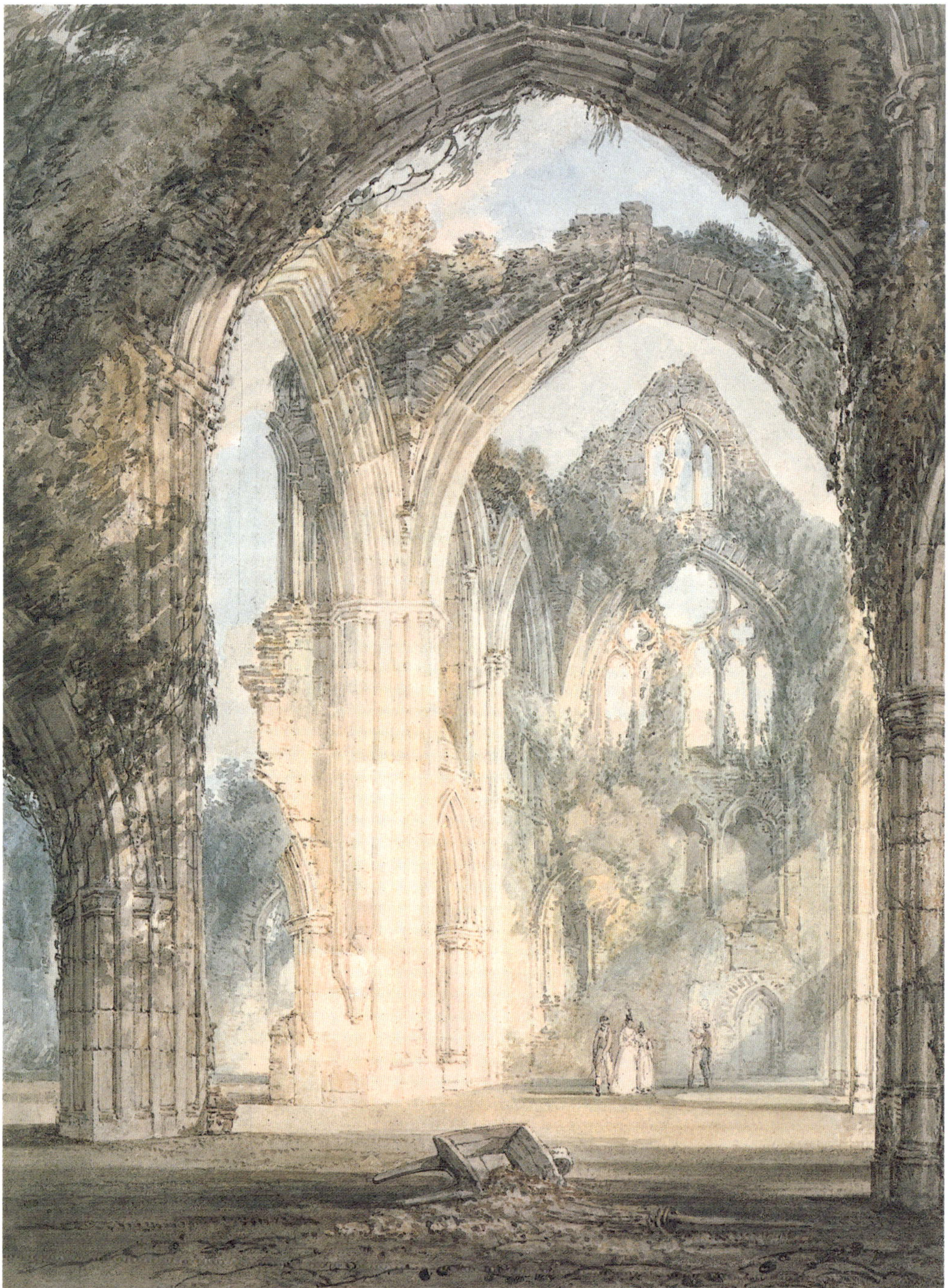

The interior of Tintern Abbey by J.M.W. Turner, 1794.
Genteel tourists are shown talking to a local labourer.

Such was the rich cultural background against which Wordsworth came to write 'Tintern Abbey'. As his friend John Thelwall, a writer and political reformer, had put it two months earlier in the *New Monthly Magazine*:

> The enchanting beauties of the River Wye are by this time pretty generally known among the lovers of the picturesque. They have acquired a due celebrity from the descriptions of GILPIN, and curiosity has been inflamed by poetry and by prose, by paintings, prints and drawings, till they have been rendered a subject of universal conversation ... An excursion on the Wye has become an essential part of the education, as it were, of all who aspire to the reputation of elegance, taste and fashion.

Visitors came to the Wye valley to enjoy themselves, to row pleasantly down the river and then picnic in the grounds of Tintern Abbey. But they also came, more self-consciously, as fashionable connoisseurs, ready to select, adapt and embellish the landscape in the preconceived ways suggested to them in contemporary literature and art, most of all by Gilpin. 'Repeated descriptions of it have been given to the world,' summed up Richard Warner, 'but the elegant pen of Mr. Gilpin, directed by taste, and enlivened by fancy, seems alone to have done justice to its inexhaustible and beautiful varieties.'

Wordsworth was well acquainted with Mr Gilpin's elegant pen, and in fact may well have taken a copy of his *Observations of the River Wye* with him on his walking tour, but he was well aware of its limitations. Gilpin had seen his pursuit of picturesque beauty as an amusement, a tasteful and agreeable game. It could not withstand its elevation to a cult, let alone a fully worked-out theory. The writer Hannah More, who also toured the Wye in the summer of 1789, told Horace Walpole that she had been dutifully 'looking at abbeys and castles, with Mr Gilpin in my hand to teach me to criticize', but added that the effect of Gilpin's 'cant of connoisseurship' had been to 'subdue my imagination, which had been not a little disordered with this enchanting scenery'. The effects of slavishly following the picturesque, of, as it were, the over-culturalisation of the landscape, were obvious: the over attachment to visual rules; the jargon ('sublime', 'beautiful', 'awesome'); the stock, contrived emotional responses ('pleasurable sadness'); the endless comparisons to the pictures of Claude Lorrain, Salvator Rosa and Gaspard Poussin; the well-trod paths and preordained viewing stations. All were described by Wordsworth in Book XI of *The Prelude* (1805), as 'a strong infection of the age', that:

Was never much my habit—giving way
To a comparison of scene with scene,
Bent overmuch on superficial things,
Pampering myself with eager novelties
Of colour and proportion, to the moods
Of Nature, and the spirit of the place,
Less sensible.

Contemporary readers of Wordsworth's 'Lines written a few miles above Tintern Abbey' might, from its title, have expected a work similar to the 'Poetical Description' of the abbey in Heath's guide, with its descriptions of 'mournful ruins' that 'fill the soul with awe' and 'fine old windows, arches, walls' that 'fill the mind with pity and delight'. But from the opening lines it is clear that the poem is something quite different:

Five years have passed; five summers, with the length
Of five long winters! and again I hear
These waters, rolling from their mountain-springs
With a sweet inland murmur. Once again
Do I behold these steep and lofty cliffs,
Which on a wild secluded scene impress
Thoughts of more deep seclusion; and connect
The landscape with the quiet of the sky.

Despite the title, there are no references either to the abbey, or to any recognisable part of the Wye valley. The description is strikingly unspecific and, what is more, hints at profound personal resonances that impress Wordsworth's thoughts and feelings upon the landscape. It is these thoughts and feelings, not the outward forms of the scenery, that are the subject of the poem.

Wordsworth wrote 'Tintern Abbey' at a turning point in his life. On his previous, solitary visit to the Wye in 1793 he had been in an agitated and restless state, and had felt a stranger in his own country. He had witnessed the French Revolution at first hand, and become devoted to its cause, and was anguished by the injustice of Britain's war with France and his own political impotence. He was separated from Annette Vallon, with whom he had had a love affair in France, and their child Caroline, whom he had never seen. The intervening five years had been years of recovery. The first two had been spent at remote Racedown in Dorset with his closest companion, his sister

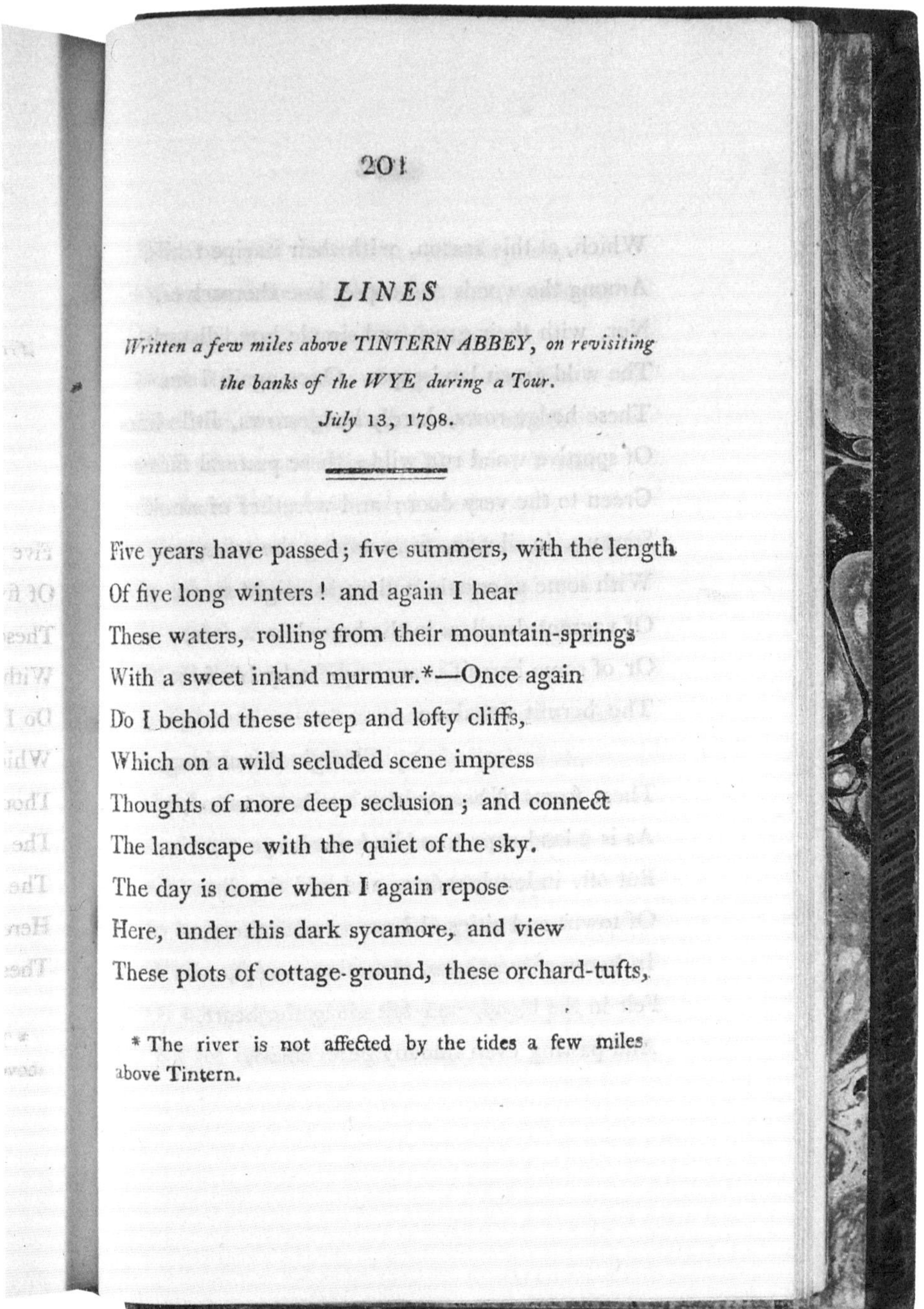

201

LINES

Written a few miles above TINTERN ABBEY, *on revisiting the banks of the* WYE *during a Tour.*

July 13, 1798.

Five years have passed; five summers, with the length
Of five long winters! and again I hear
These waters, rolling from their mountain-springs
With a sweet inland murmur.*—Once again
Do I behold these steep and lofty cliffs,
Which on a wild secluded scene impress
Thoughts of more deep seclusion; and connect
The landscape with the quiet of the sky.
The day is come when I again repose
Here, under this dark sycamore, and view
These plots of cottage-ground, these orchard-tufts,

* The river is not affected by the tides a few miles above Tintern.

The first publication of 'Tintern Abbey', in *Lyrical Ballads*, 1798.

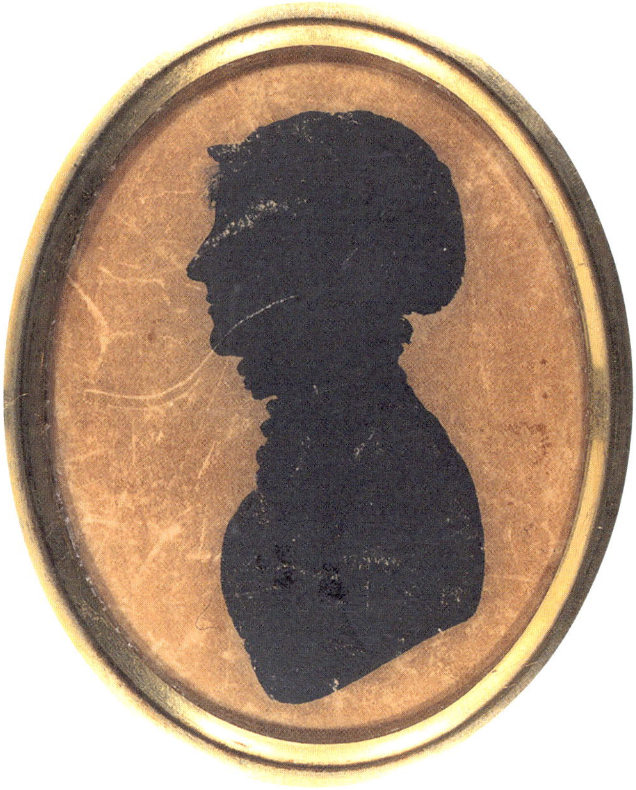

Dorothy Wordsworth by an unknown artist, *c.*1806.

Dorothy. Then he had met Samuel Taylor Coleridge, and in 1797 had moved to Alfoxden in the Quantock hills, Somerset, to be near him. Over the next twelve months he and Coleridge had written the great poetry that would make up *Lyrical Ballads*, and Coleridge had recognised Wordsworth as, potentially, the greatest philosophical poet since Milton. To this end Wordsworth had begun a great poem, 'The Recluse', in which, he had written to a friend, 'I continue to convey most of the knowledge of which I am possessed ... I know not anything which will not come into the scope of my plan.'

'Tintern Abbey' was not only a meditation on the past but also a confident look to the future, and the landscape, no longer merely pictorial, becomes part of the interplay between the poet's memories and the progress of his thoughts. Amid the loneliness and the din of towns and cities, the Wye valley and its 'forms of beauty' remained with Wordsworth, not just as a simple recollection, but as something deeper and more elusive, 'Felt in the blood, and felt along the heart', and leading to:

that serene and blessed mood,
In which the affections gently lead us on,
Until, the breath of this corporeal frame,
And even the motion of our human blood
Almost suspended, we are laid asleep
In body, and become a living soul:
While with an eye made quiet by the power
Of harmony, and the deep power of joy,
We see into the life of things.

In the poem, Wordsworth looks back on his life and sees it as a series of changing responses to nature. First there were the 'coarser pleasures' and 'glad animal movements' of his childhood, when

The sounding cataract
Haunted me like a passion: the tall rock,
The mountain, and the deep and gloomy wood,
Their colours and their forms, were then to me
An appetite: a feeling and a love,
That had no need of a remoter charm,
By thought supplied, or any interest
Unborrowed from the eye.

Then, in adulthood, the landscape becomes interfused with something more internal and intangible. The 'aching joys' and 'dizzy raptures' of youth are lost, but 'other gifts' have followed. Wordsworth now wonderfully expresses these gifts in what he called 'impassioned music'. He gives what amounts to a declaration of faith, a visionary belief in the sustaining power of the natural world that will act as a foundation to his future poetry:

For I have learned
To look on nature, not as in the hour
Of thoughtless youth, but hearing oftentimes
The still, sad music of humanity,
Nor harsh nor grating, though of ample power
To chasten and subdue. And I have felt
A presence that disturbs me with the joy
Of elevated thoughts; a sense sublime

Of something far more deeply interfused,
Whose dwelling is the light of setting suns,
And the round ocean, and the living air,
And the blue sky, and in the mind of man,
A motion and a spirit, that impels
All thinking things, all objects of all thought,
And rolls through all things. Therefore am I still
A lover of the meadows and the woods,
And mountains; and of all that we behold
From this green earth; of all the mighty world
Of ear and eye, both what they half-create,
And what perceive; well pleased to recognize
In nature and the language of the sense,
The anchor of my purest thoughts, the nurse,
The guide, the guardian of my heart, and soul
Of all my moral being.

By the end of 'Tintern Abbey', the landscape has become not only inseparable from the past, but also an integral part of the future. Wordsworth imagines the continuing hold of the landscape over Dorothy's mind:

If solitude, or fear, or pain, or grief,
Should be thy portion, with what healing thoughts
Of tender joy wilt thou remember me,
And these my exhortations! Nor, perchance,
If I should be, where I no more can hear
Thy voice, nor catch from thy wild eyes these gleams
Of past existence, wilt thou then forget
That on the banks of this delightful stream
We stood together; and that I, so long
A worshipper of Nature, hither came,
Unwearied in that service: rather say
With warmer love, oh! with far deeper zeal
Of holier love. Nor wilt thou then forget,
That after many wanderings, many years
Of absence, these steep woods and lofty cliffs,
And this green pastoral landscape, were to me
More dear, both for themselves, and for thy sake.

'Lines written a few miles above Tintern Abbey' was a completely original response to the landscape of the Wye valley, and it would be some time before it gained the popularity it enjoys today. By the 1830s, however, Wordsworth had replaced Gilpin as the representative voice of the Wye. For, despite the poem's few references to the actual scenery, the very fact that it had been written there was enough to associate it, more lastingly than any other work, with the area. In *The Wye and its Associations, A Picturesque Ramble*, published in 1838, Leitch Ritchie felt compelled to quote the lines of 'Tintern Abbey' in full, because, he said, 'our volume would have been incomplete without them'. 'Near this spot,' he wrote of Tintern, 'the great Druid of the Wye, the poet of nature internal and external, produced a poem which in all probability will be read, either with tears or smiles of delight, long after the works of man shall have completely obliterated those features of the grand, the beautiful, the simple, and sublime, to which it is our humble task to point the finger.'

Both the poem and the Wye Valley continued to be a treasured part of Wordsworth's own life. When, in the summer of 1812, his wife Mary visited the area, he wrote to her: 'You cannot think how much dearer the Wye is to me since you have seen it. I loved it deeply before on most tender remembrances & considerations but now that you have seen it also & know it, & we [? now] can talk of it together what a sanctity will it attain in my mind, and of all my Poems The one [in] which I speak of it will be the most beloved by me.— '

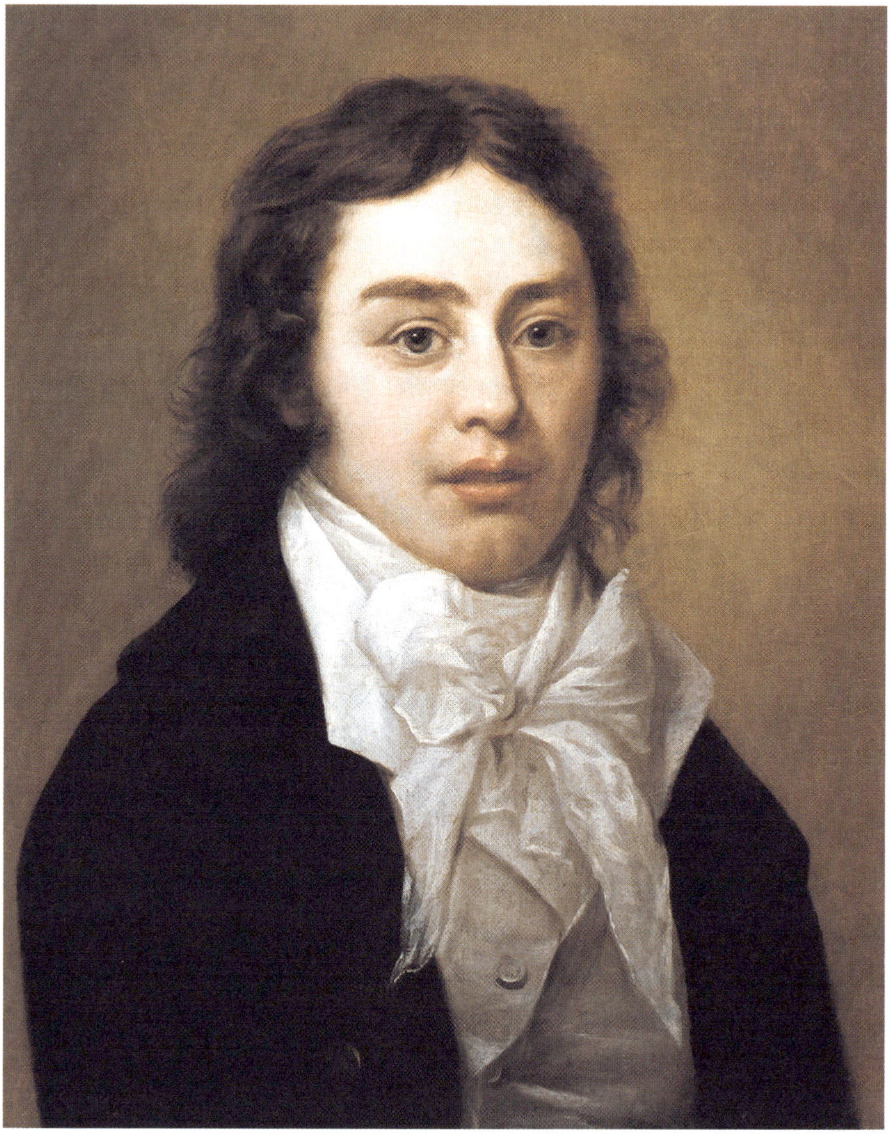

Samuel Taylor Coleridge aged twenty-three, by Peter Vandyke, 1795.

'A QUIET, SPIRIT-HEALING NOOK'

Coleridge and Rural Retirement, 1795–1804

IN JUNE 1799 a notice of *Lyrical Ballads* appeared in the *Monthly Review*. 'The reflections of no common mind,' it said of 'Tintern Abbey', 'poetical, beautiful, and philosophical: but somewhat tinctured with gloomy, narrow and unsociable ideas of seclusion from the commerce of the world: as if men were born to live in woods and wilds, unconnected with each other! Is it not to education and the culture of the mind that we owe the raptures which the author so well describes?' The reviewer was Charles Burney, successful musician and teacher, fellow of the Royal Society, member of the Literary Club, and the friend of Samuel Johnson, Joshua Reynolds, Edmund Burke and David Garrick. He was the author of the highly regarded, four-volume *A General History of Music*. His daughter, the novelist and diarist Fanny Burney, was keeper of the robes at the court of George III. It is hardly surprising that someone so close to the artistic life of London should fail to find culture on the banks of the Wye; for Burney, the landscape, though aesthetically beautiful and a relief from the city, belonged in the end to 'the savage'. It was a place to visit, not a place in which to live and work.

A secluded life in the country was, however, central to Wordsworth's devotion to poetry, to the great task of writing 'The Recluse', and he would soon return, permanently, to his native Lake District. Shortly after writing 'Tintern Abbey', he, Dorothy and Coleridge travelled to Germany, 'in order to acquire the German language, and to furnish ourselves with a tolerable stock of information in natural science'. In Hamburg Wordsworth and Dorothy parted from Coleridge and settled in Goslar, at the foot of the Hartz Mountains. They stayed there for five lonely months, and for much of the time were confined indoors by the worst winter of the century. Isolated and intensely homesick, Wordsworth's thoughts turned to his childhood in the Lake District and, inspired by the conviction that it was here that he would find the foundations for his creative adult life, he began to shape his thoughts into verse. So began, in its earliest form, his great autobiographical poem, *The Prelude*. At the end of February 1799, he and Dorothy left Goslar and, in April, after a tour of the Hartz Mountains, they met up with Coleridge at

Göttingen. Coleridge noticed that Wordsworth was full of 'impatience to return to their native country', and within a week Wordsworth and Dorothy were back in Hamburg. By the end of April they had reached England. Almost immediately they proceeded north to Sockburn-on-Tees in County Durham, the home of their friends the Hutchinsons, brothers Thomas and George, and their sisters Mary, Sara and Joanna.

Coleridge returned from Germany in July. 'I long to see what you have been doing,' he wrote to Wordsworth in October. 'O let it be the tail-piece of "The Recluse!" for of nothing but "The Recluse" can I hear patiently.' Then, without telling his wife, he hastened up to Sockburn with Joseph Cottle, the publisher of *Lyrical Ballads*. They immediately joined Wordsworth on a three-week walking tour of the Lake District. Soon after their departure, at Greta Bridge, Cottle broke off and returned to London, but further on, at Temple Sowerby near the north-east border of the Lake District, Wordsworth and Coleridge were joined by Wordsworth's sailor brother, John, who was enjoying a rare break from the sea. Together they entered the Lake District from the north, walking south through Kentmere to Troutbeck and Hawkshead. From there they proceeded north through the central fells to Ambleside and Grasmere. At Grisedale John Wordsworth left them, while Wordsworth and Coleridge continued north to Keswick. The second part of their journey took them to the wilder lakes in the west: Buttermere, Ennerdale and Wastwater, and, finally, they looped back to the north-east, ending up at Pooley Bridge on the northern shore of Ullswater.

The tour was to have a momentous effect on both poets. At Grasmere, Wordsworth had seen a small cottage available for rent and, separating from Coleridge at Pooley Bridge, he returned there to arrange a lease. By the time Wordsworth had arrived back at Sockburn on 26 November, all the necessary arrangements to take the cottage had been made, and on 17 December he and Dorothy left Sockburn for Grasmere. On the evening of 20 December, after a dramatic winter journey through the Yorkshire Dales, they arrived at their new home in Grasmere, now known as Dove Cottage.

For Coleridge, the tour had been an overwhelming introduction to a new kind of landscape – 'how deeply I have been impressed by a world of scenery absolutely new to me', he wrote afterwards to Dorothy. 'It was to me a vision of a fair Country.' While in the Lakes he had received an offer of work from Daniel Stuart, editor of the *Morning Post*. He accepted immediately, and in November took up residence in London. In his notebook he remarked on the 'harsh contrast' between the city and 'the universal motion, the harmonious

System of Motions, in the country'. In the dim winter light, London seemed like 'a huge place of Sepulchres thro' which Hosts of Spirits were gliding'. For all his attachment to the countryside, however, Coleridge loved the convivial literary life of the capital. For the next four months he applied himself, often brilliantly, to his journalistic work. He saw his old school friend Charles Lamb frequently, befriended the philosopher William Godwin (with whom he talked politics and drank punch), and enjoyed the society of well-known literary ladies like Mary 'Perdita' Robinson (one-time mistress of the Prince of Wales) and the poet Charlotte Smith. But the feeling that his proper place was in the country, and close to Wordsworth, would not go away: 'Where I next settle, I shall continue,' he told Thomas Wedgwood, '& that must be in a state of retirement & rustication.'

Coleridge's fitful but persistent devotion to the secluded rural life had begun six years earlier, in Somerset. In October 1795, after astonishing the citizens of Bristol with a series of fiery political addresses, he had married and spent his honeymoon in Clevedon, a village overlooking the Bristol Channel. 'Low was our pretty Cot,' he recalled affectionately in 'Reflections on having left a Place of Retirement':

> our tallest Rose
> Peep'd at the chamber-window. We could hear
> At silent noon, and eve, and early morn,
> The Sea's faint murmur. In the open air
> Our Myrtles blossom'd; and across the porch
> Thick Jasmins twined: the little landscape round
> Was green and woody, and refresh'd the eye.
> It was a spot which you might aptly call
> The Valley of Seclusion!

But seclusion was of little use to society. 'Was it right,' he continued,

> While my unnumber'd brethren toil'd and bled,
> That I should dream away the entrusted hours
> On rose-leaf beds, pampering the coward heart
> With feelings all too delicate for use?

It was his duty, he concluded, 'to fight the bloodless fight / Of Science, Freedom, and the Truth in Christ', and so he left his pretty cottage, its roses, myrtle and jasmine, and re-engaged with radical politics. He went to the

Midlands and gathered subscribers for a new radical journal, *The Watchman*, with its rousing motto: 'That All may know the Truth; And that the Truth may make us free!!'. He considered becoming a Unitarian minister, or perhaps a schoolmaster in Derby.

Then, abruptly, and characteristically, Coleridge changed his mind. 'I have declined my Derby connection, and determined to retire once [and] for all and utterly from cities and towns,' he wrote in October 1796 to the father of his friend Charles Lloyd. He was, he announced, 'about to take a cottage and half a dozen acres of land in an enchanting situation about eight miles from Bridgewater'. Towns were bad for his health, he said, and he was anxious that his children be brought up 'in the simplicity of peasants, their food, dress and habits completely rustic'. Lloyd Senior, a wealthy banker, pious Quaker and leading light of the Bible Society, was dubious; Coleridge's wish for retirement sounded dangerously like monasticism, Milton's 'fugitive and cloistered virtue ... that never sallies out and seeks her adversary, but slinks out of the race'. Coleridge hastened to justify himself. Yes, he said, he could become a Unitarian minister, or obtain a lucrative job as a politician, but 'the Voice within' said no. 'Can he be deemed monastic who is married, and employed in rearing his children,' he asked, 'who *personally* preaches the truth to his friends and neighbours, and who endeavours to instruct tho' Absent by the Press? In what line of life could I be more *actively* employed?'

To his friend Thomas Poole, a tanner who lived in the small village of Nether Stowey about forty miles from Bristol in the Quantocks, Coleridge wrote: 'To live in a beautiful country & to inure myself as much as possible to the labors of the field, have been for this year past my dream of the day, my Sigh at midnight ... I am anxious beyond measure to be in the country as soon as possible.' (Coleridge later admitted that this was a rather '*flighty* letter', written under the influence of some laudanum he had taken for a sudden and terrifying pain in his face and shoulder.) By the end of the year Poole had found him a possible cottage – one, in fact, close to his own house in Nether Stowey – but, like Lloyd, he had his doubts. Would he be comfortable enough? he asked Coleridge. Would he not be too far from his friends in Bristol? 'But whence comes this sudden revolution in your opinions, my dear Poole?' Coleridge replied, somewhat hurt. 'Lloyd's Father in a letter to me yesterday enquired how I should live without any companions? – I answered him, not an hour before I received your letter – "I shall have six companions – My Sara, my Babe, my own shaping and disquisitive mind, my Books, my beloved Friend, Thomas Poole, & lastly, Nature, looking at me with a

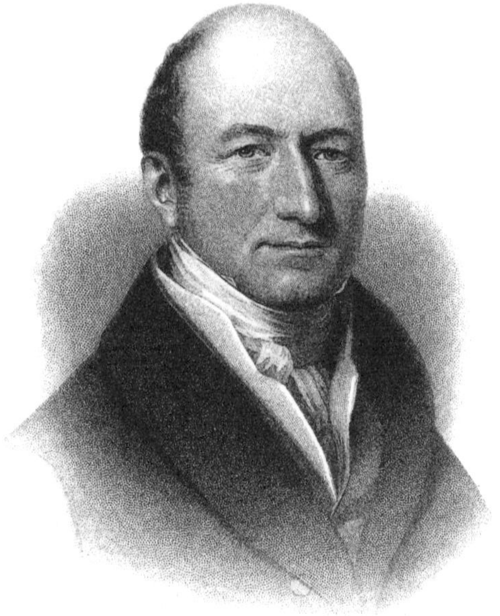

Thomas Poole, by G.J. Stodart after a painting by T. Barber, *c.*1815.

thousand looks of Beauty, and speaking to me in a thousand melodies of Love."' Poole relented, and on the last day of 1796 Coleridge, his wife Sara and baby son Hartley moved to Nether Stowey.

The cottage was indeed, as Poole had hinted, very humble: built hard against the road, it was small, dark, damp, and infested with mice – 'Our little hovel' Coleridge later called it. Within weeks, however, he was boasting to John Thelwall of his new rural life. Every day between breakfast and midday he read and composed; between tea and supper he reviewed. Otherwise, he worked in his garden: he raised potatoes and 'all manner of vegetables' and planned to raise corn; he had ducks, geese, and two pigs, but no cow, 'for we have whatever milk we want from T. Poole'. He never went to Bristol, he said. 'Is it a farm you have got?' asked Charles Lamb with good-natured scepticism, '& what does your worship know about farming? Coleridge, I want you to write an Epic poem.' For the moment, however, epic poems were not forthcoming. Instead Coleridge tinkered with existing works like 'The Destiny Of Nations'; 'I torture the poem, and myself, with corrections,' he told his publisher Joseph Cottle. And there were other distractions. Charles

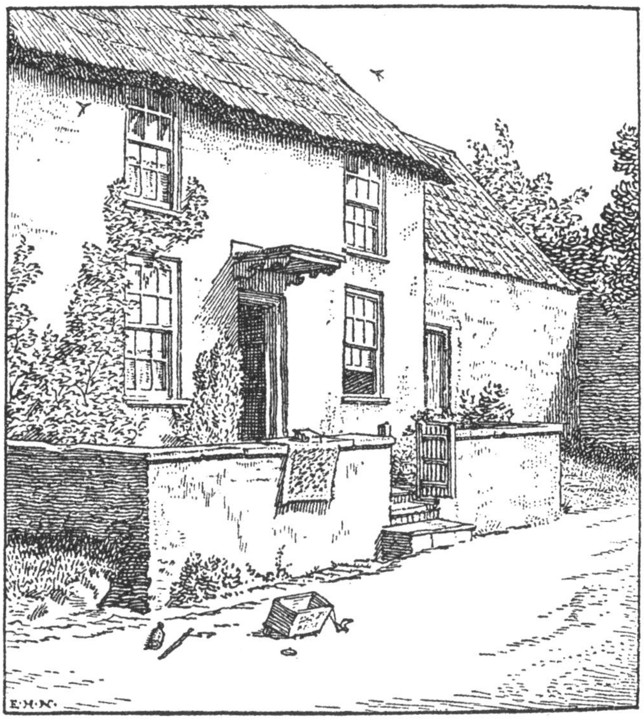

Coleridge's cottage at Nether Stowey, by Edmund H. New, 1913.

Lloyd Junior was sharing the cottage, and though a fellow poet, a keen disciple and a paying guest, he was also, it turned out, mentally unstable, and for some weeks, before Lloyd's eventual departure for a sanatorium, Coleridge was forced into the exhausting role of nurse.

Then in the spring of 1797, his retired life received an unexpected but very welcome boost. Since 1795 William Wordsworth had been living quietly at Racedown in remotest Dorset, where he read, wrote, and took morning walks with Dorothy. 'We are now at Racedown and both as happy as people can be who live in perfect solitude,' he had written to his friend William Matthews soon after his arrival. 'We do not see a soul.' In early April, after a visit to Bristol, Wordsworth stopped off in Nether Stowey on his way back to Racedown. The two poets had met occasionally in Bristol, and thought highly of each other; they now rapidly became close friends. In June, Coleridge visited Racedown, stayed for a month, then returned home bringing the Wordsworths with him (just as Charles Lamb arrived from London for a week's stay). By July, the Wordsworths had left Racedown, and taken a year's lease of Alfoxden, a large house set in its own deer park and, vitally, only a few

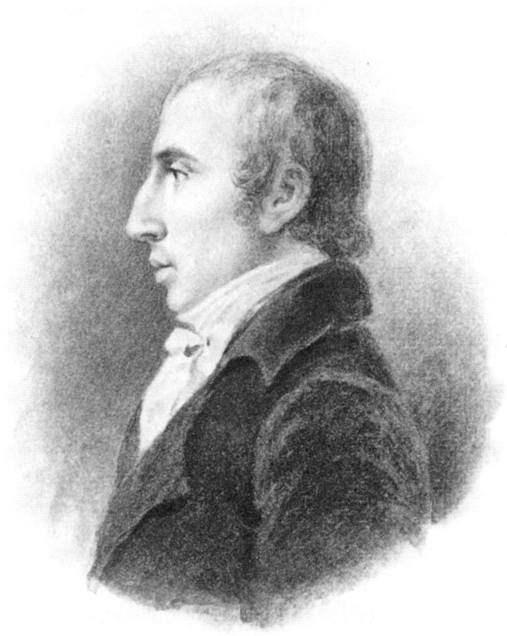

William Wordsworth, after Robert Hancock, 1798.

miles from Coleridge at Nether Stowey. 'Here I have *settled them,'* Coleridge told Robert Southey, his brother-in-law and fellow poet. 'Wordsworth is a very great man – the only man, to whom *at all times* & in *all modes of excellence* I feel myself inferior ... the London Literati appear to me to be very much like little Potatoes – i.e. *no great Things!'*

There followed twelve wonderful months of walks, reading, writing, and stimulating talk – the realisation, it must have seemed, of the productive life among nature that Coleridge had dreamt of when first moving to the Quantocks. Dorothy kept a journal, and from it we can see how deeply the landscape worked its way into their imaginations. Here, for instance, is her entry for 26 February 1798:

> Coleridge came in the morning, and Mr and Mrs Cruikshank; walked with Coleridge nearly to Stowey after dinner. A very clear afternoon. We lay sidelong upon the turf, and gazed on the landscape till it melted into more than natural loveliness. The sea very uniform, of a pale greyish blue, only one distant bay, bright and blue as a sky; had there

been a vessel sailing up it, a perfect image of delight. Walked to the top of a high hill to see a fortification. Again sat down to feed upon the prospect; a magnificent scene, *curiously* spread out for even minute inspection, though so extensive that the mind is afraid to calculate its bounds. A winter prospect shows every cottage, every farm, and the forms of distant trees such as in summer have no distinguishing mark. On our return, Jupiter and Venus before us. While the twilight still overpowered the light of the moon, we were reminded that she was shining bright above our heads, by our faint shadows going before us. We had seen her on the tops of the hills, melting into the blue sky.

'I love fields & woods & mounta[ins] with an almost visionary fondness,' Coleridge told his brother George. In 'The Eolian Harp', written at Clevedon, he had imagined nature as a series of Aeolian harps, simple stringed instruments which, when placed in a sash window, were played by the wind:

And what if all of animated nature
Be but organic Harps diversely fram'd,
That tremble into thought, as o'er them sweeps
Plastic and vast, one intellectual Breeze
At once the soul of each, and God of all?

This intimation of a religious spirit in nature imbues the series of meditative blank-verse poems that he now wrote at Nether Stowey. The first of these, 'This Lime-tree Bower my Prison', dates from the Wordsworths' and Charles Lamb's visit to Nether Stowey in June. On the second day of their stay Sara Coleridge had accidentally spilled boiling milk over her husband's foot, so confining him to the cottage, and in the poem he imagines his friends taking an evening walk over the hills:

Yes! they wander on
In gladness all; but thou, methinks, most glad,
My gentle-hearted Charles! for thou hast pined
And hunger'd after Nature, many a year,
In the great City pent, winning thy way
With sad yet patient soul, through evil and pain
And strange calamity! Ah! slowly sink
Behind the western ridge, thou glorious Sun!
Shine in the slant beams of the sinking orb,

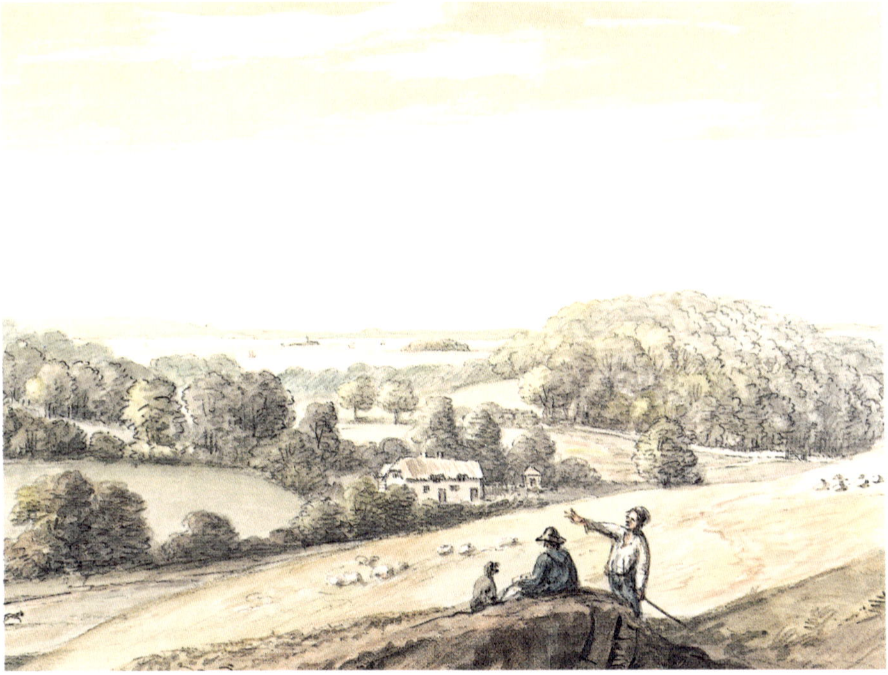

A view of Alfoxden, by Coplestone Warre Bampfylde.

Ye purple heath-flowers! richlier burn, ye clouds!
Live in the yellow light, ye distant groves!
And kindle, thou blue Ocean! So my Friend
Struck with deep joy may stand, as I have stood,
Silent with swimming sense; yea, gazing round
On the wide landscape, gaze till all doth seem
Less gross than bodily; and of such hues
As veil the Almighty Spirit, when yet he makes
Spirits perceive his presence.

The second poem, 'Frost at Midnight', was composed the following February. It begins with Coleridge sitting at home late one evening, watching the fire and listening to the soft breathing of his sleeping son as 'the frost performs its secret ministry'. Thinking back to his own childhood, 'In the great city, pent 'mid cloisters dim', he imagines Hartley growing up around nature:

But *thou*, my babe! shalt wander like a breeze
By lakes and sandy shores, beneath the crags

Of ancient mountain, and beneath the clouds,
Which image in their bulk both lakes and shores
And mountain crags: so shalt thou see and hear
The lovely shapes and sounds intelligible
Of that eternal language, which thy God
Utters, who from eternity doth teach
Himself in all, and all things in himself.

In these poems man and nature are seen in complete harmony, united by 'the one intellectual breeze', or what Wordsworth would call in 'Tintern Abbey' the 'motion and spirit' that 'rolls through all things'.

Visitors came to the Quantocks and were enchanted. John Thelwall, the prominent radical with whom Coleridge had been corresponding for some time, arrived shortly after the Wordsworths' move to Alfoxden. In 1794, in a celebrated case, Thelwall had been tried and acquitted of High Treason, and had then become a star of the regional lecture circuit. But now he was exhausted and in poor health, and, relentlessly pursued by his opponents, was looking to withdraw from public affairs. The 'Academus of Stowey', as he called it, delighted him. He wrote to his wife soon after his arrival:

> We have been having a delightful ramble to-day among the plantations, and along a wild, romantic dell in these grounds, through which a foaming, rushing, murmuring torrent of water winds its long artless course. There have we … a literary and political triumvirate, passed sentence on the productions and characters of the age, burst forth in poetical flights of enthusiasm, and philosophised our minds into a state of tranquillity, which the leaders of nations might envy, and the residents of cities can never know.

'We were sitting in a beautiful recess in the Quantocks,' Coleridge recalled many years later, 'when I said to him, "citizen John, this is a fine place to talk treason in!" "Nay, citizen Samuel," replied he, "it is rather a place to make a man forget that there is any necessity for treason!"' Thelwall dreamed of settling nearby. In his poem 'Lines written at Bridgewater' he wrote fondly:

Ah! let me then, far from the strifeful scenes
Of public life (where Reason's warning voice
Is heard no longer, and the trump of Truth

Who blows but wakes The Ruffian Crew of Power
To deeds of maddest anarchy and blood)
Ah! let me, far in some sequester'd dell,
Build my low cot; most happy might it prove,
My Samuel! near to thine, that I might oft
Share thy sweet converse, best-belov'd of friends!—
Long-lov'd ere known: for kindred sympathies
Link'd, tho far distant, our congenial souls.

But even in retirement, politics would not go away. The country, fearful of a French invasion, was on edge, and Coleridge and Wordsworth, with their mildly radical pasts, had already stirred up the small rural community. Coleridge now told Thelwall that his coming to live there would cause uproar. 'Very great odium T. Poole incurred by bringing *me* here,' he wrote, 'my peaceable manners & known attachment to Christianity had almost worn it away – when Wordsworth came & he likewise by T. Poole's agency settled here – You cannot conceive the tumult, calumnies, & apparatus of threatened persecutions which this event has occasioned round about us. If *you* too should come, I am afraid, that even riots & dangerous riots might be the consequence.' Unbeknown to them at the time, Thelwall had in fact been followed to Somerset by a government spy who, after observing their animated conversations and frequent walks by both day and night, concluded that they were a 'Sett of violent democrats'. So Thelwall left Nether Stowey and eventually, after four months of searching, found a place for himself and his family at Llys-Wen, a remote village on the upper reaches of the Wye.

Another visitor, the young William Hazlitt, came to Nether Stowey the following spring. In his later essay of 1823, 'My First Acquaintance with Poets', he drew a series of vivid pictures of poetic life in the Quantocks as lit by his youthful enthusiasm: strolls through Alfoxden Park after breakfast; Coleridge reading aloud while they sat 'on the trunk of an old ash-tree that stretched along the ground'; the sound of Coleridge's voice 'as we passed through echoing grove, by fairy stream or waterfall, gleaming in the summer moonlight!'; Wordsworth noticing the beauty of a sunset – 'I thought within myself, "With what eyes these poets see nature!"' 'Thus I passed three weeks at Nether Stowey and in the neighbourhood,' Hazlitt remembered, 'generally devoting the afternoons to a delightful chat in an arbour made of bark by the poet's friend Tom Poole, sitting under two fine elm-trees, and listening to the bees humming round us, while we quaffed our *flip*.'

But the question that Coleridge had asked himself at Clevedon remained: of what use was the retired life? In 1794 Wordsworth had been left £900 by a friend, Raisley Calvert, 'from a confidence on his part', Wordsworth said, 'that I had powers and attainments that might be of use to mankind'. And in January 1798 Coleridge had been given an annuity by the Wedgwoods, the famous potters, of £150 a year for life, to give him a permanent income and to free him from everyday distractions. These gifts brought independence, but also a sense of personal responsibility; retirement had to be justified, not by occasional poems, but by philosophical work on a grand scale – the epic poem that Lamb had requested. Coleridge began a projected long work, 'The Brook', but soon abandoned it. More promisingly, Wordsworth started on 'The Recluse', but by this time the lease on Alfoxden was about to expire and Coleridge was anxious that Wordsworth should find other accommodation nearby: 'we must', he wrote to Cottle, 'for the hills, and the woods, and the streams, and the sea, and the shores would break forth into reproaches against us, if we did not strain every nerve, to keep their Poet among them'. Wordsworth had become part of the landscape.

In the meantime, however, there was their trip to Germany, and shortly before setting sail from Yarmouth, Coleridge rapidly put together a further collection: *Fears in Solitude*. It contained just three poems: 'France: An Ode', 'Frost at Midnight', and the title poem, written from 'a green and silent spot, amid the hills', and a celebration of his life in the Quantocks:

Oh! 'tis a quiet spirit-healing nook!
Which all, methinks, would love; but chiefly he,
The humble man, who, in his youthful years,
Knew just so much of folly, as had made
His early manhood more securely wise!
Here he might lie on fern or withered heath,
While from the singing lark (that sings unseen
The minstrelsy that solitude loves best),
And from the sun, and from the breezy air,
Sweet influences trembled o'er his frame;
And he, with many feelings, many thoughts,
Made up a meditative joy, and found
Religious meanings in the forms of Nature!

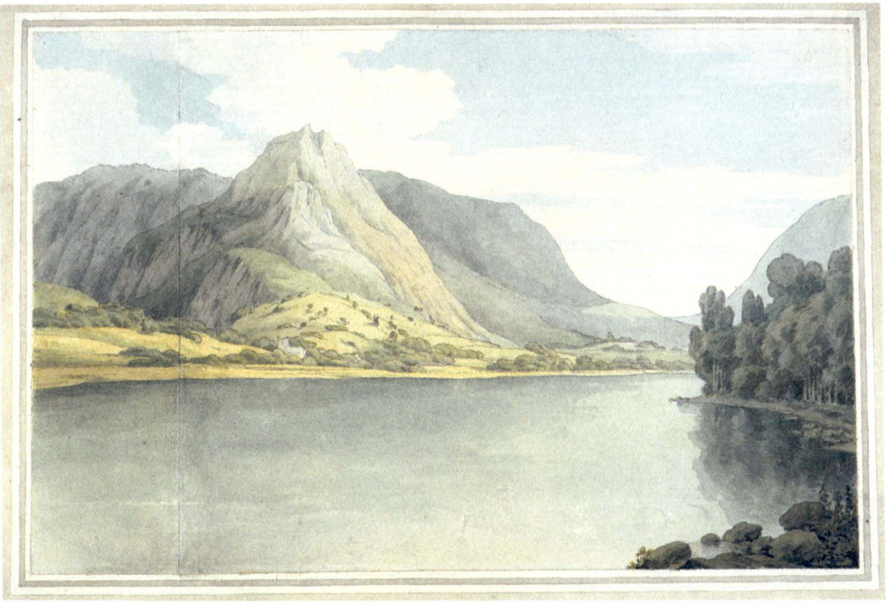

A watercolour of Grasmere, by John White Abbott, 1812.

'I would to God, I could get Wordsworth to re-take Alfoxden,' Coleridge told Poole after his return from Germany, 'the Society of so great a Being is of priceless Value.' But since their tour of the Lakes together he had realised that the chances of luring him away from his native north were small: 'he will never quit the north of England – his habits are more assimilated with the inhabitants there – there he & his Sister are exceedingly beloved, enthusiastically. Such difference do small Sympathies make – such as Voice, Pronunciation, &c – for from what other Cause can I account for it – .'

Accordingly, on 2 April, Coleridge travelled to Grasmere. His London friends were sorry to see him go. 'Coleridge has left us, to go into the North,' grumbled Charles Lamb, 'on a visit to his God, Wordsworth.' Godwin called on Lamb and they stayed up till midnight drinking punch and talking about their absent friend. 'He [Godwin] seems, above all men, mortified at your going away,' Lamb told Coleridge. But Coleridge's mind was made up. 'If I cannot procure a suitable house at Stowey, I return to Cumberland & settle at Keswick ... I shall be in a beautiful country ... and you must come and write your next work at my house,' he wrote to Godwin (who would successfully resist this and repeated invitations to come north). On 4 May Coleridge went to Bristol to pick up Sara and Hartley, made one last, half-hearted attempt to find a house in the West Country, and then on Sunday 29 June 'rearrived

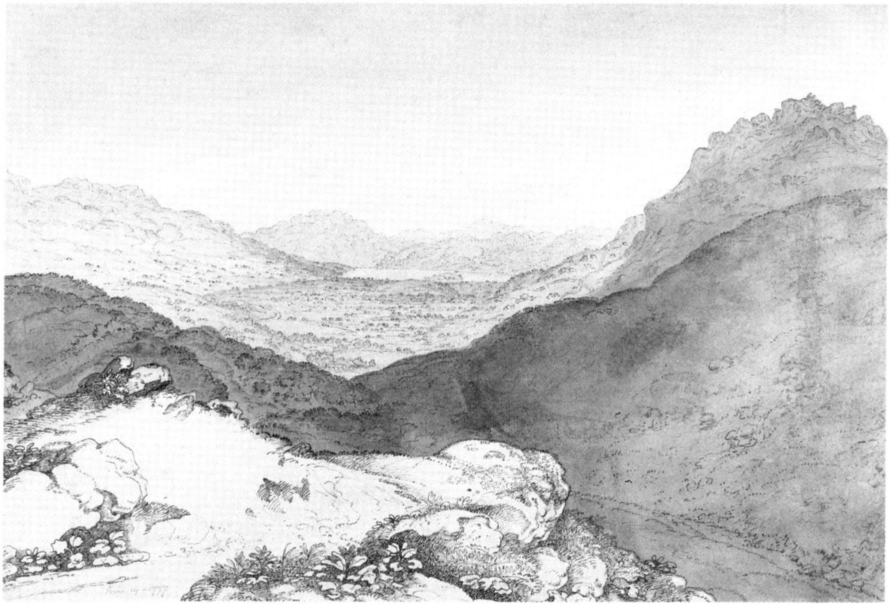

Grasmere, looking south from Dunmail Raise, by Joseph Farington, 1777.

at Grasmere' with the intention of settling at Greta Hall, the house he had found at Keswick. He remained in Grasmere for another month, and with Wordsworth began work on a second edition of *Lyrical Ballads*. Shortly before his departure he and the Wordsworths rowed out to the island on the lake, where they drank tea. Later that day they made a bonfire on the shore:

> I lay & saw the wood, & mountains, & lake all trembling, & as it were *idealized* thro' the subtle smoke which rose up from the clear red embers of the fir-apples which we had collected. Afterwards, we made a glorious Bonfire on the Margin, by some alder bushes, whose twigs heaved & sobbed in the uprushing column of smoke – & the Image of the Bonfire, & of us that danced round it – ruddy laughing faces in the twilight – the Image of this in a Lake smooth as that sea, to whose waves the Son of God has said, PEACE!

Coleridge was not the first, or last, person to see Grasmere as a kind of rural paradise. Lying in the centre of the Lake District, midway between Windermere in the south and Derwentwater in the north, its village and lake are enclosed on all sides by fells: Loughrigg, Silver How, Helm Crag, Seat Sandal, Stone Arthur. It was a place that had poets and travellers dreaming of blissful retirement, the apparent embodiment of a literary ideal of rural life that went back to Horace and Theocritus. Approaching Grasmere over Dunmail Raise from the north, in 1769, the poet Thomas Gray looked down into the valley and saw 'one of the sweetest landscapes, that art ever attempted to imitate. ... not a single red tile, no flaring Gentleman's house, or garden-walls, break in upon the repose of this little unsuspected paradise, but all is peace, & rusticity, & happy poverty in its neatest most becoming attire'. William Hutchinson, in his account of his tour of the Lakes in 1776, described how he and his companion happily renewed 'a succession of pastoral images we had collected from the poets in our early years, when the young mind was charmed with romance, and the most fantastic ideas of rural innocence, retirement and love'. Grasmere was perfect: 'a retirement surrounded by hills on every hand ... It seemed to be the vale of peace.' While still a schoolboy at Hawkshead Grammar School, Wordsworth had walked over the fells until he found himself on the top of a fell, looking down upon the vale of Grasmere, and he too had thought it a paradise:

> Once on the brow of yonder Hill I stopped
> While I was yet a School-boy (of what age
> I cannot well remember though the year be gone),
> And, with a sudden influx overcome
> At sight of this seclusion, I forgot
> My haste, for hasty had my footsteps been
> As boyish my pursuits; and sighing said,
> 'What happy fortune were it here to live!
> And if I thought of dying, if a thought
> Of mortal separation could come in
> With paradise before me, here to die.'

Wordsworth had now come to this 'abiding place' of 'Perfect Contentment, Unity entire' to devote himself to 'The Recluse'. It was a struggle that would preoccupy him over the coming years as he sought to justify, as a poet, his retreat to Grasmere, and would eventually result in his greatest poetry. Between his arrival in December 1799 and October the following year, he composed a series of poems that he grouped together as 'Poems on the Naming of Places'. They see him bringing the local landscape into his imagination, naming, according to rural custom, places that were connected with particular incidents, friends or feelings. In 'It was an April Morning', he comes

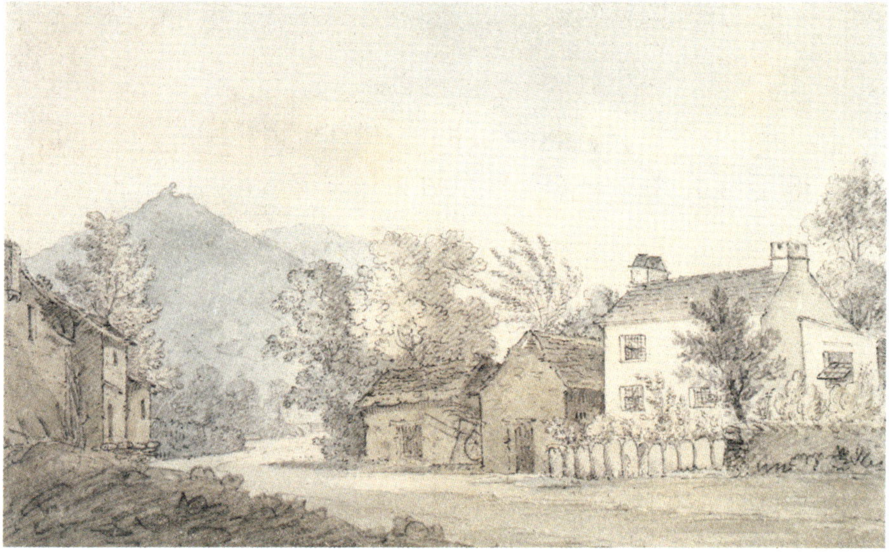

A watercolour by Dora Wordsworth, showing Helm Crag (left) and Dove Cottage (right).

upon a 'wild nook' of waterfall, rocks and trees and names it Emma's Dell (Emma being, in the poem, his name for Dorothy). 'To Joanna' is rich with local place names: the River Rothay, Silver How, Helvellyn, Hammar-Scar, Fairfield, Skiddaw, Glaramara, Kirkstone, and Helm Crag with the 'ancient Woman' formed by the outcrop of rocks on its summit. 'A narrow circle of rough stones and crags' describes an encounter between Wordsworth, Coleridge and Dorothy, and a fisherman on the shore of Grasmere lake. After expressing surprise that someone should be so idle in mid harvest, they approach to find a sick man 'Too weak to labour in the harvest field', and so 'using his best skill to gain / A pittance from the dead unfeeling lake'. Suitably admonished, they name the spot 'POINT RASH-JUDGEMENT'. And in 'To M.H.', Wordsworth names a favourite nook among beech trees after Mary Hutchinson, his future wife:

> And if a man should plant his cottage near,
> Should sleep beneath the shelter of its trees,
> And blend its waters with his daily meal,
> He would so love it that in his death-hour
> Its image would survive among his thoughts,
> And therefore, my sweet MARY, this still nook
> With all its beeches we have named for you.

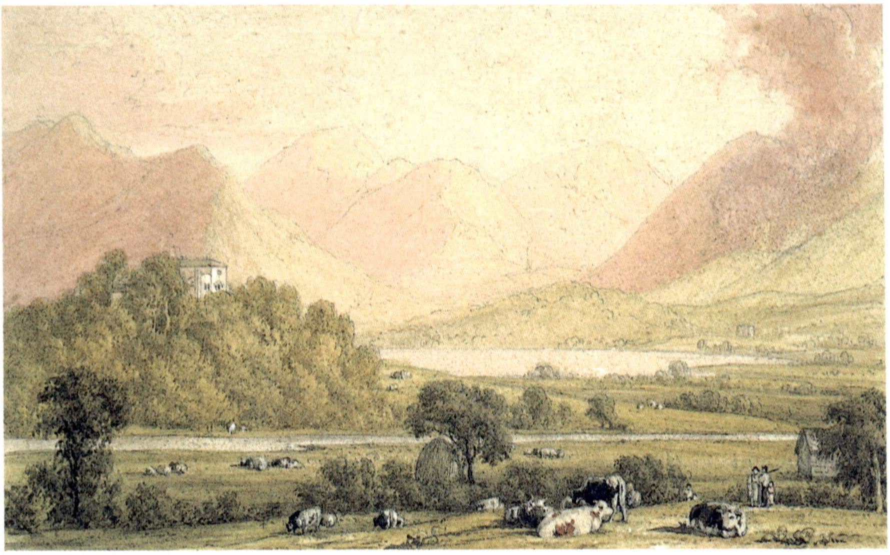

The Vale of Keswick, by William Westall. Greta Hall is shown on the left.

Coleridge saw how rooted his friend had become: 'Wordsworth remains at Grasmere till next summer (perhaps longer),' he wrote to James Webbe Tobin. 'His cottage is indeed in every respect so delightful a residence, the walks so dry after the longest rains, the heath and a silky kind of fern so luxurious a bedding on every hilltop, and the whole vicinity so tossed about on those little hills at the feet of the majestic mountains, that he moves in an eddy; he cannot get out of it.'

On 24 July, Coleridge and his family took possession of Greta Hall, a roomy house built on a hill just outside Keswick, twelve miles north of Grasmere. There was a large garden, at the bottom of which was a delightful shaded walk along the River Greta. Greta Hall had originally been an observatory, and the views were stunning: a sweeping panorama of fields, lakes and fells. 'Yes – my dear Sir! – here I am,' Coleridge wrote to Samuel Purkis in high excitement,

> with Skiddaw at my back – on my right hand the Bassenthwait Water with it's majestic *Case* of Mountains, all of simplest Outline – looking slant, direct over the feather of this infamous Pen, I see the Sun setting – my God! what a scene – ! Right before me is a great *Camp* of single mountains – each in shape resembles a Giant's Tent! – and to the left, but closer to it far than Bassenthwaite Water to my right, is the lake

> of Keswick, with it's Islands & white sails, & glossy Lights of Evening – *crowned* with green meadows, but the three remaining sides are encircled by the most fantastic mountains, that ever Earthquakes made in sport; as fantastic, as if Nature had *laughed* herself into the convulsion, in which they were made.

'I question, if there be a room in England which commands a view of Mountains & Lakes & Woods & Vales superior to that, in which I am now sitting,' he wrote to Godwin, adding pointedly, 'I say this, because it is destined for your Study, if you come.' The new landscape exhilarated him, and in letter after letter, notebook entry after notebook entry, he tried to put the mercurial effects of weather, light and water into words: 'The water leaden white, even as the grey gleam of water in latest Twilight. – Now thinning the break over the road is swallowed up, & the Stars gone, the break over the House is narrowed into a rude Circle, & on the edge of its circumference one very bright Star – see! already the white mass, thinning at its edge, *fights* with its Brilliance – see! it has bedimmed it, & now it is gone – & the Moon is gone. The Cock-crowing too has ceased. The Greta sounds on, for ever. But I hear only the Ticking of my Watch, in the Pen-place of my Writing Desk, & the far lower voice of quiet change, of Destruction doing its work by little & little.' Such was the hold this view had on him, he told his friend Francis Wrangham, that he could not shave in the morning without cutting himself: 'Some Mountain or Peak is rising out of the Mist, or some slanting Column of misty Sunlight is sailing cross me so that I offer up soap & blood daily, as an Eye-servant of the Goddess Nature.' 'This grand panorama of mountain scenery,' Thomas De Quincey later wrote of this view, 'so varied, so expansive, and yet having the delightful feeling about it of a deep seclusion and dell-like sequestration from the world.'

When he wasn't gazing from his window, Coleridge went exploring. He had once told John Thelwall: 'my gait is awkward, & the walk, & the *Whole man* indicates *indolence capable of energies*', and it was with a great rush of energy that he now went clambering over the hills around Keswick. In 1800, fell walking was not the popular pursuit it is today. The first recorded walking tour of the Lakes had been made only eight years before by the intrepid Captain Joseph Budworth, writer, antiquary and one-armed veteran of the siege of Gibraltar. For Budworth, walking was a physical challenge, synonymous with good health and a hearty appetite. His ascent of Helm Crag, he tells us in his *Ramble through the Lakes*, was made after 'as good and

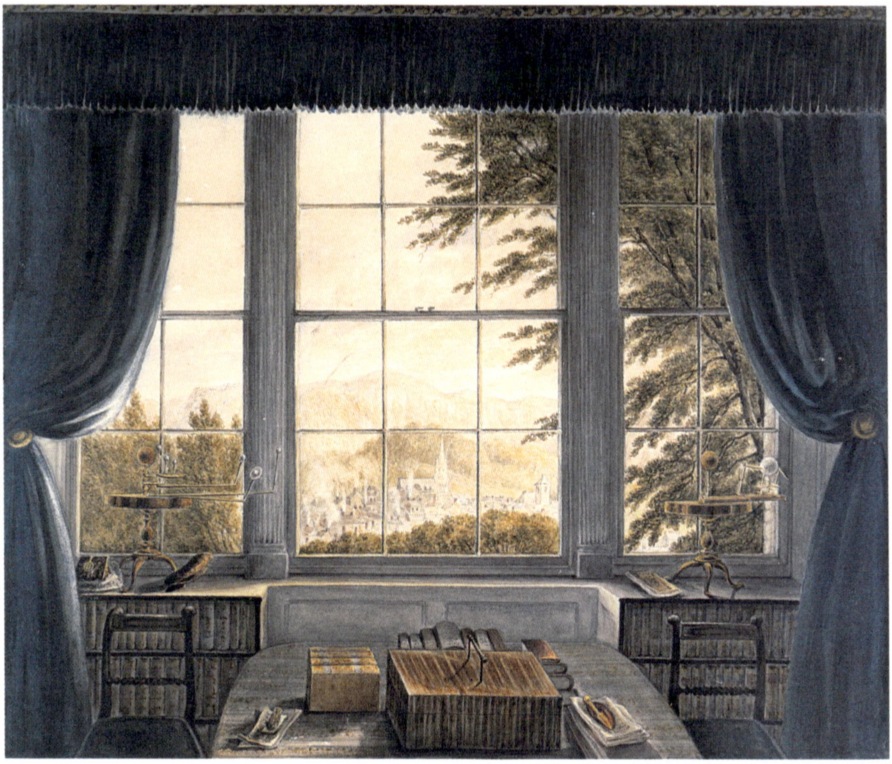

The study window at Greta Hall, by Caroline Bowles, 1841.

well-dressed a dinner … as man could wish': 'Roast pike, stuffed, A boiled fowl, Veal cutlets and ham, Beans and bacon, Cabbage, Pease and potatoes, Anchovey sauce, Parsley and butter, Plain butter, Butter and cheese, Wheat bread and oat cake, Three cups of preserved gooseberries, with a bowl of rich cream in the centre, For two people, at ten pence a head.' The ascent itself is a grand adventure, with winds, perilous ridges, and a country, he is pleased to note, that has been 'seldom frequented but by foxes, sheep and ravens: our guide was never on it but once, and neither he nor Partridge remember that it has been visited by strangers'.

Wordsworth's acquaintance from Bristol, the Reverend Richard Warner, was another devotee of walking. On his tour of Wales he had walked 462 miles in just eighteen days (an average of twenty-six miles a day). He later claimed that his account of this tour 'originated a taste, among the younger part of my countrymen, for pedestrian tours into the principality … it animated the old to resume the use of their legs; and inspired the fair sex, with a desire to emulate my exertions; or, (which I would rather believe) to follow my

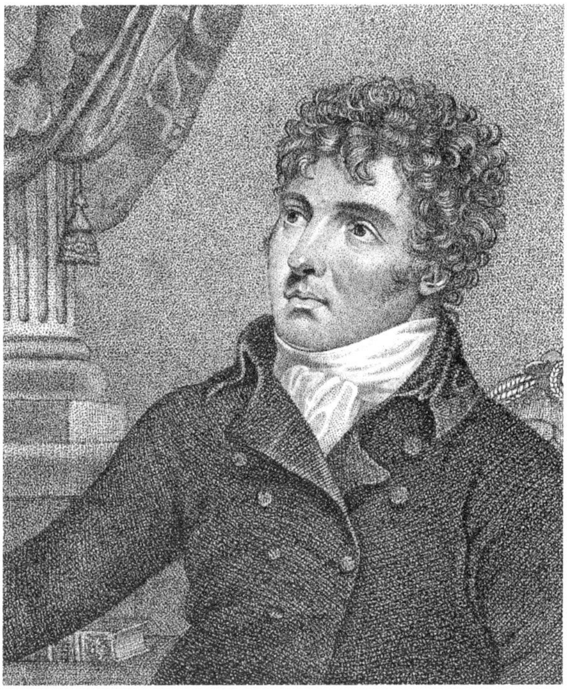

Richard Warner, by S. Harding after S. Williams, 1800.

example'. Warner delighted in the practical side of walking – for instance how best to carry one's belongings. The solution of one pedestrian party he met with in Cardiganshire particularly impressed him:

> Each of the gentlemen (for there were three of them) carried a handsome leathern bag, covered with neat net-work, which, being suspended from the right shoulder by a strap, hung under the left arm, in the manner of a shooting-bag. This was occasionally shifted from one shoulder to the other, and at the same time that it proved a most convenient conveyance for linen, &c. was no inelegant addition to the person; at least, it gave the wearer much less the appearance of a pedlar than attached to us, from the enormous side-pockets of my companion, and my own swoln Spencer. It is proper to note also, that, in addition to our stock of necessaries, we each found it convenient to provide ourselves with a small drinking-horn; for although we had no difficulty in procuring milk, and other sorts of beverage, yet the vessels from which we quaffed these potations were not always so clean as those we had been accustomed to use.

But walking for Coleridge was much more than a genteel pastime. It stimulated and enriched his extraordinary imagination; it was a deeply felt engagement with 'the grand outline & perpetual Forms, that are the guardians of Borrodale, & the presiding Majesty, yea, the very Soul of Keswick'. He went everywhere, usually alone, and in a series of scintillating notebook entries endeavoured to capture the most transient and elusive effects of light and shade, and their play on his emotions:

> I have come suddenly upon Ulswater, running straight on the opposite Bank, till the Placefell, that noble Promontory runs into it, & gives it the winding of a majestic River, a little below Placefell a large Slice of calm silver – above this a bright ruffledness, or atomic sportiveness – motes in the sun? – Vortices of flies? – how shall I express the Banks waters all fused Silver, that House too its slates rainwet silver in the sun, & its shadows running down in the water like a column – the Woods on the right shadowy with Sunshine, and in front of me the sloping hollow of sunpatched Fields, sloping up into Hills so playful, the playful Hills so going away in snow-streaked savage black mountain – But I have omitted the two island Rocks in the Lake – & the colors of the Lake all changed! the one scarce visible in the shadow-coloured Slip now bordered by the melted Silver – the other nearer to me, likewise in the glossy shadow, but far removed from the Dazzle & quite conspicuous – The Sun, it being just past noon, hangs over the Lake – clouded so that any but a weak eye might gaze on it – the clouds being in part bright white, part dusky Rain-clouds, with islets of blue Sky – How the scene changes – what tongues of Light shoot out from the Banks!

And like all serious walkers Coleridge paid careful attention to his footwear. He had casts made of the exact shape of his feet, and treated his boots with a mixture of his own: 'Mutton suet 1. Hog's Lard 2. Venice Turpentine ½ – all mixed & melted – always put on warm, Shoe or boot being held to the fire, while it is being rubbed in – The middle sole of the Boot covered with Cobbler's wax – or still better, steeped thoroughly in the above Composition – the Leather of the Boot should be stout Horse leather – if none to be had, Cow-leather – a piece of oil Silk 6 inches above the Heel, 2 inches wide with a back strap to the Boots.'

At the beginning of August, Coleridge had a memorable encounter on the summit of Skiddaw, the highest of the fells around Keswick. 'I was

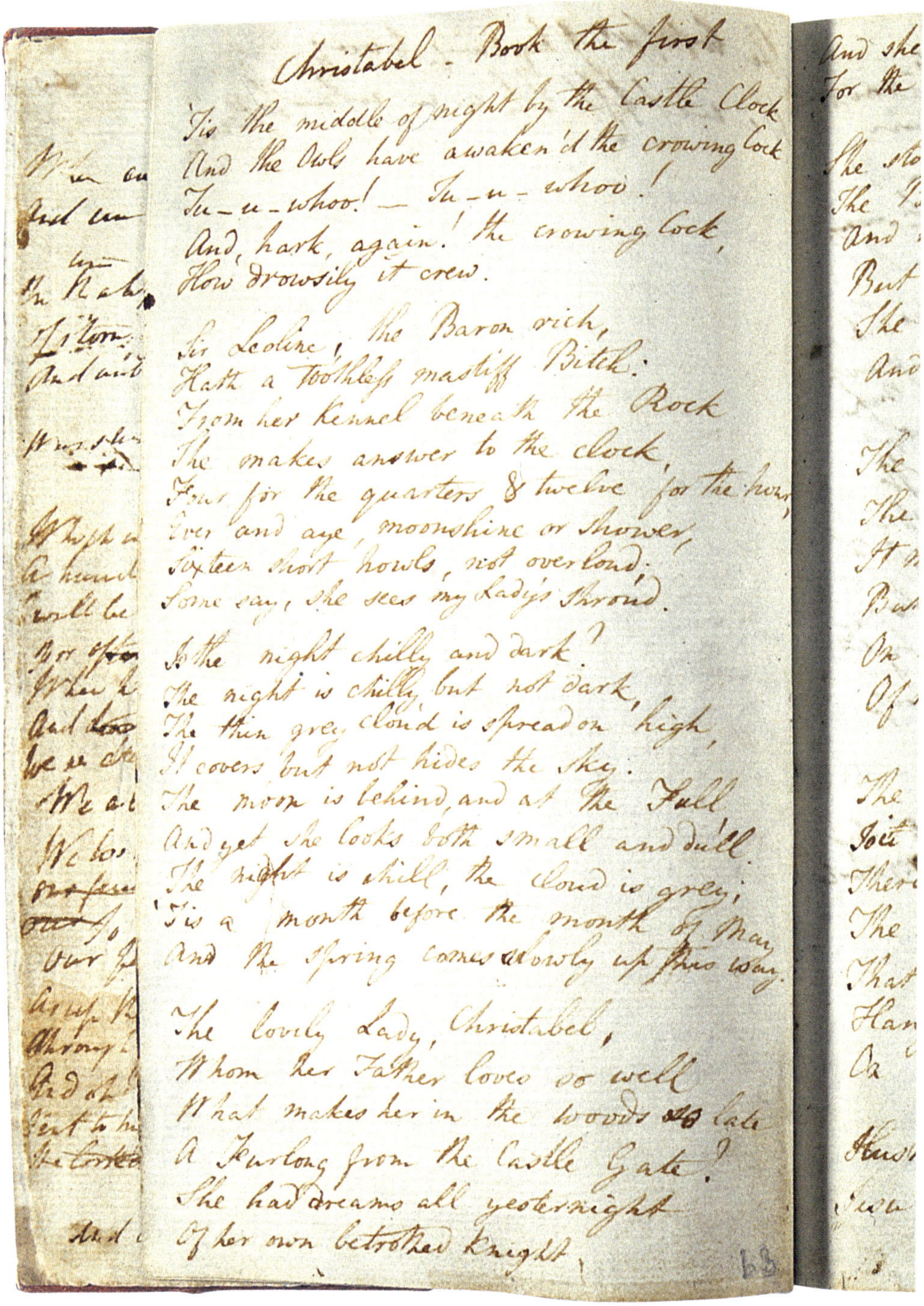
Christabel – Book the first

'Tis the middle of night by the Castle Clock
And the Owls have awaken'd the crowing Cock
Tu-u-whoo! – Tu-u-whoo!
And hark, again! the crowing Cock,
How drowsily it crew.

Sir Leoline, the Baron rich,
Hath a toothless mastiff Bitch:
From her kennel beneath the Rock
She makes answer to the clock,
Four for the quarters & twelve for the hour,
Ever and aye, moonshine or shower,
Sixteen short howls, not overloud;
Some say, she sees my Lady's Shroud.

Is the night chilly and dark?
The night is chilly, but not dark,
The thin grey cloud is spread on high,
It covers but not hides the sky.
The moon is behind, and at the Full
And yet she looks both small and dull.
The night is chill, the cloud is grey;
'Tis a month before the month of May
And the Spring comes slowly up this way.

The lovely Lady, Christabel,
Whom her Father loves so well
What makes her in the woods so late
A Furlong from the Castle Gate?
She had dreams all yesternight
Of her own betrothed Knight,

The earliest surviving manuscript of Coleridge's poem 'Christabel', 1802.

standing on the very top of Skiddaw,' he told Thomas Poole, 'by a little Shed of Slatestones on which I had scribbled with a bit of slate my name among the other names – a lean expressive-faced Man came up the Hill, stood beside me, a little while, then running over the names, exclaimed, *Coleridge!* I lay my life, that is the *Poet Coleridge.*' On 29 August, he set out for Grasmere with the manuscript of the recently completed Book II of 'Christabel' in his pocket. Walking first to the neighbouring village of Threlkeld, he then continued towards the high ridge that ran south towards Helvellyn: 'Ascended, straight up, for at least an hour – and O! how glad was I at last to see blue sky on the other side.' He trudged on towards the summit of White Pike over heathy, boggy ground, 'ground which in a wet time would, I suppose, be unsafe', he wrote in his journal. For the next few hours he walked along the ridge to Helvellyn, all the time noting his impressions and progress in his journal: 'From this point I hear swelling & sinking a murmur – is it of water? or is it of falling screes? – Fine columns of misty sunshine sailing slowly over the crags. I make for the water – it runs down that green Mountain which is so directly behind that which I first ascended & somewhat higher than it. I drank, & was refreshed ...' By the time he began his descent to Dunmail Raise and Grasmere it was growing dark:

> travelling along the ridge I came to the other side of those precipices and down below me on my left – no – no! no words can convey any idea of this prodigious wildness that precipice fine on this side was but its ridge, sharp as a jagged knife, level so long, and then ascending so boldly – what a frightful bulgy precipice I stand on and to my right how the Crag which corresponds to the other, how it plunges down, like a waterfall, reaches a level steepness, and again plunges!
>
> The Moon is above Fairfield almost at the full! – now descended over a perilous peat-moss then down a Hill of stones all dark ...

From Dumail Raise he walked by road to Dove Cottage. Dorothy recorded his arrival in her journal:

> At 11 o'clock Coleridge came when I was walking in the still, clear moonshine in the garden – he came over Helvellyn – Wm was gone to bed & John also, worn out with his ride round Coniston. We sate & chatted till ½ past three W in his dressing gown. Coleridge read us a part of Christabel. Talked much about the mountains &c &c ...

It was the high point of the summer and, perhaps, of Coleridge's life in the Lake District. For as winter approached his life began to unravel, and the second book of 'Christabel' was, perhaps, his last great poetic achievement. The new edition of *Lyrical Ballads* was published in two volumes in January 1801, but it was largely the work of Wordsworth. All the new poems that made up the second volume were his, and the unfinished 'Christabel' had been rejected as unsuitable for inclusion. 'The Rime of the Ancient Mariner', Coleridge's main contribution to the first edition of *Lyrical Ballads*, was no longer the opening poem but had been repositioned to near the back of the first volume. There was a lengthy preface, 'more than half a child of my own brain', Coleridge later said, but on the title page Wordsworth was attributed as the sole author. 'As to poetry, I have altogether abandoned it,' a dispirited Coleridge wrote to John Thelwall, 'being convinced that I never had the essentials of poetic Genius, & that I mistook a strong desire for original power.'

On top of Coleridge's doubts as a poet, was a serious physical decline. The Lake District winter, with its seemingly endless days of mist, drizzle and biting winds, did nothing for his health, and this, coupled with a growing addiction to opium, led to a series of ghastly physical ailments which he described in all their frightful detail in letters to friends: boils, swollen eyes, stomach fits, bowel attacks and rheumatic pains. And added to physical suffering was emotional torment. He had fallen obsessively in love with Sara Hutchinson, whom he had first met in Sockburn on his first trip to the north of England in October 1799, and subsequently seen many times in Grasmere. His marriage had been under strain for some time; 'we are not suited to each other', he told Robert Southey. 'If my wife loved me, and I my wife, half as well as we both love our children, I should be the happiest man alive – but this is not – will not be!'

'You would not know me – !' Coleridge wrote to Godwin in March 1801,

> The Poet is dead in me – my imagination (or rather the Somewhat that had been imaginative) lies, like a Cold Snuff on the circular Rim of a Brass Candle-stick, without even a stink of Tallow to remind you that it was once cloathed & mitred with Flame. That is past by! – I was once a Volume of Gold Leaf, rising & riding on every breath of Fancy – but I have beaten myself back into weight & density, & now I sink in quicksilver, yea, remain squat and square on the earth amid the hurricane, that makes Oaks and Straws join in one Dance, fifty yards high in the Element.

Godwin replied suggesting that his ill health might be due to 'uninterrupted rural retirement'. Coleridge dismissed the idea. 'What uninterrupted rural retirement can have had to do in these outward & visible evils, I cannot guess!' he wrote back. 'What share it has had in consoling me under them I know with a tranquil mind, & feel with a grateful Heart. O that you had now before your eyes the delicious picture of Lake, & River, & Bridge, & Cottage, & spacious Field with it's pathway, & woody Hill with it's spring verdure, & mountain with the snow yet lingering in fantastic patches upon it – this, even the same which I had from my sick bed, even without raising my head from the Pillow! – O God! All but dear & lovely Things seemed to be known to my Imagination only as Words – even the Forms which struck terror into me in my fever-dreams were still forms of Beauty.' Besides, he added with some asperity, 'I have had, during the last three weeks, such numerous interruptions of my "uninterrupted rural Retirement", such a succession of Visitors both indigenous & exotic, that I verily wanted both the time & the composure necessary to answer your Letter.' A month later he wrote to Godwin again. The spring weather had arrived, and for the first time in three weeks he was out of bed, but the winter had been a truly hard one: 'one ugly Sickness has followed another, fast as phantoms before a vapourish Woman'.

'Nature indeed looks prettily in rhyme,' William Cowper had written in his poem 'Retirement', 'He likes the country, but in truth must own, / Most likes it, when he studies it in town.' For Coleridge, winter, ill health and an unhappy domestic situation had all thrown into sharp relief the hard reality and isolation of rural retirement. Such too had been John Thelwall's experience when, inspired by his visit to the Quantocks in 1798, he had gone to live at Llys-Wen in Wales. In 1801 he published *Poems chiefly written in Retirement*, together with a 'prefatory memoir of the life of the author', written by himself, in which he recounted (in the third person) his subsequent trials. 'Such a retreat could not but appear, to an enthusiastic imagination, as a sort of enchanted dormitory,' he wrote, 'where the agitations of political feeling might be cradled to forgetfulness, and the delicious day dreams of poesy might be renewed.' But, he goes on, 'in his hopes of consequent tranquility he was most woefully disappointed'. As an intellectual-looking teetotaller who enjoyed solitary walks, Thelwall aroused the suspicions of the local inhabitants of 'those rude parts'; and his political views, when they became known, earned him their outright hostility. His letters were intercepted, and he felt the absence of a library keenly. Bad harvests ruined his agricultural ambitions, and he missed the lively discourse of the city:

> From 'Theatres and Halls of Assembly' to a little Village of only twenty miserable cottages – from the friendly, the enlightened, the animated circles of Norwich – from the elegant and highly intellectual society of Derby, to the sordid ignorance of a neighbourhood whose boorish inhabitants hash up a barbarous jargon of corrupted Welsh, with still more corrupted English, utterly indigestible to unaccustomed organs, was another of those sudden transitions by which the faculties are necessarily stunned and stupified. The new Recluse, accordingly, (with the exception only of a few transient efforts) resigned himself up, for a considerable time, to mere inanity; and his first succeeding attempt at serious composition (some specimens of which were handed about among his friends) exhibited only a mournful picture of the soreness and irritability of a mind equally out of humour with himself and with all the world.

Charles Lamb, meanwhile, had been none too pleased with being called 'gentle-hearted' in Coleridge's poem 'This Lime-Tree Bower my Prison', nor with the idea that 'In the great city pent', he had 'pined / And hunger'd after Nature'. Watching his friends disappear into the Lake District, he felt called upon to defend the city life he loved so much. 'For my part, with reverence to my friends northward, I must confess that I am not romance-bit about *Nature,*' he wrote to Thomas Manning in December 1800. 'The earth, and sea, and sky (when all is said) is but as a house to dwell in.' And to Wordsworth a month later he wrote: 'Separate from the pleasure of your company, I dont much care if I never see a mountain in my life. – I have passed all my days in London, until I have formed as many and intense local attachments, as any of you Mountaineers can have done with dead nature. ... So fading upon me from disuse, have been the Beauties of Nature, as they have been confinedly called; so ever fresh & green and warm are all the inventions of men and assemblies of men in this great city.' In February 1802, Lamb contributed an article to the *Morning Post* as 'The Londoner'. He had been born and bred, he said, 'in a *crowd*':

> This has begot in me an entire affection for that way of life, amounting to an almost insurmountable aversion from solitude and rural scenes. This aversion was never interrupted or suspended, except for a few years in the younger part of my life, during a period of which I had set my affections upon a charming young woman.

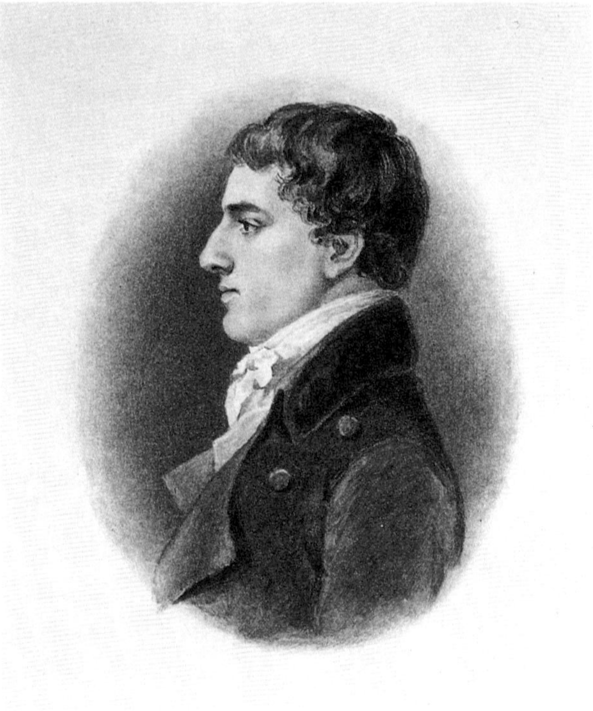

Charles Lamb, after Robert Hancock, 1798.

> Every man while the passion is upon him, is for a time at least addicted to groves and meadows and purling streams. During this short period of my existence, I contracted just enough familiarity with rural objects to understand tolerably well ever after the *poets*, when they declaim in such passionate terms in favor of a country life.
>
> For my own part, now the fit is past, I have no hesitation in declaring, that a mob of happy faces up at the pit door of Drury-lane Theatre, just at the hour of five, give me ten thousand finer pleasures, than I ever received from all the flocks of silly sheep that have whitened the plains of Arcadia or Epsom Downs.

'Nine dreary months – and Oh me! have I had even a fortnight's full and continuous health?' Coleridge wrote in July 1801. He made plans for wintering abroad, but in the end it was to Lamb's London that, in November, he turned. 'Poor C. left us,' wrote Dorothy Wordsworth in her journal, 'Every sight and every sound reminded me of him dear dear fellow – of his many walks to us by day and by night, of all dear things. I was melancholy and could not talk, but at last I eased my heart by weeping – nervous blubbering says William. It is not so, O how many, many reasons have I to be anxious for him!' But, as usual, once he had settled in the metropolis Coleridge began to enjoy himself. He saw old friends, and attended Humphry Davy's lectures on chemistry at the Royal Institution. He wrote to William Godwin: 'I saw so many People on Monday and walked to & fro so much, that I have been ever since like a Fish in air, who, as you perhaps know, lies panting & dying from excess of Oxygen. ... A great change from the society of W. & his sister – for tho' we were three persons, it was but one God – whereas here I have the amazed feeling of a new Polytheist, meeting Lords many, & Gods many.' 'I am quite a man of *fashion*,' he told his wife, 'so many titled acquaintances.'

Then, at the end of February 1802, hearing that Sara Hutchinson was ill at Gallow Hill, the Hutchinson farm near Scarborough, Coleridge again hastened north. After ten days with Sara, he returned to Greta Hall. In April, more depressed than ever, he poured all his feelings into a verse letter to Sara Hutchinson: his failed marriage, his loss of creativity and, fundamentally, his changing relationship with the landscape:

> O dearest Sara! In this heartless Mood,
> All this long Eve, so balmy & serene,
> Have I been gazing on the western Sky
> And it's peculiar Tint of Yellow Green—
> And still I gaze—& with how blank an eye!
> And those thin Clouds above, in flakes & bars,
> That give away their Motion to the Stars;
> Those Stars, that glide behind them, or between,
> Now sparkling, now bedimm'd, but always seen;
> Yon crescent Moon, as fix'd as if it grew
> In it's own cloudless, starless Lake of Blue—
> A boat becalm'd! dear William's Sky Canoe!
> —I see them all, so excellently fair!
> I see, not feel, how beautiful they are.

In the Quantocks, Coleridge had seen the mind, like an Aeolian harp in the breeze, as the passive instrument of nature. Now he believed the contrary: it was the active mind that projected itself onto the landscape, and he lacked the necessary joy to respond to its beauty:

These Mountains too, these Vales, these Woods, these Lakes,
Scenes full of Beauty & of Loftiness
Where all my Life I fondly hop'd to live—
I were sunk low indeed, did they *no* solace give;
But oft I seem to feel, & evermore I fear,
They are not to me now the Things, which once they were.

O Sara! we receive but what we give,
And in *our* Life alone does Nature live.
Our's is her Wedding Garment, our's her Shroud—
And would we aught behold of higher Worth
Than that inanimate cold World allow'd
To the poor loveless ever-anxious Crowd,
Ah! from the Soul itself must issue forth
A Light, a Glory, and a luminous Cloud
    Enveloping the Earth!
And from the Soul itself must there be sent
A sweet & potent Voice, of it's own Birth,
Of all sweet Sounds the Life & Element.

Coleridge still believed in the essential unity of nature and the mind: 'A Poet's *Heart & Intellect* should be *combined, intimately* combined & *unified*, with the great appearances in Nature – & not merely held in solution & loose mixture with them, in the shape of formal Similes.' Yet the external forms of the landscape, in which he had so delighted, now existed in a fraught relationship with darker thoughts and moods, as seen in this fragmentary note to Sara:

> – the thick black Cloud indeed is still over my head, and all the Landscape around me is dark & gloomy with it's shadow – but the wind has risen, Darling! it blows this way a strong & steady gale, & I see already with the eye of confident anticipation the laughing blue sky, & no black thick Cloud! –

On 20 April, Coleridge walked over to Grasmere to read the verse letter to the Wordsworths. 'I was affected with them & was on the whole, not being well, in miserable spirits,' wrote Dorothy. 'The sunshine – the green fields & the fair sky made me sadder; even the happy sporting lambs seemed but sorrowful to me.' While Coleridge's life in the Lakes had grown ever more fraught, Wordsworth had, by contrast, thrived. The years at Dove Cottage were his most fruitful period as a poet, and he was shortly to marry Sara Hutchinson's sister, Mary. When a shortened version of Coleridge's letter to Sara was published as 'Dejection: An Ode' in the *Morning Post*, it was on 4 October 1802 – his wedding anniversary, and Wordsworth's wedding day.

The writing of 'Dejection' in April 1802 seems to have been a kind of catharsis for Coleridge, and he was to make two final, remarkable walking tours. The first, a nine-day, 100-mile circuit of the western fells, he made between 1 and 9 August 1802. He called it his 'circumcursion', and it is perhaps the first great recorded walk of the Lake District. He set out from Keswick shortly after midday, with a shirt, a cravat, two pairs of stockings, 'a little paper and half a dozen pens', a book of German poetry, tea and sugar, his night cap and an oil skin all packed into his knapsack, and a broom handle for a walking stick. Heading south-west through Newlands, he walked to Buttermere, and from there past Ennerdale to St Bees on the coast. From St Bees he walked south, via Calder Abbey, to remote Wastwater. There he ascended Scafell, England's highest peak, and on the summit wrote, to Sara Hutchinson, 'surely the first Letter ever written from the Top of Sca' Fell!':

> But O! what a look down just under my Feet! The frightfullest Cove that might ever be seen / huge perpendicular Precipices, and one Sheep upon it's only Ledge, that surely must be crag! ... Just by it & joining together, rise two huge Pillars of bare lead-colored stone – I am no measurer but their height & depth is terrible.

He descended, perilously, by the great stone steps of Broadstand, and for one heart-stopping moment he became stuck, unable to go either up or down. 'My Limbs were all in a tremble,' he wrote afterwards to Sara:

> I lay upon my Back to rest myself, & was beginning according to my Custom to laugh at myself for a Madman, when the sight of the Crags above me on each side, & the impetuous Clouds just over them, posting so luridly & so rapidly northward, overawed me / I lay in a state of almost prophetic Trance & Delight – & blessed God aloud, for the powers of Reason & the Will, which remaining no Danger can overpower us! O God, I exclaimed aloud – how calm, how blessed am I now / I know not how to proceed, how to return but I am calm and fearless and confident ...

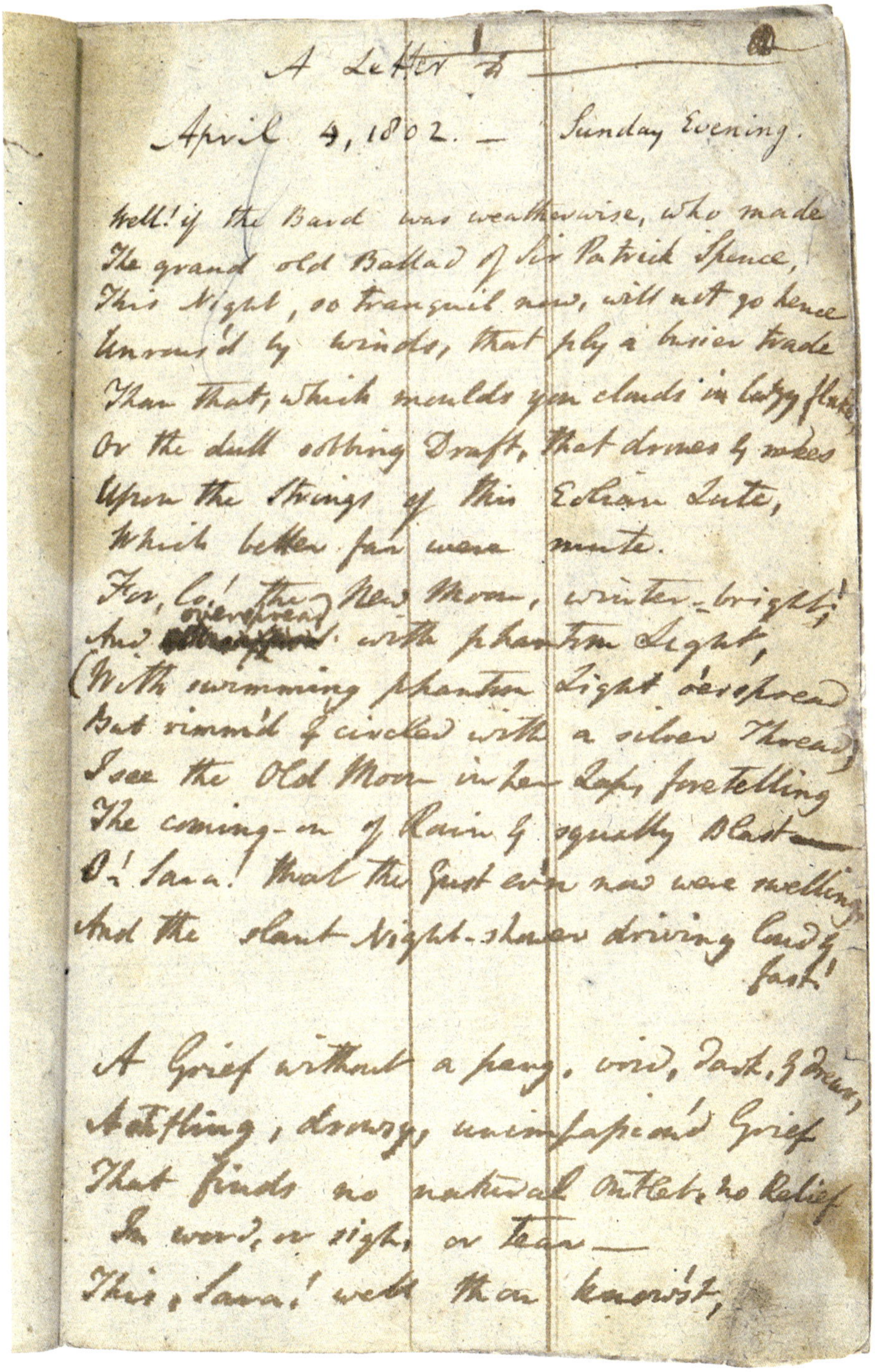
A Letter to —

April 4, 1802. — Sunday Evening.

Well! if the Bard was weatherwise, who made
The grand old Ballad of Sir Patrick Spence,
This Night, so tranquil now, will not go hence
Unrous'd by winds, that ply a busier trade
Than that, which moulds yon clouds in lazy flakes,
Or the dull sobbing Draft, that drones & rakes
Upon the Strings of this Eolian Lute,
Which better far were mute.
For, lo! the New Moon, winter-bright!
And overspread with phantom Light,
(With swimming phantom Light o'erspread
But rimm'd & circled with a silver Thread)
I see the Old Moon in her Lap, foretelling
The coming-on of Rain & squally Blast—
O! Sara! that the Gust ev'n now were swelling,
And the slant Night-shower driving loud & fast!

A Grief without a pang, void, dark, & drear,
A stifling, drowsy, unimpassion'd Grief
That finds no natural Outlet, no Relief
In word, or sigh, or tear—
This, Sara! well thou know'st,

Samuel Taylor Coleridge, manuscript of his verse letter to Sara Hutchinson, 1802. Later revised as 'Dejection – An Ode'.

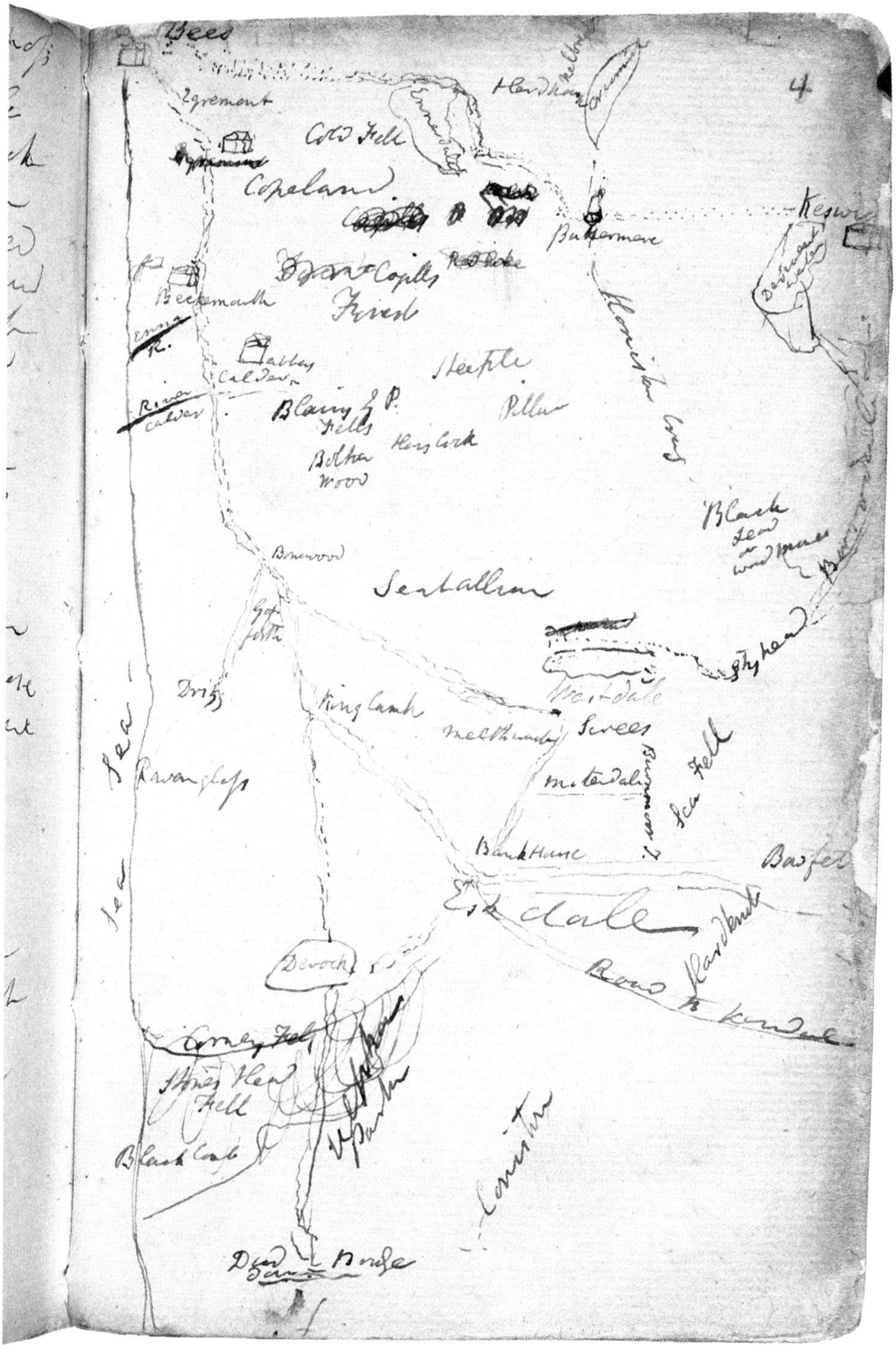

A page from Coleridge's notebook, mapping out part of his Lakes walk of August 1802.

From Scafell he walked down to Broughton and the Duddon valley, and circled back to Keswick through Coniston, Hawkshead, Ambleside and Grasmere. He arrived back at Greta Hall at eight o'clock in the evening, and began a letter to Robert Southey. '[I] must defer all account of my very interesting Tour,' he wrote, 'saying only that of all earthly things which I have beheld, the view *of* Sca' fell & *from* Sca' fell, (*both* views from it's own summit) is the most heart-exciting.'

The second tour was made the following summer. In the middle of August 1803, he accompanied Wordsworth and Dorothy on a trip to Scotland. Both poets hoped it would improve their health; Coleridge had diagnosed his complaint as '*atonic Gout*', and had been told by his doctor that 'if I can only get on, the Exercise & the Excitement will be of so much service as to outweigh the chances of Injury from Wet or Cold'. They considered going on foot, but in the end they went by 'jaunting car', an open, horse-drawn vehicle, with 'a Dicky Box for the Driver' and room for three people to sit each side, back-to-back, on hanging seats, their feet almost level with the ground. In this curious manner they travelled north, and by 19 August they had reached the Falls of the Clyde. The next day they had an amusing encounter which showed the limitations of picturesque description. Dorothy recalled in her later account of the tour, *Recollections of a Tour made in Scotland 1803*:

> We sat upon a bench, placed for the sake of one of these views, whence we looked down upon the waterfall, and over the open country, and saw a ruined tower, called Wallace's Tower, which stands at a very little distance from the fall, and is an interesting object. A lady and gentleman, more expeditious tourists than ourselves, came to the spot; they left us at the seat, and we found them again at another station above the Falls. Coleridge, who is always good-natured enough to enter into conversation with anybody whom he meets in his way, began to talk with the gentleman, who observed that it was a *majestic* waterfall. Coleridge was delighted with the accuracy of the epithet, particularly as he had been settling in his own mind the precise meaning of the words grand, majestic, sublime etc., and had discussed the subject with William the day before. 'Yes, sir,' says Coleridge, 'it *is* a majestic waterfall.' 'Sublime and beautiful,' replied his friend. Poor Coleridge could make no answer, and, not very desirous to continue the conversation, came to us and related the story, laughing heartily.

From the Falls of Clyde they continued on to Glasgow, and shortly afterwards, near Inverary, they agreed to part. Anxious about Coleridge's state of health, the Wordsworths suggested that Coleridge make his own way to Stirling, and catch the coach to Edinburgh. But there was also clearly some tension between them. Coleridge seems to have become annoyed with what he sees as Wordsworth's egotism and hypochondria, 'living wholly among *Devotees* – having every the minutest Thing, almost his very Eating & Drinking, done for him by his Sister, or Wife', as he later wrote to Thomas Poole.

'Our thoughts were full of Coleridge,' wrote Dorothy. 'I shivered at the thought of his being sickly and alone, travelling from place to place.' But in fact Coleridge was invigorated by his new solitude. 'I must be alone, if either my Imagination or Heart are to be excited or enriched,' he wrote later that year in his journal, dismissing a convivial excursion through Borrowdale with Southey and Hazlitt as 'a mere walk'. He now travelled with great pace and stamina, 'in the hope of forcing the Disease into the extremities'. Walking through Glencoe, he continued to Fort Augustus, then along the western shore of Loch Ness to Inverness. He then headed south through Aviemore, arriving at Perth on 10 September. He had covered, he calculated, 263 miles in just eight days.

His companion on this extraordinary journey along the remote Scottish roads was his notebook, which he filled with some brilliant descriptive writing. Here the internal world of his agitated state of mind, and the external world of the wild Highland landscape, achieved the imaginative fusion that he had earlier explored in the 'Dejection' ode:

> having mounted a litle & seen that there was not probably anything more to be noticed, I turned back – & now my mind being as it were leisurely and of[f] the stretch with what delight did I look at a floatage of Shadows on the water, made by wavelets of the Stream, with what delight that most exquisite net at the bottom / sandy + pebbly river, all whose loops are wires of sunshine, gold finer than silk, beside yon Stone the breeze seems to have blown them into a Heap, a rich mass of light, light spreading from the loop holes into the interstices / O we turn from novelties & rarities to old Delights & simple Beauty!

The phrases are spontaneous, richly detailed and have a wonderful immediacy, but at the same time they are carefully wrought. Coleridge knew that the landscape, if it was to be fully appreciated and held in the memory, had to be

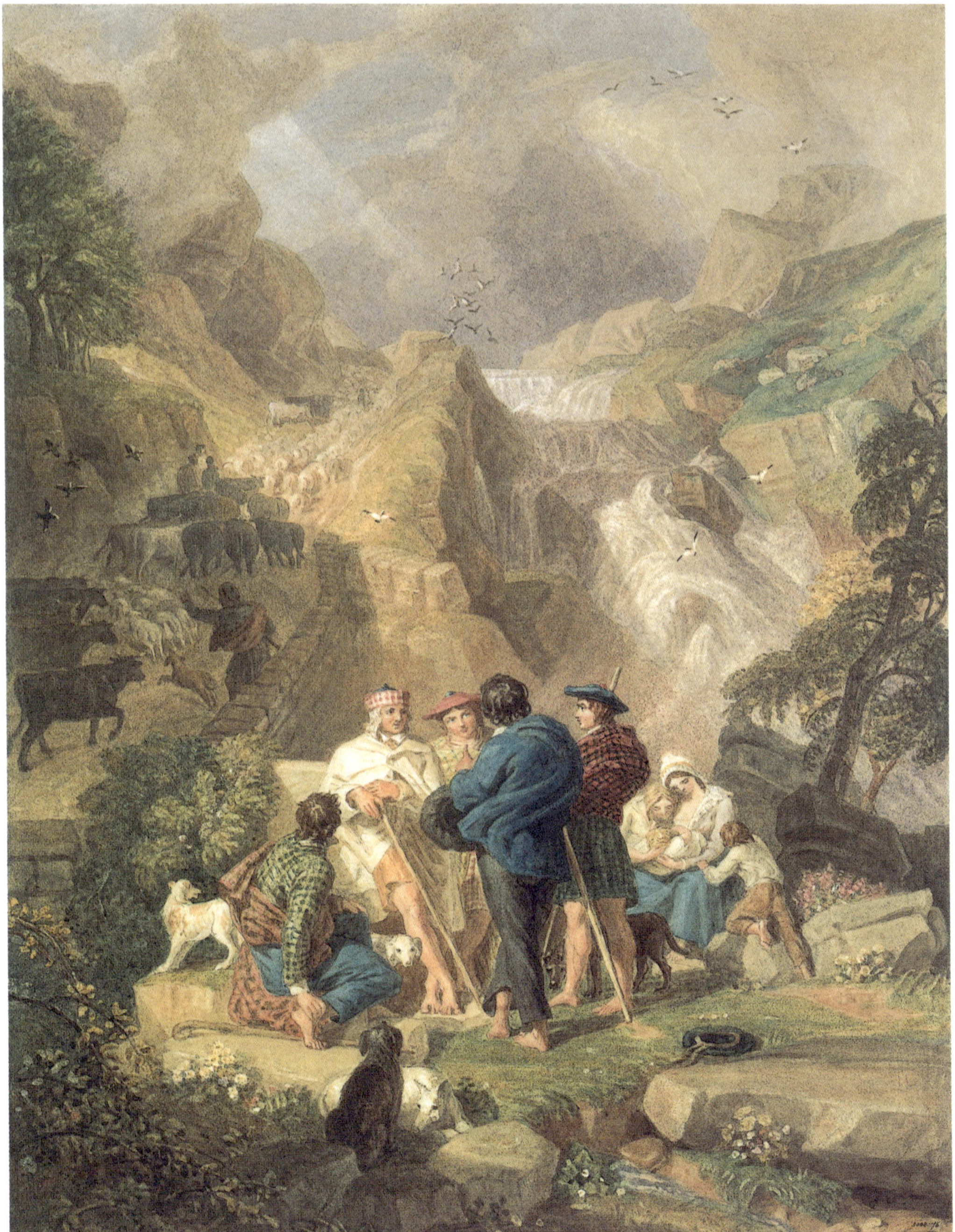

Highland Drovers near Inverary, by Joshua Cristall (undated).

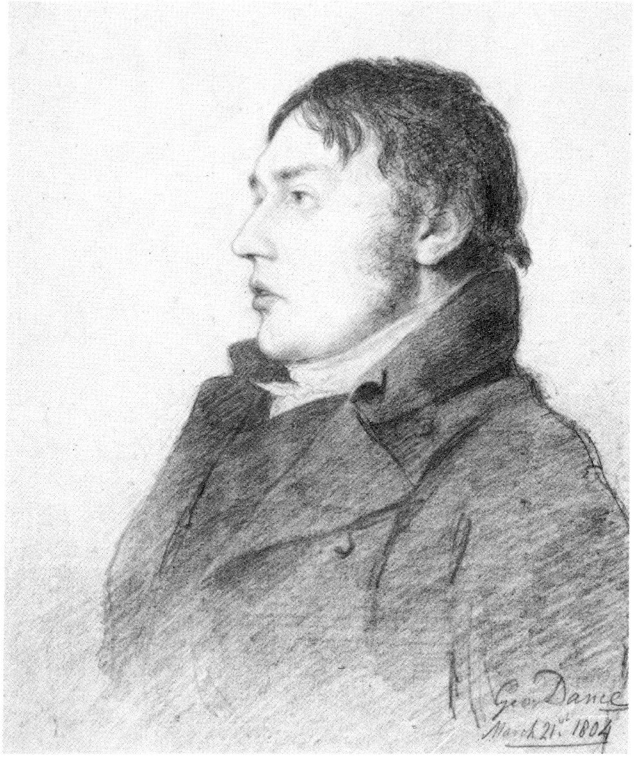

Samuel Taylor Coleridge, by George Dance, March 1804.

organised and arranged into artful shapes by the mind: 'Those who hold it undignified to illustrate Nature by Art – how little would the truly dignified say so – how else can we bring the forms of Nature within our voluntary memory! – the first Business is to subjugate them to our Intellect & voluntary memory – then comes their Dignity by Sensation of Magnitude, Forms & Passions connected therewith.'

Coleridge arrived back at Greta Hall on 15 September. 'It has been an instructive tho' melancholy Tour,' he had written to his wife from Perth, but his mental and physical health had not improved, and he suffered from appalling night terrors which he described in his poem 'The Pains of Sleep':

> ... yesternight I pray'd aloud
> In Anguish and in Agony,
> Awaking from the fiendish Crowd
> Of Shapes & Thoughts that tortur'd me!

By 1804, it had become clear that only a complete change of scene and climate would restore Coleridge's ruined health and depressed state of mind. In March that year he booked a place on the *Speedwell*, bound for Malta. From London he wrote bleakly to the Wordsworths of 'a wish to retire into stoniness & to stir not, or to be diffused upon the winds & have no individual Existence'. His physical appearance, so different from only a few years before, was captured in portraits by James Northcote and George Dance, made while he was suffering from 'a diarrhoea of incessant fury'.

In the Lake District, Dorothy and Mary Wordsworth filled a notebook with Wordsworth's poems, for Coleridge to take with him to Malta. 'Thinking of his banishment, his loneliness, the long distance he will be from all the human beings that he loves, it is one of my greatest consolations that he has those poems with him,' Dorothy told her friend Catherine Clarkson. 'I am very anxious to have your notes for the Recluse,' Wordsworth wrote to him, 'I cannot say how much importance I attach to this, if it should please God that I survive you, I should reproach myself for ever in writing the work if I had neglected to procure this help.' 'God in heaven bless you, my dear dear Friend!' Mary added at the bottom of the letter. 'I am just going to get ready to go with W. to see the beautiful scenery beyond Rydale. O, that you were here to accompany us!'

Robert Southey's pompous friend John Rickman, Secretary to the Speaker to the House of Commons, thought he knew the reason for Coleridge's condition: he had spent too long in the countryside, without society and with no regular employment. If Coleridge died in Malta, he wrote to Southey, then it would be the result of 'a sulky imagination', produced by the lack of 'regular work or application'. Coleridge's fault, Rickman maintained, was 'to admire Nature in the country too much'. The appreciation of landscape was better treated as an occasional recreation: 'Why should not the beauties of Nature be to a grown thinking man, what play hours are at school? Then no harm would be done, and the world would not lose men capable of being the most usefull members of society.'

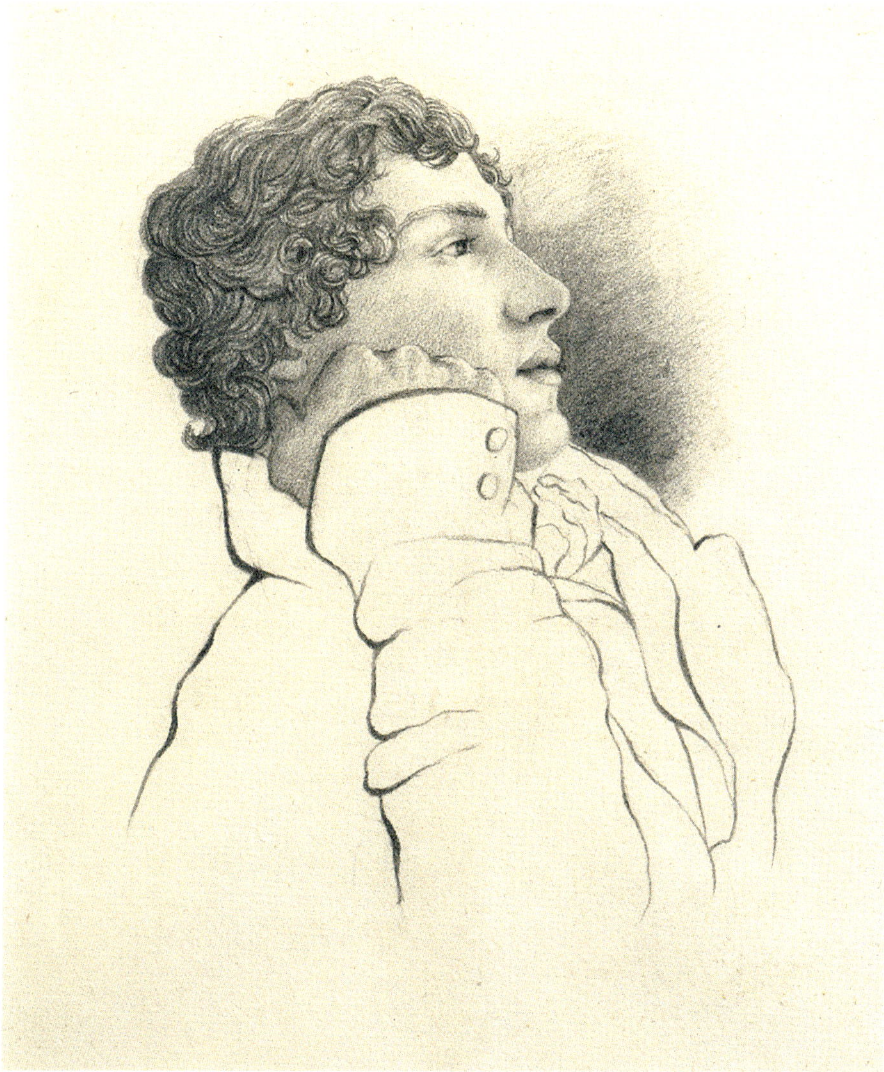

John Keats, by Charles Armitage Brown, 1819.

‘THROUGH THE CLOUDS’

Keats’s Tour North, 1818

IN JULY 1818, fifteen years after Coleridge’s tour of Scotland, a young poet, John Keats, was walking through the Lake District. With his friend Charles Armitage Brown, he intended to walk north into the Highlands, through to John O’ Groats, and then return south, via the Lake District, by a different route. His motive, he told his artist friend Benjamin Robert Haydon, was ‘to make a sort of prologue to the Life I intend to pursue – that is to write, to study and to see all Europe at the lowest expence. I will clamber through the clouds and exist.’

The idea for the tour had been conceived amid the clouds and rain of Devon. Keats had spent March and April in Teignmouth, looking after his youngest brother Tom, who was gravely ill with tuberculosis. Situated on the south coast at the mouth of the River Teign, in the latter part of the eighteenth century Teignmouth had grown into one of the most fashionable watering and bathing spots in the south-west of England. But, unfortunately, Keats saw very little of his surroundings. He had travelled by coach from London in a violent storm, and in the weeks that followed it rained steadily; ‘bye the bye you may say what you will of devonshire’, he wrote to his friend Benjamin Bailey, ‘the truth is, it is a splashy, rainy, misty snowy, foggy, haily floody, muddy slipshod County – the hills are very beautiful, when you get a sight of ’em – the Primroses are out, but then you are in – the Cliffs are of a fine deep Colour, but then the Clouds are continually vieing with them’. The next day he wrote to his friend John Hamilton Reynolds promising him a good dose of picturesque description in the manner of the fashionable novelist and travel writer Ann Radcliffe: ‘Buy a girdle – put a pebble in your Mouth – loosen your Braces – for I am going among Scenery whence I intend to tip you the Damosel Radcliffe – I’ll cavern you, and grotto you, and waterfall you, and wood you, and water you, and immense-rock you, and tremendous sound you, and solitude you.’ But for the moment he was prevented by the weather: ‘I would have taken a walk in the first day, but the rain wod not let me; and the second, but the rain wod not let me; and the third; but the rain forbade it – Ditto 4 ditto 5 – ditto.’

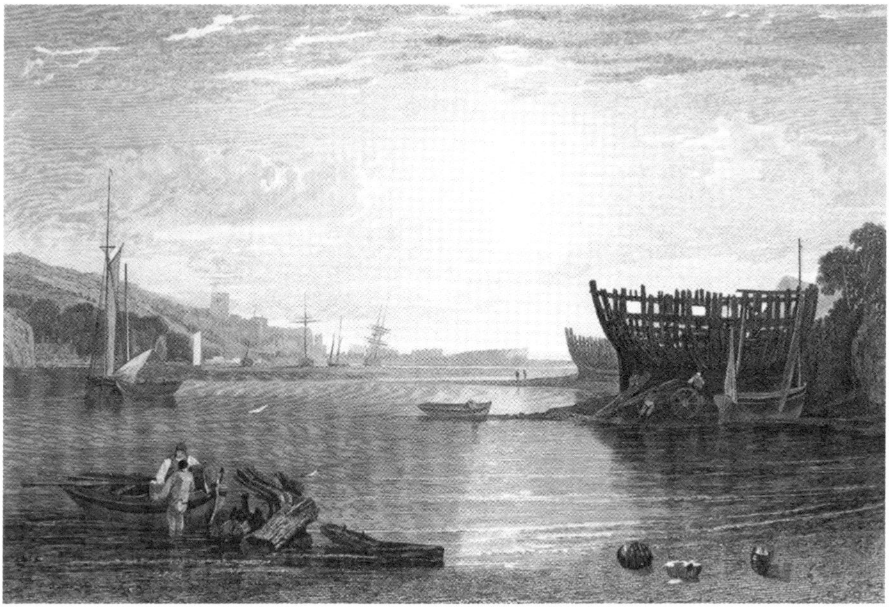

Teignmouth, by George Cooke after J.M.W. Turner, 1815.

So, instead, Keats sat indoors, watched the rain beat against the windows, and brooded. It was a defining period of his life. Two years before he had given up a promising medical career to concentrate on poetry, and had been welcomed into the literary and artistic circles of Hampstead: he became friendly with the poet and journalist Leigh Hunt, the historical painter Benjamin Robert Haydon, fellow poets Percy Bysshe Shelley and J.H. Reynolds, the publisher John Taylor, and the critic William Hazlitt. A first collection of Keats's poems, dedicated to Hunt, had been published in 1817, but had barely been noticed. He had followed this with a long and ambitious poem in four books, *Endymion*; 'it will be a test, a trial of my Powers of Imagination and chiefly of my invention which is a rare thing indeed', he had told his other brother, George, 'by which I must make 4000 Lines of one bare circumstance and fill them with Poetry'. Now *Endymion* was almost ready for publication, and as Keats went through the proofs of its final book, all he could see were the poem's many faults. The trial was over, and he wanted to move on. 'I wish it was all done,' he told Reynolds, 'for I want to forget it and make my mind free for something new.' What preoccupied him was not the literary world, still less the reading public, but his own lack of knowledge and experience. Sitting down to compose a preface for *Endymion*, he practically disowned the poem: '... this Poem must rather be considered as an endeavour than a thing accomplished; a poor prologue to what, if I live, I humbly hope to do. In duty to the Public I should have kept it back for a year or two, knowing it to be so faulty: but I really cannot do so: – by repetition my favourite Passages sound vapid in my ears, and I would rather redeem myself with a new Poem should this one be found of any interest. ... I here declare that I have not any particular affection for any particular phrase, word or letter in the whole affair.' A few days later Keats learned that this preface had been rejected, but he was defiant: 'a Preface is written to the Public; a thing I cannot help looking upon as an Enemy, and which I cannot address without feelings of Hostility', he told Reynolds. 'I never wrote one single Line of Poetry with the least Shadow of public thought ... I could not live without the love of my friends – I would jump down Aetna for any great Public good – but I hate a Mawkish Popularity. – I cannot be subdued before them – My glory would be to daunt and dazzle the thousand jabberers about Pictures and Books.' He did, however, send a revised preface the following day.

Meanwhile, the Devon rain continued to fall: 'As the drops beat against the window, they give me the same sensation as a quart of cold water offered to revive a half drowned devil – No feel of the clouds dropping fatness, but as if the roots of the Earth were rotten cold and drench'd.' Haydon, a Devonian, wrote to Keats asking him to give the Devon landscape a chance: 'Stay till the summer, and then bask in its deep blue summer sky, and lush grass, & tawny banks, and silver bubbling rivers – you must not leave Devonshire without seeing some of its Scenery rocky, mossy, craggy with roaring rivers & as clear as crystal – it will do your mind good.' But Keats had in mind a very different kind of physical and mental landscape.

Every summer his friend and near neighbour Charles Armitage Brown toured his native Scotland on foot, and he proposed that Keats join him that summer. Keats agreed. He promised Haydon that he would revisit Devon 'at some more favourable time of year', then told him of his plan to go north: 'I purpose within a Month to put my knapsack at my back and make a pedestrian tour through the North of England, and part of Scotland ... I will get such an accumulation of stupendous recollolections [*sic*] that as I walk through the suburbs of London I may not see them – I will stand upon Mont Blanc and remember this coming Summer when I intend to straddle ben Lomond.' The wild Scottish landscape would be an inspiration for the great epic poem he still aimed to write, its mountainous austerity an antidote to the cosy sociability of Hampstead Heath. 'I have many reasons for going wonder-ways,' he told Reynolds, 'to make my winter chair free from spleen – to enlarge my vision – to escape disquisitions on Poetry and Kingston Criticism. – to promote digestion and economise shoe leather – I'll have leather buttons and belt; and if Brown holds his mind, over the Hills we go. – If my Books will help me to it, – thus will I take all Europe in turn, and see the Kingdoms of the Earth and the glory of them.'

On his return, he would work with a new seriousness and sense of purpose. 'I find cavalier days are gone by,' he told his publisher John Taylor. 'I find that I can have no enjoyment in the World but continual drinking of Knowledge – I find there is no worthy pursuit but the idea of doing some good for the world – some do it with their society – some with their wit – some with their benevolence – some with a sort of power of conferring pleasure and good humour on all they meet and in a thousand ways all equally dutiful to the command of Great Nature.' Keats had his own plan: in the manner of Milton and Wordsworth he would retire from the world and prepare himself for an epic work: 'the road lies through application study and thought. I will pursue it and to that end purpose retiring for some years. I have been hovering for some time between an exquisite sense of the luxurious and a love for Philosophy – were I calculated for the former I should be glad – but as I am not I shall turn all my soul to the latter.'

His great poetic examplars, Milton and Wordsworth, were the subject of a letter Keats then wrote to Reynolds, his last from Teignmouth. Who was greater? he asked. Who saw further? Keats then compared life to 'a large Mansion of Many Apartments'. The first he called 'the infant or thoughtless Chamber, in which we remain as long as we do not think'; then, 'imperceptibly impelled by the awakening of the thinking principle', people moved into the 'Chamber of Maiden Thought'. Here, although at first 'intoxicated by the light and atmosphere', they were convinced 'that the World is full of Misery and Heartbreak, Pain, Sickness and oppression'. In this manner, wrote Keats, the Chamber of Maiden Thought 'becomes gradually darken'd and at the same time on all sides of it many doors are set open – but all dark – all leading to dark passages – We see not the ballance of good and evil. We are in a Mist – *We* are now in that state – We feel the "burden of the Mystery". To this point was Wordsworth come, as far as I can conceive when he wrote "Tintern Abbey" and it seems to me that his Genius is explorative of those dark Passages.' Wordsworth, Keats concluded, was a greater poet than Milton, who 'did not think into the human heart, as Wordsworth has done'.

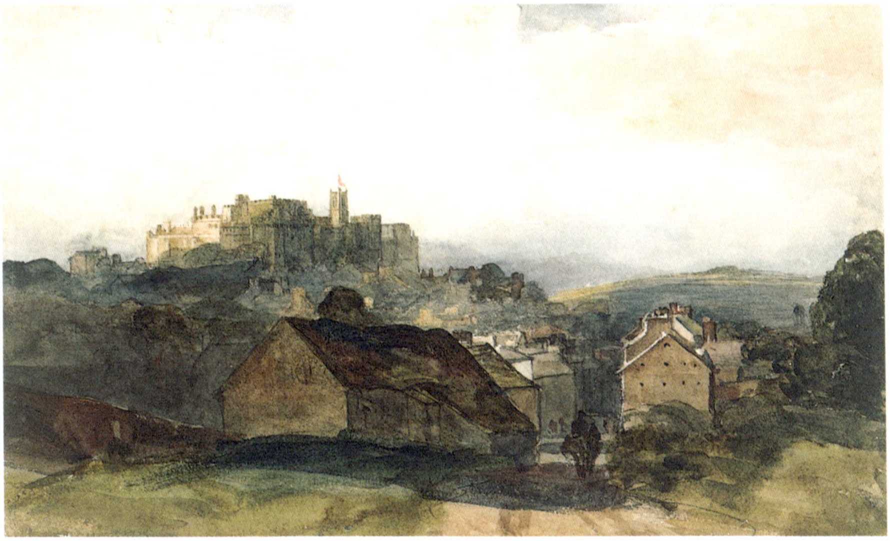

A view of Lancaster by Peter De Wint. 'Tell De Wint I will return an expert in landskip,' Keats wrote to John Taylor shortly before leaving London.

Keats and Tom left Teignmouth in the first week in May, and returned to their home in Hampstead. A month later, on the morning of 22 June, Keats and Brown boarded a coach at the Swan and Two Necks inn in Cheapside, bound for Liverpool. With them were Keats's brother George and George's new wife Georgiana, who were to emigrate to America. 'You know my Brother George has been out of employ for some time,' Keats had written to Bailey. 'It has weighed very much upon him, and driven him to scheme and turn things over in his Mind. The result has been his resolution to emigrate to the back settlements of America, become farmer and work with his own hands.' The following day they arrived at Liverpool, from where George and Georgiana were to set sail. Early the next morning, with George and Georgiana still sleeping, Keats and Brown took a coach to Lancaster, the starting point of their journey.

It was election day and the town was in uproar. After waiting two hours for dinner they were told that there were no beds available, but luckily they found room in a private house – 'better than a public one on such roaring occasions', wrote Brown. They rose at four the next morning and, after three hours of rain, during which time they read Milton's *Samson Agonistes*, they left Lancaster in a fine Scotch mist. 'Just out of the town,' Brown later recalled, 'we overheard a labourer rather sarcastically observe to his companion – "There go a couple of gentlemen! – having nothing to do, they are finding out hard work for themselves!"' As their journey progressed, however, Keats and Brown would look less and less like gentlemen, and were instead taken for pedlars, travelling jewellers, razor sellers, linen drapers, excisemen and even spies.

After seventeen miles of walking Keats and Brown spent the first night at Endmoor, a village near Kendal, where Keats began the journal he would send in instalments to his brother Tom. The following day they walked through Kendal and on into the Lake District. As they descended into the village of Bowness, by Lake Windermere, they got their first sight of lakes and fells. Brown afterwards remembered Keats's ecstatic reaction:

> His bright eyes darted on a mountain-peak, beneath which was gently floating on a silver cloud; thence to a very small island, adorned with the foliage of trees, that lay beneath us, and surrounded by water of a glorious hue, when he exclaimed – 'How can I believe in that? – surely it cannot be!' He warmly asserted that no view in the world could equal this – that it must beat all Italy – yet, having moved onward but a few hundred yards – catching the further extremity of the lake, he thought it 'more and more wonderfully beautiful!'

Arriving in Bowness, they took a boat out on to Windermere, pulled up some local trout, and then dined in a room overlooking the lake. The view of water, shore, islands, mountains and clouds surpassed Keats's expectations, but the popularity of the place surprised and disappointed him. 'The disfigurement I mean is the miasma of London,' he told Tom. 'I do suppose it contaminated with bucks and soldiers, and women of fashion – and hat-band ignorance.' Brown showed contempt for a certain type of fashionable tourist, and later in the day, at Ambleside, they came upon a man dressed like themselves, whose ambition, Brown said, was 'to be regarded as an important gentleman in disguise'. He was, they suspected, 'a London sharper'. Further north, at Keswick, Brown was offended by a late riser: 'When wound up to enthusiasm for natural objects, it is like enduring a direct act of hostility to meet with something brought from the depths of sophistication. At the inn here, near mid-day, came a yawning dandy from his bed-room, and sat at his breakfast reading a bouncing novel!' Keats was less critical and showed the self-deprecating humour and quick intelligence that never allowed him to accept a single point of view. He was, after all, a visitor from London himself, sitting by Windermere, enjoying the local trout and looking at the view: 'The border inhabitants are quite out of keeping with the romance about them, from a continual intercourse with London rank and fashion. But why should I grumble? They let me have a prime glass of soda water – O they are as good as their neighbors.'

What was harder to accept was the idea of Wordsworth, whose home was at nearby Rydal, living among tourists. 'Lord,' Keats said to Tom, 'Wordsworth, instead of being in retirement, has himself and his house full in the thick of fashionable visitors quite convenient to be pointed at all summer long.' To a younger generation of writers, the thought of the older poet deep in contemplation among the mountains had been an inspiration. In 1803 a young admirer, Thomas De Quincey, had written to Wordsworth from Everton, near Liverpool: 'your name is with me for ever linked to the lovely scenes of nature; and that not yourself only but that each place and object you have mentioned – and all the souls in that delightful community of your's – to me "Are dearer than the sun!".' The names of the hills and valleys of the Lake District, De Quincey later wrote, and the thought of Wordsworth in his rural solitude, had acted like a spell upon him:

> The very names of the ancient hills – Fairfield, Seat Sandal, Helvellyn, Blencathra, Glamara; of the sequestered glens – such as Borrowdale, Martindale, Mardale, Wasdale, and Ennerdale; but, above all, the shy pastoral recesses, not garishly in the world's eye, like Windermere or Derwentwater, but lurking half unknown to the traveller of that day – Grasmere, for instance, the lovely abode of the poet, himself, solitary, and yet sowed, as it were, with a thin diffusion of humble dwellings – here a scattering, and there a clustering, as in the starry heavens ...

In 1811 the young Percy Bysshe Shelley, recently expelled from Oxford, had lived briefly in Keswick with his wife Harriet, and her sister Eliza. There, his garden experiments with hydrogen gas had flared through the night and disconcerted the local inhabitants, who asked him to leave – 'Strange prejudices have these country people!' he wrote indignantly to his friend Elizabeth Hitchener – but for a while he had enjoyed his retired situation: 'Oh! how you will delight in this Scenery,' he told her:

> The lake as I see it hence is glassy & calm. Snow vapours tinted by the loveliest colors of refraction pass far below the summits of these giant rocks. The scene even in a winter sunset is inexpressibly lovely. The

> clouds assume shapes which seem peculiar to these regions; what will it be in summer, what when *you* are here. Oh! give me a little cottage in *that* scene, let all live in peaceful little houses, let temples and palaces rot with their perishing masters.

Shelley had hoped to see Wordsworth and Coleridge, but in the end saw only Robert Southey, then at Greta Hall, and living largely among his books.

In November 1814 another young poet, John Hamilton Reynolds, who was yet to meet Keats, had sent Wordsworth a copy of his poem *The Eden of the Imagination*. 'Will you accept of the accompanying little Sketch of Rural Scenery?' he asked. 'Written not from the objects themselves before my eyes, but from the images of them on my mind. It may appear presumptuous in me to send the offspring of but an ill-stored memory to One who lives in a very friendship with nature and thinks daily over the wandering streams & in the silent fields: – But I have long wished to thank you for the deep pleasure your Poems have given me ... Living as I do in the bustle of London – opportunities occur but seldom of feeding my mind in the fresh, clear, & calm Country: – When they do, I lose no time in improving my stock of reflections and preparing for retirement – I look at beautiful scenery in the boldness of Sunshine and in the delicacy of Moonlight with great mental pleasure – Though where you would find a harvest, I can but glean.'

In 1816 Keats had composed a sonnet in which he imagined Wordsworth *in situ* on the summit of Helvellyn:

> Great spirits now on earth are sojourning;
>   He of the cloud, the cataract, the lake,
>   Who on Helvellyn's summit, wide awake,
> Catches his freshness from Archangel's wing.

Haydon had sent Keats's sonnet on to Wordsworth, and the following year Keats had met the elder poet several times in London. But Wordsworth had not been in an approachable mood, and Keats was disappointed. 'It has as yet been a Mystery to me how and when Wordworth went,' he had written to Haydon after Wordsworth's return to the north. 'I cant help thinking he has returned to his Shell – with his beautiful Wife and his enchanting Sister – It is a great pity that People should by associating themselves with the finest things, spoil them – Hunt has damned Hampstead Masks and Sonnets and italian tales – Wordsworth has damned the lakes ...'

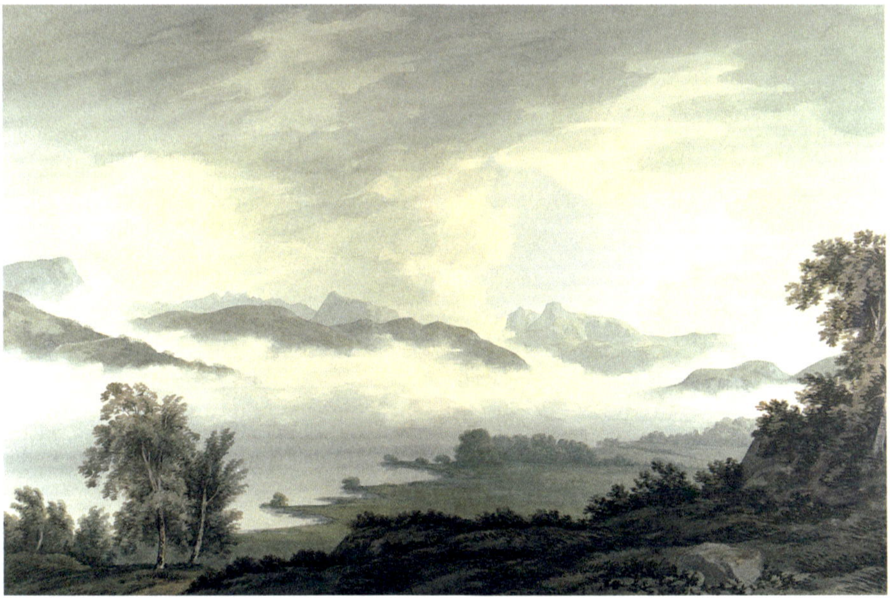

View of Windermere, by John 'Warwick' Smith, *c.*1790. 'I have an amazing partiality for mountains in the clouds,' Keats wrote to his brother, Tom, from Bowness.

Now, at Bowness, Keats was shocked to discover from the waiter that Wordsworth was campaigning in the local election for the Tory Lord Lowther against the Whig candidate, Henry Brougham: 'What think you of that,' he wrote to Tom, 'Wordsworth versus Brougham!! Sad – sad – sad – and yet the family has been his friend always. What can we say?' But he still recognised Wordsworth as by far the greatest contemporary poet, 'deeper than Milton', whose poem *The Excursion* he had declared to be one of the principal things 'to rejoice at in this age'. He and Brown planned to call on him at Rydal the following day.

From Windermere, Keats and Brown walked along the road by the lake, 'a winding lane, wooded on each side, and green overhead, full of Foxgloves', to Ambleside, where they spent the night. Early the following morning they went to see the nearby waterfalls, and of this Keats gave a rapturous description to Tom:

> What astonishes me more than any thing is the tone, the coloring, the slate, the stone, the moss, the rock-weed; or, if I may so say, the intellect, the countenance of such places. The space, the magnitude of mountains and waterfalls are well imagined before one sees them; but

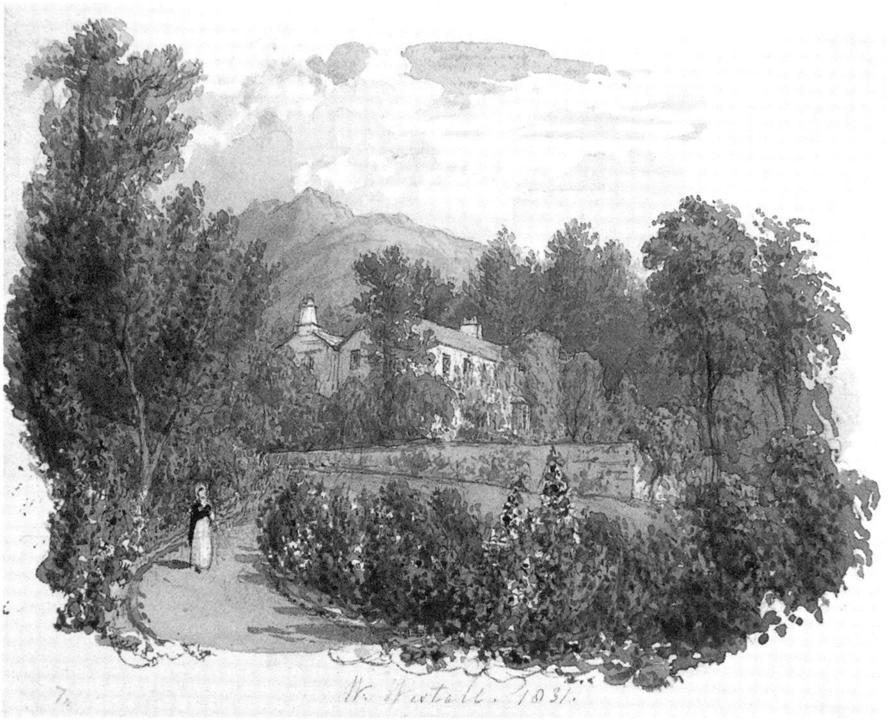

Wordsworth's later home, Rydal Mount, by William Westall, 1831.

> this countenance or intellectual tone must surpass every imagination and defy any remembrance. I shall learn poetry here and shall henceforth write more than ever, for the abstract endeavor of being able to add a mite to that mass of beauty which is harvested from these grand materials, by the finest spirits, and put into etherial existence for the relish of one's fellows.

Keats was to give few extended natural descriptions like this. For increasingly, as he walked further north, it was the effect the landscape, and the local people, had on his mind and imagination that mattered. 'Let any of my friends see my letters,' he concluded this first travel letter to Tom, 'they may not be interested in descriptions – descriptions are bad at all times – I did not intend to give you any; but how can I help it? I am anxious you should taste a little of our pleasure; it may be not an unpleasant thing, as you have not the fatigue.' 'For myself I hate descriptions,' he wrote later to George and Georgiana from Staffa. 'I would not send it were it not mine.' Dorothy Wordsworth had expressed the same opinion when, after her tour of Scotland in 1803, she wrote to her friend Catherine Clarkson: 'Bye the Bye I am writing not a journal, for we took no notes, but *recollections* of our Tour in the form of a journal, you will be amused with it for our sakes, but I think journals of Tours except as far as one is interested in the travellers are very uninteresting things.'

At Rydal, Keats found to his disappointment that neither Wordsworth nor any of his family was at home, and so, after leaving a note on the mantelpiece, propped against a portrait of what they took to be Dorothy, he and Brown continued to Grasmere. Here Keats picked out landmarks familiar to him from Wordsworth's 'Poems on the Naming of Places', which had been published in the second, 1800 edition of *Lyrical Ballads*, and then in his 1815 collected poems. 'I have seen Loughrigg and Silver How,' he wrote to George and Georgiana, 'and discovered without a hint "that ancient woman seated on Helm Craig".' Leaving Grasmere by Dunmail Raise, they looked back to admire the famous view first described by Thomas Gray in 1765. They walked on to Thirlmere, and then to Wythburn at the foot of Helvellyn, perhaps the best-known Lakeland peak, where, two years earlier, Keats had imagined Wordsworth 'wide awake'. Here they spent the night, in flea-ridden beds.

They awoke to a morning of cloud and drizzling rain, and were thus prevented from ascending Helvellyn. So they continued into Keswick, duly pausing to appreciate the view of Derwentwater and the surrounding fells – Skiddaw and Borrowdale – on the way. After breakfast they took in the customary sights: a walk around Derwentwater, including the famous Lodore Falls (which disappointed them), and then in the evening the famous prehistoric stone circle at Castlerigg. 'Nothing was wanting in the town, at least by attempts, to please a London taste,' Brown later wrote. 'It was full of lures to pass away the time – a circulating library, a fossil museum, an exhibition of Mr Green's drawings, and a camera obscura.' In 1800, upon arriving at Greta Hall, Coleridge had described the town as being quiet for two thirds of the year, but during the other third 'alive & swarm[ing] with Tourists of all shapes & sizes, & characters – it is the very place I would recommend to a novelist or farce writer'.

At four o'clock the next morning Keats and Brown were roused by a guide, and joined a small party to ascend Skiddaw. 'It promised all along to be fair,' Keats later wrote to Tom, '& we had fagged & tugged nearly to the top, when at halfpast six there came a mist upon us & shut out the view; we did not however lose anything by it, we were high enough without mist, to see the coast of Scotland; the Irish Sea; the hills beyond Lancaster; & nearly

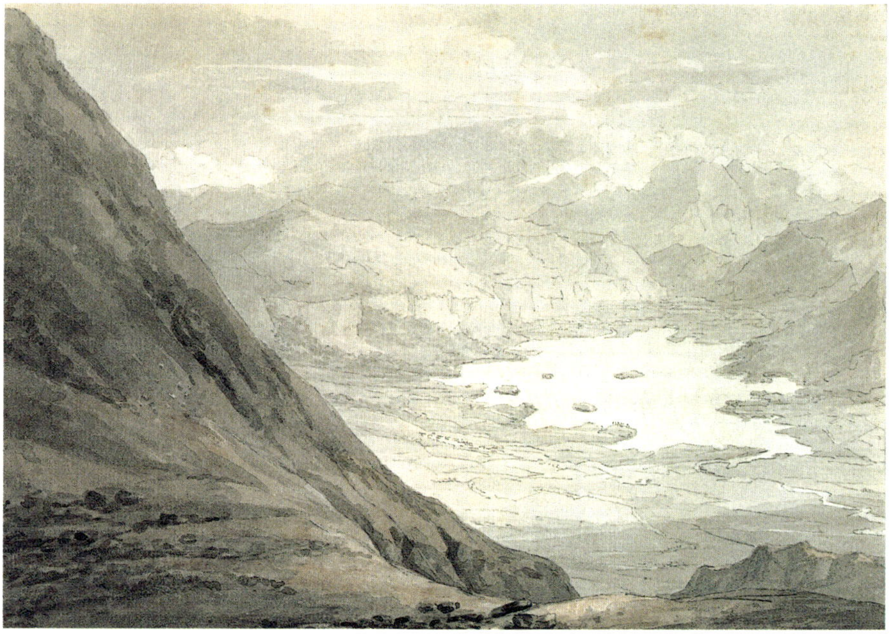

A view of Derwentwater from Skiddaw, by Thomas Hearne, 1777.

all the large ones of Cumberland & Westmoreland, particularly Helvellyn & Scawfell.' Descending, they left Keswick, and the Lake District, and continued north towards Carlisle. So far they had followed a fairly conventional route, and Keats had described their progress to Tom in what he knew was equally conventional language. Now, as he moved into less frequented areas, his alert eye began to notice distinctive things around him. At Ireby ('a dull beggarly looking place', said Brown), on their way to Carlisle, they came across a country dancing school at the local inn: 'there was as fine a row of boys & girls as you ever saw, some beautiful faces, & one exquisite mouth', Keats told Tom. 'I never felt so near the glory of Patriotism, the glory of making by any means a country happier. This is what I like better than scenery. I fear our continued moving from place to place, will prevent our becoming learned in village affairs; we are mere creatures of Rivers, Lakes, & mountains.' Eventually they reached Carlisle. By Keats's calculation they had now walked 114 miles, but were 'merely a little tired in the thighs, & a little blistered'. Here they decided to take a coach to Dumfries. 'Aware there was nothing interesting in the country between Carlisle and Dumfries,' wrote Brown, 'and that, consequently, it would be toil without numeration, we coached the distance.' By such means they entered Scotland.

Until quite late in the eighteenth century, southern England had looked upon Scotland with a kind of fascinated horror. 'The native Caledonians preserved in the northern extremity of the island their wild independence, for which they were not less indebted to their poverty than their valour,' Edward Gibbon wrote in the first volume of his *Decline and Fall of the Roman Empire*, published in 1776. 'Their incursions were frequently repelled and chastised, but their country was never subdued. The masters of the fairest and most wealthy climates of the globe, turned with contempt from gloomy hills assailed by the winter tempest, from lakes concealed in a blue mist, and from cold and lonely heaths, over which the deer of the forest were chased by a troop of naked barbarians.' 'Shall I tire you with a description of this unfruitfull country?' wrote Oliver Goldsmith from Edinburgh in 1753, 'where I must lead you over their hills all brown with heath, or their valleys scarce able to feed a rabbet? ... every part of the country presents the same dismall landscape, no grove nor brook lend their musick to cheer the stranger, or make the inhabitants forget their poverty.'

But by the end of the eighteenth century, Scotland had become a popular destination for lovers of the picturesque. In contrast to the much-visited landscapes of the Wye Valley, the Peak District and the Lake District, it seemed primitive and unspoiled. Travellers were thrilled by its sublime mountains and desolate heaths – here was nature in all its naked simplicity. William Gilpin published his picturesque observations on the Highlands in 1789, and in 1801 John Stoddart, *Times* journalist, William Hazlitt's brother-in-law and acquaintance of Wordsworth, published his *Remarks on Local Scenery and Manners in Scotland During the Years 1799 and 1800*. 'Tours are the mushroom produce of every summer, and Scotland has had her share,' Stoddart wrote in his preface. 'Tours are read, as much as any other ephemeral productions; and some of them live.' Tourists also got a taste of Scotland from its literature: the poems and novels of Walter Scott, the melancholy strains of the supposed primitive poet Ossian, and the songs and ballads of that 'animated painter of Scottish feelings', Robert Burns.

Burns had died in 1796, and was buried in Dumfries. The Wordsworths and Coleridge had been to see his grave in August 1803. 'He lies at a corner of the churchyard,' recollected Dorothy. 'There is no stone to mark the spot; but a hundred guineas have been collected, to be expended on some sort of monument.' In 1813 a subscription was opened to raise money for a mausoleum, and in 1815 Burns's remains were moved to a more conspicuous monument. Keats went to see it while he was in Dumfries, and pronounced it 'not very much to my taste, though on a scale large enough to show they wanted to honour him – Mrs Burns lives in this place, most likely we shall see her tomorrow'. He wrote a sonnet, 'On visiting the Tomb of Burns', 'in a strange mood, half asleep. I know not how it is, the Clouds, the sky, the Houses, all seem anti Grecian & anti Charlemagnish'. There was a horse fair that day, and Keats noticed that 'the women were nearly all barefoot, with their shoes & clean stockings in hand, ready to put on and look smart in town'. He gave his young sister Fanny a quick summary of their journey: 'We set off from Lancaster with our knapsacks on, and have walked a little zig-zag through the mountains and Lakes of Cumberland and Westmoreland – We came from Carlisle yesterday to this place – We are employed in going up Mountains, looking at Strange towns prying into old ruins and eating very hearty breakfasts.'

Keats and Brown left Dumfries and spent the next four days walking steadily along the western coast of Galloway, through Dalbeattie, Auchencairn, Kirkcudbright, Creetown and Newton Stuart to Glenluce. There were fine views of wooded hills and craggy mountains to the right, with the sea a constant presence on the left. 'For the most part, our track lay through cornfields, or skirting small forests,' wrote Keats. It was the country of Walter Scott's novel *Guy Mannering*, which had been published three years before, and as soon as Brown learned that Keats had not read it, he started to point out scenes connected with the story, concentrating on its gypsy protagonist Meg Merrilies: 'I enjoyed the recollection of the events as I described them in their own scenes. There was a little spot, close to our pathway, where, without a shadow of doubt, old Meg Merrilies had often boiled her kettle, and, haply, cooked a chicken. It was among fragments of rock, and brambles, and broom, and most tastefully ornamented with a profusion of honeysuckle, wild roses, and fox glove, all in the very blush and fullness of blossom.' One morning, after breakfast at Auchencairn, Brown noticed that Keats was writing poetry – it was his song 'Old Meg she was a Gipsey'; 'We are now in Meg Merrilies country and have this morning passed through some parts exactly suited to her,' Keats wrote to Tom after copying the poem for him. 'Kirkudbright Country is very beautiful, very wild with craggy hills somewhat in the Westmoreland fashion.'

The country began to feel more foreign. Very few southerners passed that way, their landlady at Creetown had told them, and the children jabbered away 'as in a foreign language'. 'The barefooted Girls look very much in keeping,' Keats wrote to Tom, 'I mean with the Scenery about them – Brown

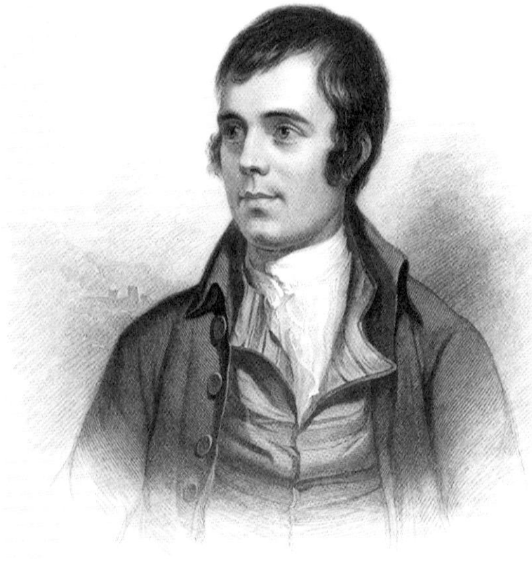

Robert Burns, after Alexander Nasmyth, 1787.

praises their cleanliness and appearance of comfort – the neatness of their cottages &c It may be – they are very squat among trees and fern and heath and broom, on levels slopes and heights – They are very pleasant because they are very primitive.' But if the locals were in keeping with the landscape, they were also, he noticed, miserably poor, and their spirit was weighed down by the strictures of the Scottish church: 'A Scotch Girl stands in awe of the Elders – poor little Susannas – They will scarcely laugh – they are greatly to be pitied and the kirk is greatly to be damn'd … These kirkmen have done Scotland harm – they have banished puns and laughing and kissing.' Keats's thoughts returned to Burns, whose poetic sensibility seemed out of keeping with this austere northern world: 'Poor unfortunate fellow – his disposition was southern – how sad it is a when a luxurious imagination is obliged in self defence to deaden its delicacy in vulgarity, and riot in thing[s] which are not. No Man in such matters will be content with the experience of others.'

On Sunday 5 July Keats and Brown arrived at Glenluce, and the next day started for Stranraer. By lucky chance they managed to catch a ride with a passing mail coach, on its way to meet the Irish mail boat at Portpatrick, from where they planned to make a detour to Ireland.

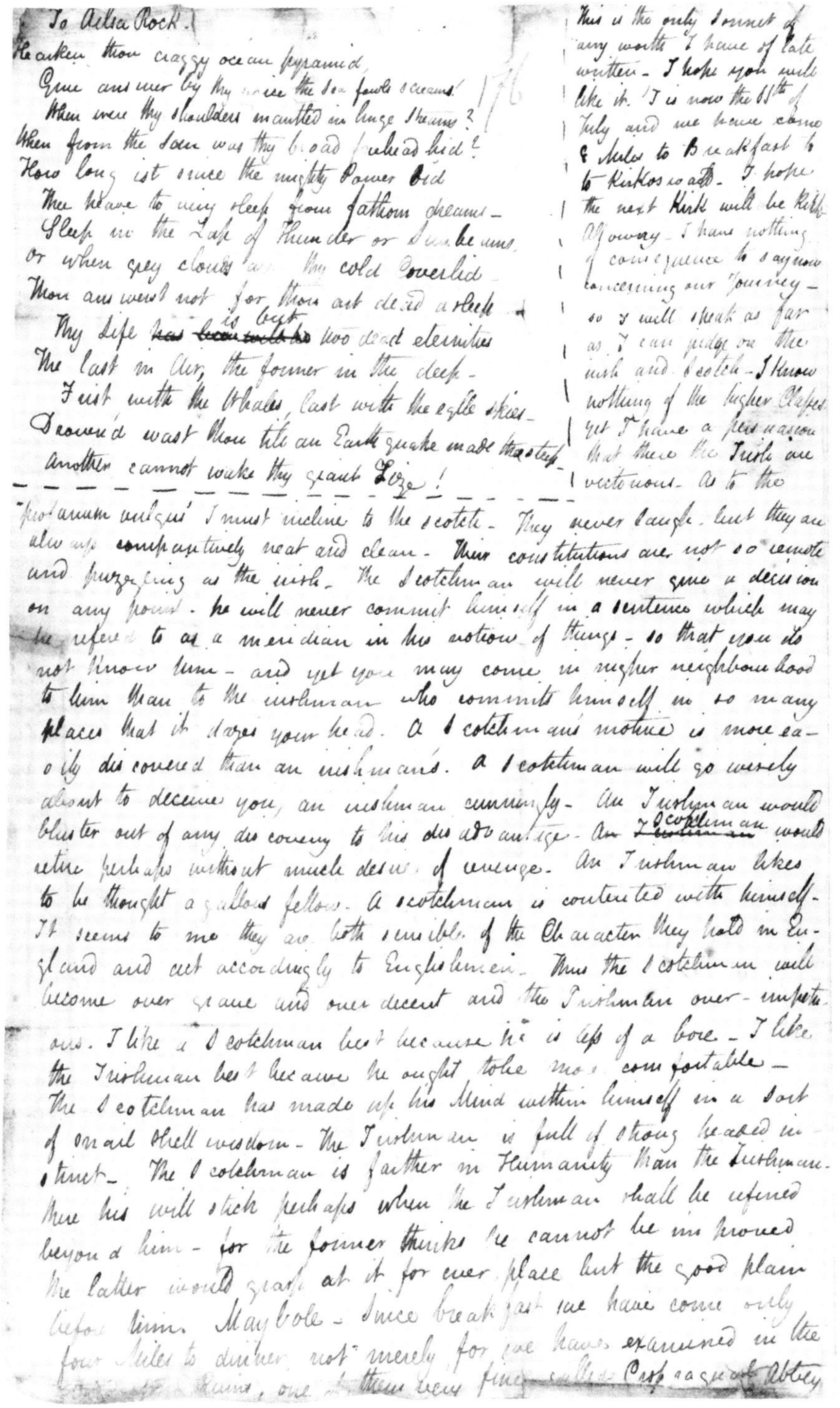

To Ailsa Rock.

Hearken thou craggy ocean pyramid,
Give answer by thy voice the Sea fowls screams!
When were thy shoulders mantled in huge Streams?
When from the Sun was thy broad forehead hid?
How long is't since the mighty Power bid
Thee heave to airy sleep from fathom dreams —
Sleep in the Lap of Thunder or Sunbeams,
Or when grey clouds are thy cold Coverlid —
Thou answerst not for thou art dead asleep —
Thy Life ~~has been with the~~ is but two dead eternities
The last in Air, the former in the deep —
First with the Whales, last with the eagle skies —
Drown'd wast thou till an Earthquake made thee steep —
Another cannot wake thy giant Size!

This is the only Sonnet of any worth I have of late written — I hope you will like it. T'is now the 11th of July and we have come 8 Miles to Breakfast to Kirkoswald — I hope the next Kirk will be Kirk Alloway — I have nothing of consequence to say now concerning our Journey — so I will speak as far as I can judge on the Irish and Scotch — I know nothing of the higher Classes yet I have a persuasion that there the Irish are victorious. As to the 'profanum vulgus' I must incline to the scotch. They never laugh — but they are always comparatively neat and clean. Their constitutions are not so remote and puzzling as the irish. The Scotchman will never give a decision on any point — he will never commit himself in a sentence which may be refered to as a meridian in his notion of things — so that you do not know him — and yet you may come in nigher neighbourhood to him than to the irishman who commits himself in so many places that it dazes your head. A Scotchman's motive is more easily discovered than an irishman's. A Scotchman will go wisely about to deceive you, an irishman cunningly. An Irishman would bluster out of any discovery to his disadvantage. An ~~Irishman~~ Scotchman would retire perhaps without much desire of revenge. An Irishman likes to be thought a gallous fellow. A scotchman is contented with himself. It seems to me they are both sensible of the Character they hold in England and act accordingly to Englishmen. Thus the Scotchman will become over grave and over decent and the Irishman over-impetuous. I like a Scotchman best because he is less of a bore — I like the Irishman best because he ought to be more comfortable — The Scotchman has made up his Mind within himself in a Sort of snail shell wisdom — The Irishman is full of strong headed instinct — The Scotchman is farther in Humanity than the Irishman — there his will stick perhaps when the Irishman shall be refined beyond him — for the former thinks he cannot be improved the latter would grasp at it for ever place but the good plain before him. Maybole — Since breakfast we have come only four Miles to dinner, not merely for we have examined in the ... Ruins, one of them very fine called Crossraguel Abbey

One of Keats's Scotttish letters to his brother, Tom, with the sonnet 'To Ailsa Rock'.

In the end they spent only two nights in Ireland, in Donaghdee and in Belfast, for the country was ruinously expensive, three times more so than Scotland, said Keats. At Donaghdee he was pleased to see that the chambermaid was refreshingly cheerful, being 'out of the horrible dominion of the Scotch kirk', but in a subsequent walk around Belfast he was appalled by the living conditions of the Irish poor: the wretched cottages and the suburbs dominated by 'that most disgusting of all noises worse than the bagpipe': the sound of the shuttles from the cotton factories. One hideous sight in particular took hold of Keats's imagination, something that could have come from Dante's *Inferno*:

> On our return from Bellfast we met a Sadan – the Duchess of Dunghill – It is no laughing matter tho – Imagine the worst dog kennel you ever saw placed upon two poles from a mouldy fencing – In such a wretched thing sat a squalid old Woman squat like an ape half starved from a scarcity of Biscuit in its passage from Madagascar to the cape, – with a pipe in her mouth and looking out with a round-eyed skinny lidded, inanity – with a sort of horizontal idiotic movement of her head – squat and lean she sat and puff'd out the smoke while two ragged tattered Girls carried her along – What a thing would be a history of her Life and sensations.

On 8 July Keats and Brown sailed from Portpatrick back to Scotland, and over the course of the following week walked up the coast to Ayr, then to Glasgow and Loch Lomond. The first day was a twenty-seven-mile hike through Stanraer and into Ayrshire. Keats described this part of the journey in some detail for Tom, again echoing Dorothy Wordsworth's comment to Catherine Clarkson about journal writing: 'I shall endeavour that you may follow our steps in this walk – it would be uninteresting in a Book of Travels – it can not be interest[ing] but by my having gone through it.' For most of the next day they had a view of Ailsa Rock, a thousand-foot-high rocky outcrop fifteen miles off the coast, which had come upon them suddenly out of the mist – 'The effect of ailsa with the peculiar perspective of the Sea in connection with the ground we stood on, and the misty rain then falling gave me a complete Idea of a deluge – Ailsa struck me very suddenly – really I was a little alarmed,' Keats wrote to Tom. He wrote a questioning sonnet, 'Hearken thou craggy ocean pyramid' – 'the only Sonnet of any worth I have written – I hope you will like it'.

At lunchtime the following day the two walkers reached Maybole. 'I have nothing of consequence to say now of our journey,' Keats told Tom, and in a letter he now began to Reynolds he was even more dismissive of travel writing. He said nothing of the landscapes he had seen since leaving Lancaster, and instead ran summarily through the usual picturesque clichés: 'My Dear Reynolds, I'll not run over the Ground we have passed, that would be merely as bad as telling a dream – unless perhaps I do it in the manner of the Laputan printing press – that is I put down Mountains, Rivers Lakes, dells, glens, Rocks, and Clouds, With beautiful enchanting, gothic picturesque fine, delightful, enchancting, Grand, sublime – a few Blisters &c – and now you have our journey thus far.'

They were now walking through Burns country, and Keats was looking forward to visiting the house in Alloway where the great poet had been born. Literary shrines, though not as prevelant as they are today, were still popular destinations. The poet John Clare wrote of his frequent desire 'to see places which poets and novelists and Essayists have rendered classical by their descriptions of the[ir] presence and other localitys rendered sacred by genius'. On his first journey to London in 1820 he made a point of stopping at William Cowper's former home at Huntington and saw the stretch of the River Ouse 'where he wandered with his dog which doubtless there cropt him the white water lily and won a song for its pains'. For Keats, approaching a literary shrine was 'One of the pleasantest means of annulling self', and he thought back to an earlier visit, with Bailey, to Stratford-upon-Avon.

This part of the Scottish landscape was as synonymous with Burns as, in time, parts of the Lake District would be with Wordsworth and, just as he had earlier done in Grasmere, Keats counted off those landmarks already familiar to him from the poetry. Of the Mountains of Annan he wrote to Tom: 'As soon as I saw them so nearly I said to myself "How is it they did not beckon Burns to some grand attempt at Epic".' 'I had no conception that the native place of Burns was so beautiful,' he told Reynolds. 'We came down upon every thing suddenly – there were in our way, the "bonny Doon," with the Brig that Tam O'Shanter cross'd – Kirk Alloway, Burns's Cottage and then the Brigs of Ayr.' Unlike the steady, methodical Brown, Keats could not find the measured pace suitable for a travel journal, as he tried to explain to Reynolds: 'my head is sometimes in such a whirl in considering the million likings and antipathies of our Moments – that I can get into no settled strain in my letters – My Wig! Burns and sentimentality coming across you and Frank Floodgate in the office – O scenery that thou shouldst be crush'd between two Puns.'

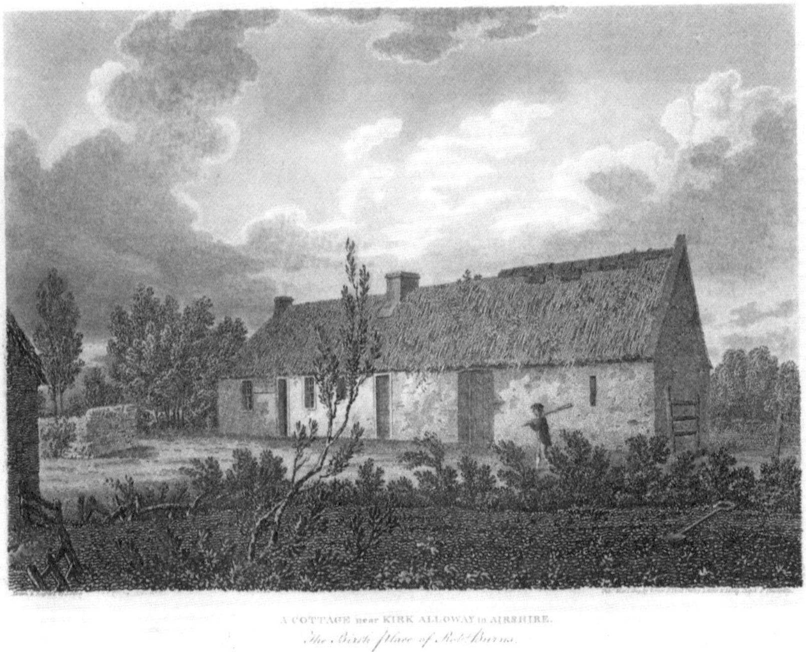

A view of Burns's birthplace, published in 1811.

Burn's birthplace had been built, largely from clay, by the poet's father in 1757. For some years the 'auld clay biggin' had been a tavern, and so was open to visitors. The public also knew it from descriptions in guidebooks, and from engravings in volumes such as *Views in North Britain Illustrative of the Works of Robert Burns*, published in handsome quarto in 1811, which contained a series of stipple engravings depiciting well-known scenes from the poet's life and work. The view of Burns's birthplace was accompanied by the following text:

> The person who occupies it at present has turned it into a snug public house; at this house, yearly, on the birth-day of Burns, a social party meet, and celebrate it with festivity and rejoicing; scarcely a traveller passes who does not there pay a tribute to the memory of the poet; and the possessor has contrived that none shall pass without knowing who once inhabited it, by placing the following inscription near the door: 'Halt, passenger, and read: This is the humble cottage, that gave birth to the celebrated poet, Robert Burns.'

The cottage turned out to be a disappointment, for the local guide rambled drunkenly in an unintelligible Scottish accent and told endless anecdotes. Keats wrote a sonnet 'for the mere sake of writing something under the roof', which was so bad he did not even transcribe it for Reynolds.

Two days later, at Kingswell past Kilmarnock, Keats took up his unfinished letter to Reynolds and reflected upon this visit. He returned to his musings at Teignmouth, on memory, the imagination and reality:

> The Man at the Cottage was a great Bore with his anecdotes – I hate the rascal ... o the flummery of a birthplace! Cant! Cant! Cant! It is enough to give a spirit the guts-ache – Many a true word they say is spoken in jest – this may be because his garb hindered my sublimity – The flat dog made me write a flat sonnet – My dear Reynolds – I cannot write about scenery and visitings – Fancy is indeed less than a palpable reality, but it is greater than remembrance – you would lift your eyes from Homer only to see close before you the real Isle of Tenedos. – you would rather read Homer afterwards than remember yourself – One song of Burns's is of more worth to you than all I could think for a whole year in his native country – His Misery is a dead weight upon the nimbleness of one's quill – I tried to forget it – to drink Toddy without any Care – to write a merry Sonnet – it wont do – he talked with Bitches – he drank with Blackguards, he was miserable – We can see horribly clear in the works of such a man his whole life, as if we were God's spies.

Concluding, Keats commended Reynolds on his forthcoming marriage, and spoke of the pleasure he got from his new sister-in-law, Georgiana. This was the kind of thing that now seemed real to him: 'upon my soul, I have been getting more and more close to you every day, ever since I knew you, and now one of the first pleasures I look to is your happy Marriage – the more, since I have felt the pleasure of loving a sister in Law – Things like these, and they are real, have made me resolve to have a care of my health.'

That evening Keats and Brown entered Glasgow 'under the most oppressive Stare a body could feel'. 'When we had crossed the Bridge Brown look'd back and said its whole population had turned to wonder at us,' wrote Keats, 'we came on till a drunken Man came up to me – I put him off with my Arm – he returned all up in Arms saying aloud that, "he had seen all foreigners bu-u-u t he never saw the like o' me ["] – I was obliged to mention the word Officer and Police before he would desist.' They left the city the following

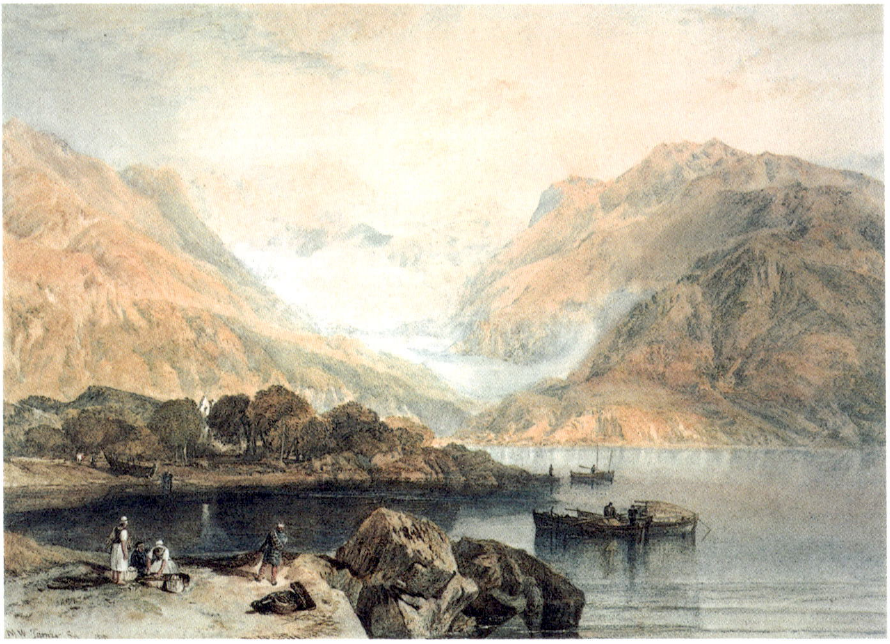

Loch Fyne, by J.M.W. Turner, 1815.

morning and spent the next few days walking north along the western shore of Loch Lomond to Inverary, the eighteenth-century new town on Loch Fyne. 'Here's Brown going on so that I cannot bring to Mind how the last two days have vanished,' Keats wrote to Tom from 'Cairn-something'. The walk had been in beautiful weather, he reported, but the landscape was somewhat spoiled by the number of tourists both around and on the loch: 'I told you last how we were stared at in Glasgow – we are not out of the Crowd yet – Steam Boats on Loch Lomond and Barouches on its sides take a little from the Pleasure of such romantic chaps as Brown and I.' He had been bathing in the Loch – 'quite pat and fresh but for the cursed Gad flies – damn 'em they have been at me ever since I left the Swan and two necks'.

They arrived at Inverary on 17 July. Brown was 'knock'd up from new shoes', but Keats explored the local attractions. Across the loch he could see Inverary Castle, the recently rebuilt ancestral home of the Dukes of Argyll, from whence came the sound of bagpipes: 'I must say I enjoyed two or three common tunes,' he told Tom, 'but nothing could stifle the horrors of a solo on the Bag-pipe – I thought the Beast would never have done – Yet I was doomed to hear another.' In the evening he went to see a play at the local theatre, *The Stranger* by Augustus von Kotzebue, which had recently been produced at

Drury Lane Theatre in London, and been given the most damning notices. In this local production, moments of high drama were accompanied by, of all things, more bagpipes: 'I saw the Stranger accompanied by a Bag pipe – There they went on about "interesting creaters" and "human nater" – till the Curtain fell and then Came the Bag pipe – When Mrs Haller fainted down went the Curtain and out came the Bagpipe – the heartrending, shoemending reconciliation the Piper blew amain.' Keats had neither seen nor read the play before, and found it even worse than the 'wretched players'.

After the performance, Keats returned to the inn and began a searching, very personal letter to Benjamin Bailey: 'And here Bailey I will say a few words written in a sane and sober mind, a very scarce thing with me … I carry all matters to an extreme – so that when I have any little vexation it grows in five Minutes into a theme for Sophocles.' He apologised for not going to see the Reynolds family in Hampstead, but explained:

> I am certain that our fair friends are glad I should come for the mere sake of my coming; but I am certain I bring with me a vexation they are better without … I am certain I have not a right feeling towards women – at this moment I am striving to be just to them but I cannot – Is it because they fall so far beneath my Boyish imagination? … Is it not extraordinary? When among Men I have no evil thoughts, no malice, no spleen … When I am among women I have evil thoughts, malice, spleen – I cannot speak or be silent – I am full of Suspicions and therefore listen to no thing – I am in a hurry to be gone – You must be charitable and put all this perversity to my being disappointed since boyhood.

He must, he wrote, 'get over this', and unravel his 'gordian complication of feelings'. He explained to Bailey that the walking tour was much more than a physical adventure, it was an integral part of this unravelling:

> You appeared to wish to avoid any words on this subject – don't think it a bore my dear fellow – it shall be my Amen – I should not have consented to myself these four Months tramping in the highlands but that I thought it would give me more experience, rub off more Prejudice, use me to more hardship, identify finer scenes load me with grander Mountains, and strengthen more my reach in Poetry, than would stopping at home among Books even though I should reach Homer …

Now, 'comparitively a mountaineer', he was too familar with wildness and mountains 'too much to break out much about their Grandeur'. The landscape itself, despite its sublimity, had less hold on Keats's mind now than his knotted feelings: 'The first Mountains I saw, though not so large as some I have since seen, weighed very solemnly upon me. The effect is wearing away – yet I like them mainely,' he continued in his letter.

The following morning, a Saturday, Keats and Brown left Inverary and started to walk along the southern shore of Loch Awe towards Cladich. Picking up his current journal-letter to Tom, Keats confessed that he had 'not been at all in the cue to write'. It had been an exhausting two days. The Scottish diet of eggs and oatcake was becoming terribly monotonous – 'we have lost the sight of white bread entirely – Now we had eaten nothing but Eggs all day – about 10 a piece and they had become sickening' – and during the twenty-mile trudge along the Loch, Brown's feet had become so blistered that he was barely able to walk. But as they continued north towards Oban and the Inner Hebrides, the landscape, at least, grew increasingly dramatic:

> the near Hills were not very lofty but many of their steeps beautifully wooded – the distant Mountains in the Hebrides very grand and Saltwater Lakes coming up between Crags and Islands fulltided and scarcely ruffled – sometimes appearing as one large Lake, sometimes as th[r]ee distinct ones in different directions – At one point we saw afar off a rocky opening opening into the main Sea – We have also seen an Eagle or two. They move about without the least motion of Wings when in an indolent fit – I am for the first time in a country where a foreign Language is spoken – they gabble away Gaelic at a vast rate ...

Keats was writing from an inn at Ford. Downstairs, an old grandmother, in old shoes and no stockings, was mixing them some snuff. The previous evening they had seen a donkey pass by laden with tin pots and, to their great annoyance, a group of 'Whisky Men sat up clattering Gaelic till I am sure one o'Clock'. They were surrounded by hills shrouded in mist, and there were the usual wretched stone cottages, where the smoke from the peat fire had to make its way out through the door or a hole in the roof. Here and there was a barefooted girl, including one 'driving Cows down a slope like a mad thing', another, with a rather pretty face, standing at the cowhouse door up to her ankles in dirt.

The following day, Thursday 21 July, Keats and Brown walked fifteen miles through rain to Oban, directly opposite the Isle of Mull. Further out to sea were two celebrated destinations, Iona, with its ancient ruins, and the Isle of Staffa with its famed Fingal's Cave. They were fashionable places, and the prices to get there reflected this: the cost of the passage to Staffa was seven guineas – ''tis like paying sixpence for an apple at a playhouse', Keats complained to Tom that afternoon, 'this irritated me and Brown was not best pleased – we have therefore resolved to set northward for fort William tomorrow morning'. But the next day one of the guides they had been haggling with offered them a cheaper alternative – a walk through the Isle of Mull to Iona. 'So we had a little talk,' said Keats, 'and finally agreed that he should be our guide across the Isle of Mull.'

In a fine breeze they took one ferry to the nearby Isle of Kerrara, and then a second to Mull itself, the two journeys together taking no more than forty minutes. The subsequent walk through the interior, however, proved to be the most difficult of the entire trip. 'The rough road through the Island, or rather the track is the most dreary you can think of – betwe[e]n dreary Mountains – over bog and river with our Breeches tucked up and our Stockings in hand,' said Keats. 'There's a wild place!' Brown wrote later to his friend Charles Wentworth Dilke. 'Thirty-seven miles of jumping and flinging over great stones along no path at all, up the steep and down the steep, and wading thro' rivulets up to the knees, and crossing a bog, a mile long, up to the ancles.' At one point their guide lost the way, and they enquired at a local cottage for directions: 'a young Woman without a word threw on her cloak and walked a Mile in a missling rain and splashy way to put us right again'.

At eight o'clock that evening the party came to an isolated shepherd's hut, and here they spent the night. It was extremely humble, and they had to stoop to get through the door. Inside, the single, earth-floored room was thick with smoke from the peat fire, which over time had blackened the rafters and thatched roof. Peering through the smoke, Keats finished the letter to Bailey he had begun at Inverary:

> We have come over heath and rock and river and bog to what in England would be called a horrid place ... The family speak not a word but gaelic and we have not yet seen their faces for the smoke which after visiting every cranny (not excepting my eyes very much incommoded for writing), finds its way out at the door. I am more comfortable than I could have imagined in such a place, and so is Brown.

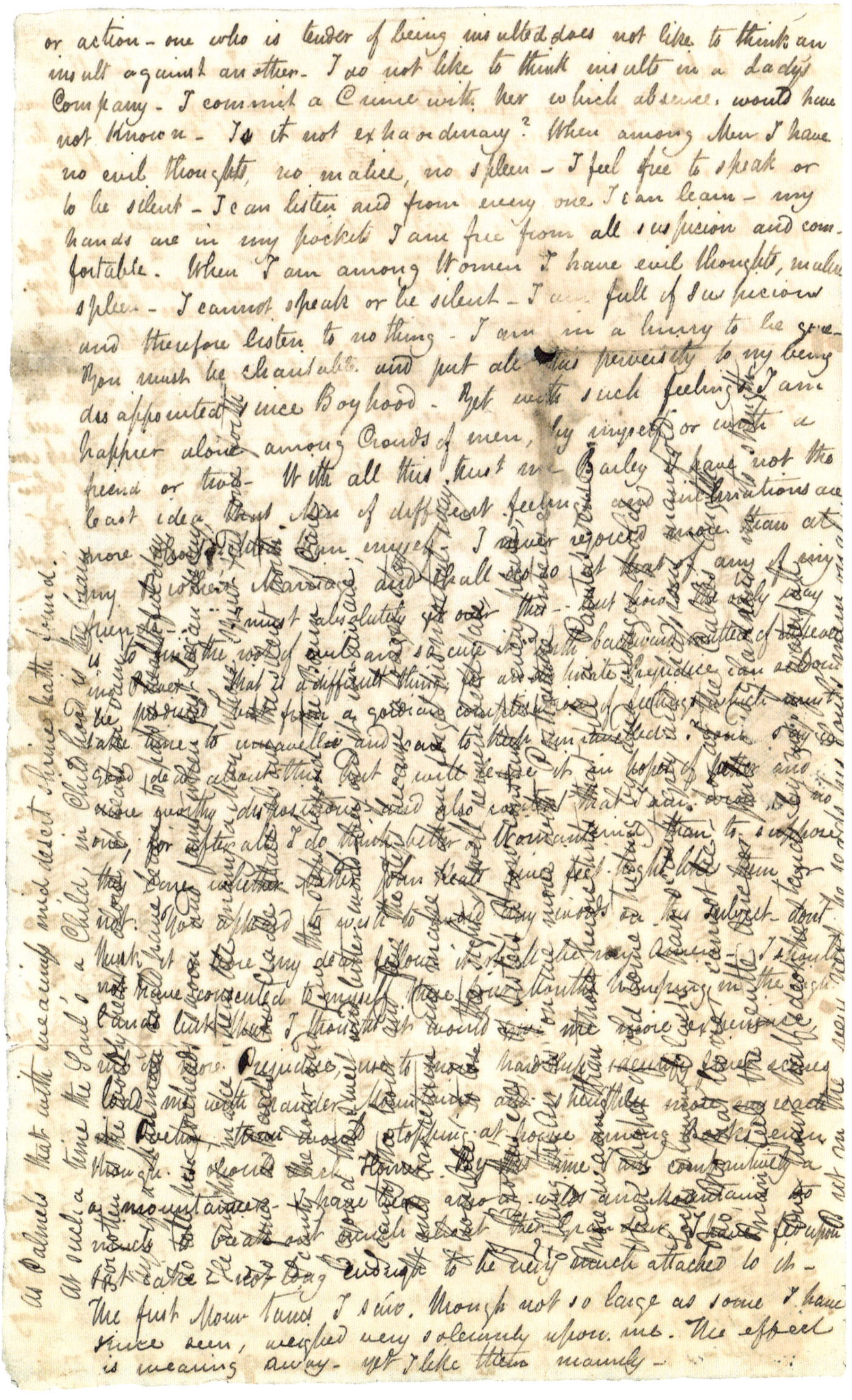
or action – one who is tender of being insulted does not like to think an insult against another – I do not like to think insults in a Lady's Company – I commit a Crime with her which absence would have not known – Is it not extraordinary? When among Men I have no evil thoughts, no malice, no spleen – I feel free to speak or to be silent – I can listen and from every one I can learn – my hands are in my pockets I am free from all suspicion and comfortable. When I am among Women I have evil thoughts, malice spleen – I cannot speak or be silent – I am full of Suspicions and therefore listen to nothing – I am in a hurry to be gone – You must be charitable and put all this perversity to my being disappointed since Boyhood – Yet with such feelings I am happier alone among Crowds of men, by myself or with a friend or two – With all this trust me Bailey I have not the least idea that Men of different feelings and inclinations are more short sighted than myself – I never rejoiced more than at my Brother's Marriage and shall do so at that of any of my friends – I must absolutely get over this – but how? The only way is to find the root of evil, and so cure it with backward mutters of dissevering Power – That is a difficult thing; for an obstinate Prejudice can seldom be produced but from a gordian complication of feelings, which must take time to unravel and care to keep unravelled. I could say a good deal about this but I will leave it in hopes of better and more worthy dispositions – and also content that I am wronging no one, for after all I do think better of Womankind than to suppose they care whether Mister John Keats five feet high likes them or not. You appeared to wish to avoid any words on this subject – don't think it a bore my dear fellow – it shall be my amen – I should not have consented to myself these four Months tramping in the highlands but that I thought it would give me more experience, rub off more Prejudice, use to more hardship, identify finer scenes load me with grander Mountains, and strengthen more my reach in Poetry, than would stopping at home among Books even though I should reach Homer – By this time I am comparatively a mountaineer – I have been among wilds and Mountains too much to break out much about their Grandeur. I have fed upon oat cake – not long enough to be very much attached to it – The first Mountains I saw, though not so large as some I have since seen, weighed very solemnly upon me. The effect is wearing away – yet I like them mainly –

John Keats's letter to Benjamin Bailey, completed on 22 July 1818, on the Isle of Mull.

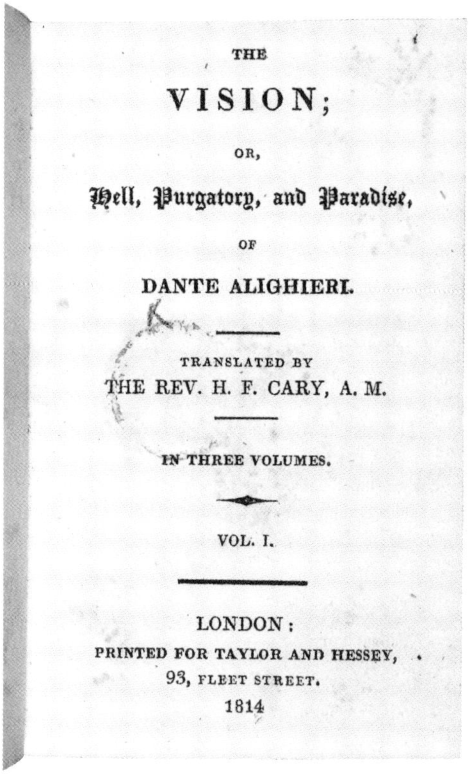

THE

VISION;

OR,

Hell, Purgatory, and Paradise,

OF

DANTE ALIGHIERI.

TRANSLATED BY

THE REV. H. F. CARY, A. M.

IN THREE VOLUMES.

VOL. I.

LONDON:

PRINTED FOR TAYLOR AND HESSEY,

93, FLEET STREET.

1814

Henry Cary's translation of Dante, the only reading Keats took with him to Scotland.

Keats went on to write about his sister Fanny, and his brother and sister-in-law in America, and said that he looked forward to seeing Bailey, then residing in Carlisle, on his return trip south. 'I hope you will have a nice convenient room for a Library ... You say I must study Dante – well the only Books I have with me are those three little Volumes. I read that fine passage you mention a few days ago.' The 'three little volumes' were a miniature edition of Dante's *Divine Comedy*, translated by Henry Cary, and published in 1814. The first serviceable and accurate English translation of Dante's great work, it had recently been extravagantly praised by Coleridge and become a best-seller. In part, Keats's choice was a practical one – 'they will fit into the aptest corner' he had said before setting out. But it was in keeping with his physical and mental journey, his 'clamber through the clouds' after experience and knowledge, that he should take with him not a guidebook advising on the best routes and inns, but Dante's extraordinary imaginative ascent through Hell and Purgatory to Paradise.

His letter went on to talk about his unsatisfactory visit to Burns's cottage, and even more unsatisfactory sonnet. He then transcribed a more recent poem, 'There is a joy in footing slow across a silent plain':

O horrible! to lose the sight of well remember'd face,
Of Brother's eyes, Of Sister's Brow, constant to every place;
Filling the Air as one we move with Portraiture intense
More warm than those heroic tints that fill a Painter's sense –
When Shapes of old come striding by and visages of old,
Locks shining black, hair scanty grey and passions manifold.
No, No that horror cannot be – for at the Cable's length
Man feels the gentle Anchor pull and gladdens in its strength –
One hour half ideot he stands by mossy waterfall,
But in the very next he reads his Soul's memorial:
He reads it on the Mountain's height where chance he may sit down
Upon rough marble diadem, that Hills eternal crown.
Yet be the Anchor e'er so fast, room there is for a prayer
That Man may never loose his Mind on Mountains bleak and bare;
That he may stray league after League some great Berthplace to find,
And keep his vision clear from speck, his inward sight unblind –

This is something more than the conventional 'horror' enjoyed by tourists. It shows the deep effect the Scottish mountains were having on Keats's mind; on the nervous sensibility that carried everything 'to extremes'.

When Keats had finished the letter he wrapped himself in a blanket and, still fully dressed, went to sleep to the sound of the guide snoring an arm's length away. The following day the group made another exhausting trudge through Mull, with their guide diverting them with Gaelic folk songs, and Brown, who fancied that his ancestors came from Mull, talking to local inhabitants. The next morning they finally reached Iona and its ancient Christian settlement. A local schoolmaster, barely four feet tall and 'an ignorant little man but reckoned very clever', said Keats, showed them round the ruins. Keats relayed the antiquarian information on to Tom: 'It is rich in the most interesting antiquities. Who would expect to find the ruins of a fine Cathedral Church, of Cloisters, Colleges, Monasteries and Nunneries in so remote an Island?' They took a boat to Staffa, which, at a bargain price, would then take them back to Mull at Loch na Keal, and thus allow them a better route back across Mull to the mainland. Taking advantage of a break in the weather,

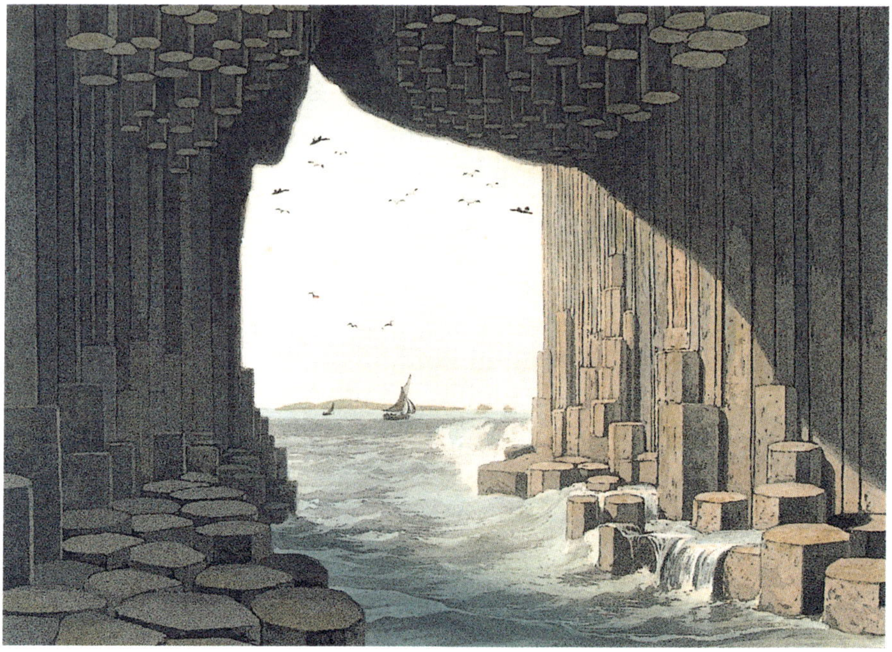

In Fingal's Cave, Staffa, by William Daniell, 1817.

they sailed to Fingal's Cave, with its extraordinary black basalt pillars rising out of the sea. 'I am puzzled how to give you an Idea of Staffa,' Keats wrote to Tom. 'It can only be represented by a first rate drawing.' But he went on to give a remarkable description of the cave:

> One may compare the surface of the Island to a roof – this roof is supported by grand pillars of basalt standing together as thick as honey combs. The finest thing is Fingal's Cave – it is entirely a hollowing out of Basalt Pillars. Suppose now the Giants who rebelled against Jove had taken a whole Mass of black Columns and bound them together like bunches of matches – and then with immense Axes had made a cavern in the body of these columns – of course the roof and floor must be composed of the broken ends of the Columns – For solemnity and grandeur it far surpasses the finest Cathedrall – The length of the Cave is 120 feet and from its extremity the view into the sea through the large Arch at the entrance – the colour of the columns is a sort of black with a lurking gloom of purple therin ... As we approached in the boat there was such a fine swell of the sea that the pillars appeared rising immediately out of the crystal – But it is impossible to describe it ...

Keats had caught a severe cold on Mull, and a sore throat that would plague him over the coming weeks. He was exhausted, and looked forward to returning home to Hampstead and his books. 'I assure you I often long for a seat and a Cup o' tea at well Walk,' he confessed to Tom, 'especially now that mountains, castles and Lakes are becoming common to me – yet I would rather summer it out for on the whole I am happier than when I have time to be glum – perhaps it may cure me – Immediately on my return I shall begin studying hard with a peep at the theatre now and then – and depend upon it I shall be very luxurious – With respect to Women I think I shall be able to conquer my passions hereafter better than I have yet done.' He had no more energy for journal writing, unlike Brown, who continued to record 'every little circumstance' in his letters. 'I should like to do the same but I confess myself too indolent and besides next winter every thing will come up in prime order as we verge on such and such things,' he told Tom. He had earlier complained to Bailey about Brown's methodical habits: 'Brown keeps on writing volumes of adventures to Dilke – when we get in of an evening and I have perhaps taken my rest on a couple of chairs he affronts my indolence and Luxury by pulling out of his knapsack 1st his paper – 2nd his pens and last his ink – Now I would not care if he would change about a little – I say now, why not Bailey take out his pens first sometimes – But I might as well tell a hen to hold up her head before she drinks instead of afterwards.'

Keats and Brown rested in Oban, and then, despite their fatigue and Keats's sore throat, continued doggedly, if more slowly, on their way. At the beginning of August they reached Fort William, and on Sunday, 2 August, they climbed Ben Nevis, Britain's highest peak and, as it turned out, the highpoint of their tour. With a guide suitably dressed 'in the Tartan and Cap', they set off at about five in the morning. They ascended slowly, rise by rise, occasionally taking a glass of whisky each and resting. Soon all vegetation dropped away and the ascent became rocky and more formidable, then, towards the top, a mist came down, and from there to the top they walked in semi-obscurity. Through the mist Keats could make out endless loose stones, patches of snow and huge chasms: 'They appear great rents in the very heart of the mountain though they are not, being at the side of it, but other huge crags arising round it give the appearance to Nevis of a shattered heart or Core in itself.' Then the mist cleared, and was replaced by swirling cloud:

> After a little time the Mist cleared away but still there were large Clouds about attracted by old Ben to a certain distance so as to form

> as it appeard large dome curtains which kept sailing about, opening and shutting at intervals here and there and everrywhere; so that although we did not see one vast wide extent of prospect all round we saw something perhaps finer – these cloud-veils opening with a dissolving motion and showing us the mountainous region beneath as through a loop hole – these Mouldy loop holes ever varrying and discovering fresh prospect east, west north and South – Then it was misty again and again it was fair – then puff came a cold breeze of wind and bared a craggy chap we had not yet seen though in close neighbourhood – Every now and then we had over head blue sky clear and the sun pretty warm.

On the summit of Ben Nevis Keats climbed the cairn, 'and so got a little higher than old Ben himself', drank some whisky, and composed a sonnet, 'Read me a Lesson muse, and speak it loud'. Then came 'the most vile descent – shook me all to pieces', and the return to Fort William. 'I am heartily glad it is done,' Keats wrote afterwards to Tom, 'it is almost like a fly crawling up a wainscoat – Imagine the task of mounting 10 Saint Pauls without the convenience of stair cases.'

Four days later Keats and Brown arrived at Inverness. It was the farthest north Keats would get. 'He caught a violent cold in the Island of Mull, which far from leaving him, has become worse,' Brown told Dilke, 'and the Physician here thinks him too thin and fevered to proceed on our journey. It is a cruel disappointment.' And so, while Brown pushed on alone, on Saturday, 8 August, Keats boarded the smack *Cromarty* and sailed south. He arrived back in Hampstead on 19 August. 'John Keats arrived here last night as brown and as shabby as you can imagine,' wrote his friend Mrs Dilke, 'scarcely any shoes left, his jacket all torn at the back, a fur cap, a great plaid, and his knapsack.'

Keats had made his tour among the Scottish mountains in the hope that it would give him a greater capacity for hardship, enlarge his vision, and, most importantly, strengthen his reach in poetry. He returned full of resolve, and that autumn, while he nursed his brother Tom through the final, terrible stages of tuberculosis, he began his long-promised epic, 'Hyperion'. Its subject was the overthrow of the Titans by the younger gods, led by Jove, and the tone of the poem, written in the blank verse of Milton's *Paradise Lost* and

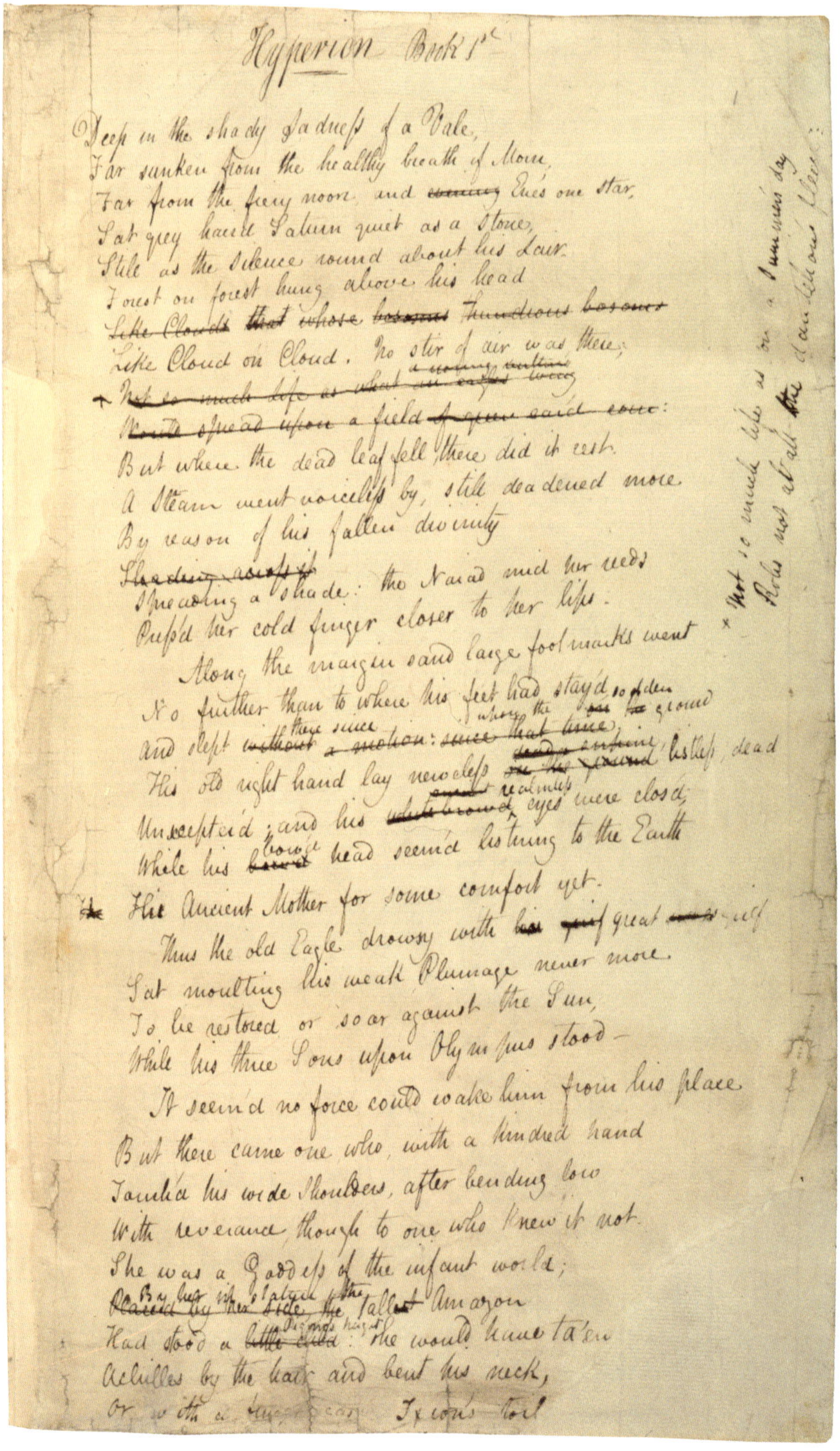

Hyperion Book 1st

Deep in the shady sadness of a Vale,
Far sunken from the healthy breath of Morn,
Far from the fiery noon and Eve's one star,
Sat grey hair'd Saturn quiet as a Stone,
Still as the silence round about his Lair.
Forest on forest hung above his head
~~Like Clouds that whose bosoms thunderous bosoms~~
Like Cloud on Cloud. No stir of air was there;
~~Not so much life as what an eagle's wing~~
~~Would spread upon a field of green ear'd corn:~~
But where the dead leaf fell there did it rest.
A Stream went voiceless by, still deadened more
By reason of his fallen divinity
~~Shading across it~~
Spreading a shade: the Naiad mid her reeds
Press'd her cold finger closer to her lips.
Along the margin sand large footmarks went
No further than to where his feet had stray'd
And slept there since. Upon the sodden ground
His old right hand lay nerveless, listless, dead,
Unsceptred; and his realmless eyes were clos'd;
While his bow'd head seem'd listening to the Earth
His ancient Mother for some comfort yet.
Thus the old Eagle drowsy with his great grief
Sat moulting his weak Plumage never more
To be restored or soar against the Sun,
While his three Sons upon Olympus stood—
It seem'd no force could wake him from his place
But there came one who, with a kindred hand
Touch'd his wide Shoulders, after bending low
With reverence, though to one who knew it not.
She was a Goddess of the infant world;
By her in stature the tall Amazon
Had stood a pigmy's height: she would have ta'en
Achilles by the hair and bent his neck,
Or with a finger stay'd Ixion's wheel

* Not so much life as on a summer's day
Robs not at all the dandelion's fleece;

John Keats, original manuscript of 'Hyperion', 1818–19.

Cary's translation of Dante, was solemn and austere. Keats told Benjamin Robert Haydon: 'in Endymion I think you may have many bits of the deep and sentimental cast – the nature of *Hyperion* will lead me to treat it in a more naked and grecian Manner'.

Then, in April the following year, he abandoned 'Hyperion' and turned instead to another kind of poetry, and another kind of landscape. He was now living at Wentworth Place, Charles Brown's home in Hampstead, and for the next few weeks enjoyed beautiful spring weather, sitting in the garden or taking walks over the Heath, on one occasion meeting Coleridge, who in two miles 'broached a thousand things'. Living in the other half of Wentworth Place, and sharing the garden, were a widow, Mrs Brawne, and her daughters. Keats, who at Inverary had written to Bailey that he had 'not a right feeling towards women', found himself falling in love with the eldest daughter, Fanny.

'Mr and Mrs Dilke are coming to dine with us to day,' Keats wrote to his sister Fanny on 1 May, 'they will enjoy the country after Westminster – O there is nothing like fine weather, and health, and Books, and a fine country, and a contented Mind, and Diligent habit of reading and thinking, and an amulet against the ennui – and, please heaven, a little claret-wine cool out of a cellar a mile deep – with a few or a good many ratafia cakes – a rocky basin to bathe in, a strawberry bed to say your prayers to Flora in.' It was in this relaxed mood that he composed, in the space of a few days, three great odes: 'On Melancholy', 'To a Nightingale' and 'To a Grecian Urn'. In contrast to the epic scale of 'Hyperion', they were short, meditative works, brimming with the landscape of Hampstead, the 'melodious plot of beechen green and shadows numberless', and the sights, sounds and smells of that wonderful spring perfectly expressed the twists and turns of Keats's thoughts:

> I cannot see what flowers are at my feet,
>   Nor what soft incense hangs upon the boughs,
> But, in embalmed darkness, guess each sweet
>   Wherewith the seasonable month endows
> The grass, the thicket, and the fruit-tree wild;
>   White hawthorn, and the pastoral eglantine;
>   Fast fading violets cover'd up in leaves;
>   And mid-May's eldest child,
>   The coming musk-rose, full of dewy wine,
>   The murmurous haunt of flies on summer eves.

At the end of June Keats travelled south to the Isle of Wight and settled at Shanklin with his friend James Rice. There he worked on a new poem, 'Lamia'. After three weeks they were joined by Charles Brown. 'Our window looks over house tops and Cliffs onto the sea, so that when the Ships sail past the Cottage Chimneys you may take them for weathercocks,' Keats wrote to his sister Fanny. 'We have Hill and Dale forest and Mead and plenty of Lobsters ... You have never seen mountains, or I might tell you that the hill at Steephill is I think almost of as much consequence as Mount Rydal on Lake Winander.'

'[M]y Scotch journey gave me a doze of the Picturesque with which I ought to be contented for some time,' Keats had told his sister from Hampstead, and at Shanklin he watched with contempt the picturesque tourists gathering around celebrated beauty spots. 'Tomorrow I shall, if my health continues to improve during the night, take a look further about the country, and spy at the parties about here who come hunting after the picturesque like beagles,' he wrote to Fanny Brawne. 'It is astonishing how they raven down scenery like children do sweetmeats. The wondrous chine here is a very great Lion: I wish I had as many guineas as there have been spy-glasses in it ... I would rather be here alone at my task than in the bustle of literary chitchat.' To Dilke he wrote at the end of July:

> If I may guess I should that there is no finer part in the Island than from this Place to Steephill – I do not hesitate to say it is fine. Bonchurch is the best. But I have been so many finer walks, with a back ground of lake and mountain instedd of the sea, that I am not much touch'd with it, though I credit it for all the Surprise I should have felt if it had taken my cockney maidenhead – But I may call myself an old Stager in the picturesque, and unless it be something very large and overpowering I cannot receive any extraordinary relish.

In August, Keats and Brown moved to Winchester. 'We ... find it an exceeding pleasant Town,' Keats told his sister, 'enriched with a beautiful Cathedrall and surrounded by a fresh-looking country.' The view from his window was as unpicturesque as could be – the blank wall of a neighbouring house – but he found it oddly reassuring. After the beauties of the south Devon coast, the lakes and fells of Westmoreland, the Scottish Highlands, and the cliffs of the Isle of Wight, he finally seemed to have found his ideal view. 'It is strange I should like it better than the view of the sea from our window at Shanklin,' he told Fanny Brawne. 'I began to hate the very posts there ... getting a great dislike of the picturesque; and can only relish it over again by seeing you enjoy it.'

At Winchester Keats enjoyed the quiet life of 'application study and thought' he had proposed to Taylor at Teignmouth. His health benefited from the fine autumn weather and the clean air of the chalk downs beside the town, 'worth sixpence a pint'. 'I enjoy the Weather I adore fine Weather as the greatest blessing I can have,' he wrote to his sister. 'Give me Books, Fruit, French wine and fine weather and a little music out of doors, played by somebody I do not know – not pay the price of one's time for a gig – but a little chance music: and I can pass a summer very quietly without caring very much about Fat Louis, fat regent or the Duke of Wellington.'

Every day before dinner Keats took his favourite walk, the first part of which he described in detail to George and Georgiana in America. Starting from the cathedral close, he left the town through one of its ancient gates, passed beside Winchester College, then, 'crossing some meadows and at last a country alley of gardens', arrived at the medieval church and hospital of St Cross. 'Then I pass across St Cross meadows till you come to the most beautifully clear river,' he told his brother and sister-in-law, 'this is only one mile of my walk I will spare you the other two till after supper when they would do you more good.'

Keats returned, briefly, to 'Hyperion', but soon abandoned it again. The poem's ornate, Miltonic verse now seemed to him self-conscious and artificial. 'I have given up Hyperion,' he wrote to Reynolds. 'Miltonic verse cannot be written but in an artful or rather artist's humour. I wish to give myself up to other sensations. English ought to be kept up.' He invited Reynolds to put a mark by those parts of the poem showing 'the false beauty proceeding from art', and another by those which showed 'the true voice of feeling'. The autumn weather, he said, reminded him of the medieval romances of the young eighteenth-century poet Thomas Chatterton: 'He is the purest writer in the English Language. He has no French idiom, or particles like Chaucer – 'tis genuine English Idiom in English words.'

'How beautiful the season is now,' he told Reynolds. 'How fine the air. A temperate sharpness about it. Really, without joking, chaste weather – Dian skies – I never lik'd stubble fields so much as now – Aye better than the chilly green of the spring. Somehow a stubble plain looks warm – in the same way that some pictures look warm – this struck me so much in my Sunday's walk that I composed upon it.' The composition was the last, and perhaps the

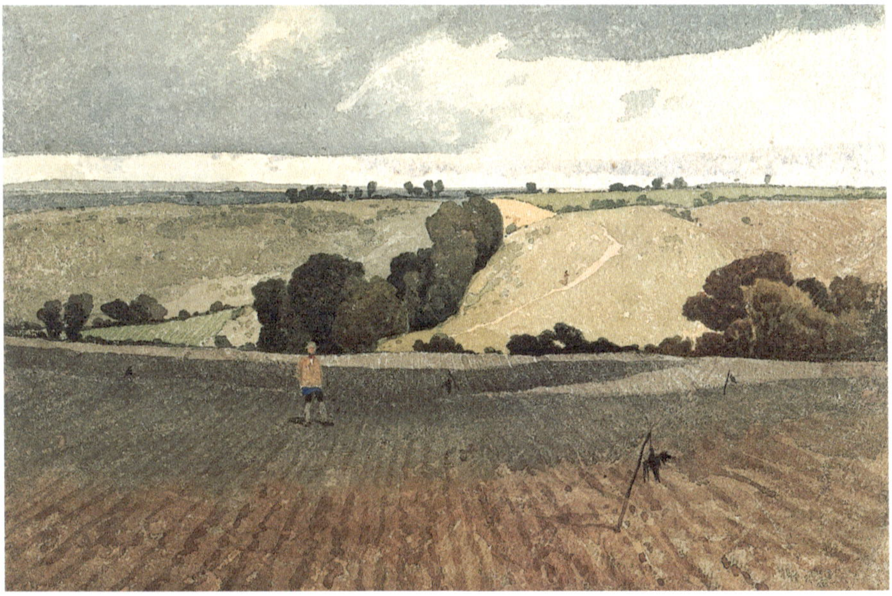

A ploughed field, by John Sell Cotman, *c.*1808.

finest of Keats's great odes, 'To Autumn'. 'If Poetry comes not as naturally as the Leaves to a tree it had better not come at all,' he had written to John Taylor in February 1818, and 'To Autumn' has a spontaneity and a tranquillity that effortlessly capture the poet's mood. Instead of the fashionable prospects and clichéd descriptions of the picturesque, we are given the intimate, more expressive details of an autumn landscape, which Keats conveys with transparent clarity:

Season of mists and mellow fruitfulness,
  Close bosom-friend of the maturing sun;
Conspiring with him how to load and bless
  With fruit the vines that round the thatch-eves run;
To bend with apples the moss'd cottage-trees,
  And fill all fruit with ripeness to the core;
    To swell the gourd, and plump the hazel shells
With a sweet kernel; to set budding more,
  And still more, later flowers for the bees,
  Until they think warm days will never cease,
    For Summer has o'er-brimm'd their clammy cells.

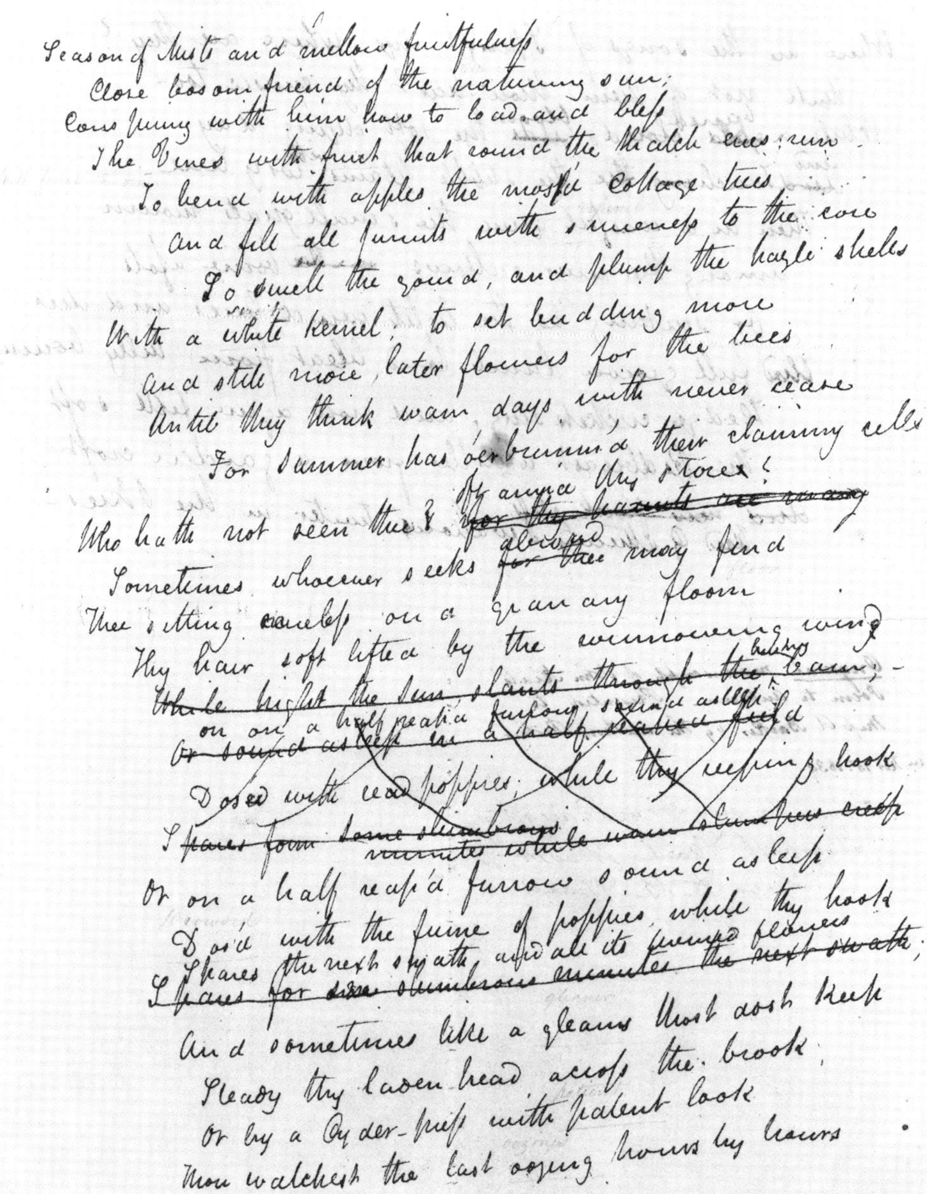
Season of Mists and mellow fruitfulness
Close bosom friend of the maturing sun;
Conspiring with him how to load and bless
The Vines with fruit that round the thatch eves run
To bend with apples the moss'd Cottage trees
And fill all fruits with sweetness to the core
To swell the gourd, and plump the hazle shells
With a white kernel; to set budding more
And still more, later flowers for the bees
Until they think warm days will never cease
For Summer has o'erbrimm'd their clammy cells.
Who hath not seen thee? Oft amid thy stores? ~~for thy haunts are many~~
Sometimes whoever seeks abroad ~~for thee~~ may find
Thee sitting careless on a granary floor
Thy hair soft lifted by the winnowing wind
~~While bright the Sun slants through the barn;~~
on on a half reap'd furrow sound asleep
~~Or sound asleep in a half reaped field~~
Dosed with red poppies; while thy reeping hook
~~Spares form some slumbrous~~ minutes while ~~warm slumbers creep~~
Or on a half reap'd furrow sound asleep
Dos'd with the fume of poppies, while thy hook
Spares the next swath and all its twined flowers
~~Spares for some slumbrous minutes the next swath;~~
And sometimes like a gleaner thou dost keep
Steady thy laden head across the brook;
Or by a Cyder-press with patient look
Thou watchest the last oozing hours by hours.

John Keats, the original manuscript of 'To Autumn', 1819.

Who hath not seen thee oft amid thy store?
  Sometimes whoever seeks abroad may find
Thee sitting careless on a granary floor,
  Thy hair soft-lifted by the winnowing wind;
Or on a half-reap'd furrow sound asleep,
  Drows'd with the fume of poppies, while thy hook
    Spares the next swath and all its twined flowers:
And sometimes like a gleaner thou dost keep
  Steady thy laden head across a brook;
  Or by a cyder-press, with patient look,
    Thou watchest the last oozings hours by hours.

Where are the songs of Spring? Ay, where are they?
  Think not of them, thou hast thy music too, –
While barred clouds bloom the soft-dying day,
  And touch the stubble-plains with rosy hue;
Then in a wailful choir the small gnats mourn
  Among the river sallows, borne aloft
    Or sinking as the light wind lives or dies;
And full-grown lambs loud bleat from hilly bourn;
  Hedge-crickets sing; and now with treble soft
The red-breast whistles from a garden-croft;
    And gathering swallows twitter in the skies.

'Did our great Poets ever write short Pieces?' Keats had asked his brother George when he was writing *Endymion*, and to his teacher and friend Charles Cowden Clarke he had said that 'epic was of all the king'. His tour north had not led to the long Miltonic epic that had once been his greatest ambition. Nor had it resulted in a love for Britain's most dramatic and celebrated landscapes. Instead, it had cleared his mind for the shorter meditative poems that are Keats's greatest poetic achievement, those written in the quiet rural settings of Hampstead and Winchester.

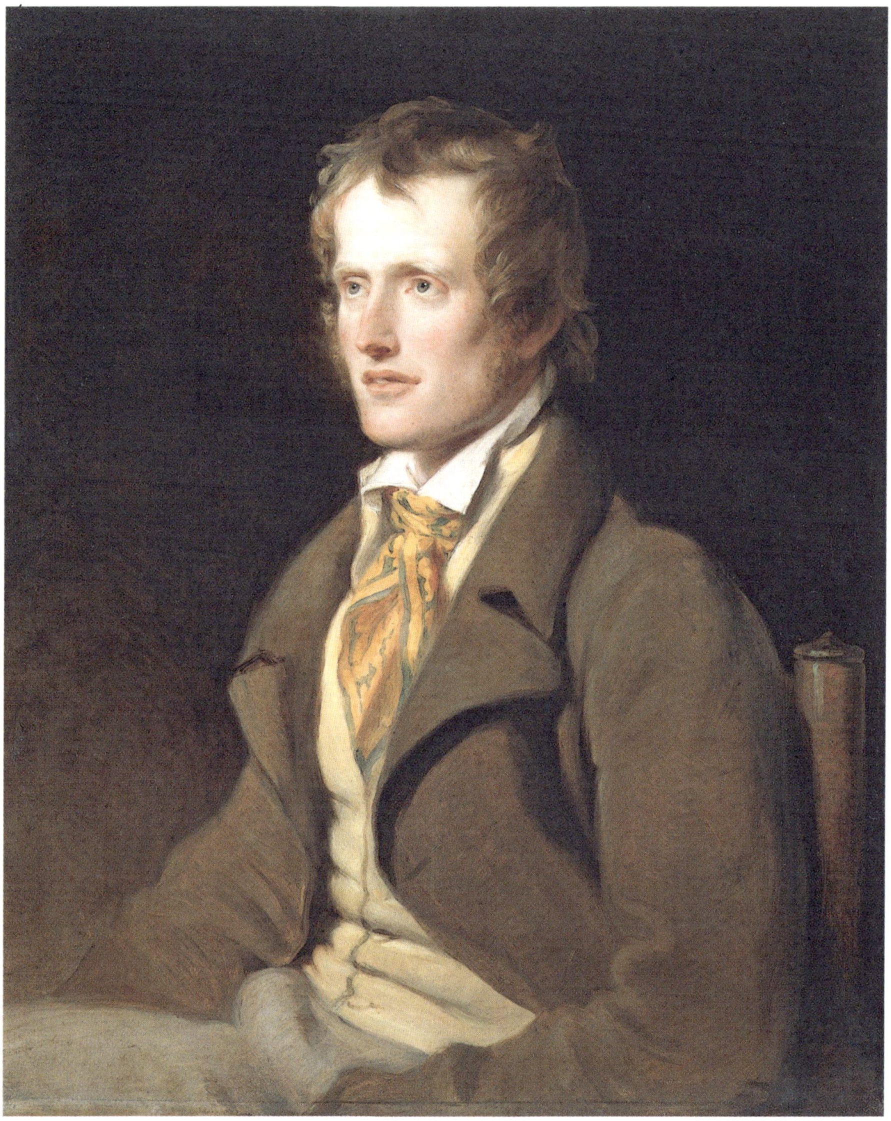

John Clare, painted during his first visit to London in 1820, by William Hilton.

'THE NORTHAMPTONSHIRE PEASANT'

Clare and Literary Society, 1818–1832

'To Autumn' was published by Taylor and Hessey at the beginning of July, 1820, in Keats's final collection, *Lamia, Isabella, the Eve of St Agnes and other Poems*. 'My book has had good success among literary people, and, I believe, has a moderate sale,' he wrote to Brown on 14 August 1820. But that was all he said about it, for by now he was mortally ill with tuberculosis, and haunted by the prospect of an imminent journey to Italy. 'A winter in England would, I have no doubt, kill me; so I have resolved to go to Italy, either by sea or land,' he told Brown.

Meanwhile, another book of poetry, also published by Taylor and Hessey, was making a much greater impact and certainly enjoying greater sales among the literary people of London – *Poems Descriptive of Rural Life and Scenery* by John Clare. The author, the title page carefully pointed out, was 'a Northamptonshire Peasant'. John Clare, then twenty-seven, was a labourer who had spent most of his life in the village of Helpston near Peterborough. This was his first collection. He had been presented to the public in the January 1820 edition of the *London Magazine* by his friend Octavius Gilchrist, a grocer, antiquary and literary critic. In his description of an early meeting he had hosted between Clare and John Taylor, Gilchrist portrayed the poet as a shy, innocent rustic, announced by 'a hesitating knock on the door': 'Nothing could exceed the meekness, and simplicity, and diffidence with which he answered the various inquiries concerning his life and habits, which we mingled with subjects calculated or designed to put him much at ease. Nothing, certainly, could less resemble splendour than the room into which Clare was shown; but there was a carpet, upon which it is likely he never previously set foot; and wine, of which assuredly he had never tasted before.'

Gilchrist then gave an account of Clare's 'melancholy' birth and 'lowly descent', his rudimentary education and subsequent work as a labourer – 'it is to the use of the spade that Clare has ever since been indebted for his precarious and narrow subsistence'. He concluded with several examples of Clare's 'innate genius for poetry', written 'at intervals stolen from his hasty meals, with a pencil, upon small slips of paper laid on the crown of his hat'.

The close connection between Clare's life and work was reinforced by John Taylor's long, considered introduction to *Poems Descriptive*. Taylor hoped that the poems would 'attract some notice by their intrinsic merit', but at the same time felt it necessary to draw attention to 'the circumstances under which they were written'. They were, he said, 'the genuine productions of a young Peasant, a day-labourer in husbandry, who has had no advantages of education beyond others of his class; and though Poets in this country have seldom been fortunate men, yet he is, perhaps, the least favoured by circumstances, and the most destitute of friends, of any that ever existed'. Clare's poverty-stricken background was not poetic fancy but 'a picture of what he has constantly witnessed and felt', a 'reality of wretchedness'.

In his introduction Taylor provided the biographical details that in the coming years would influence, to a greater or lesser extent, all critical appraisals of Clare's work. The poet had lived all his life at Helpston, with his mother and invalid father. As a child he had worked as a thresher and ploughboy, and had received a rudimentary education at the village school. When he was thirteen he had discovered Thomson's descriptive poem *The Seasons*, which had 'called forth all the passion of his soul for poetry'. It was after buying his own copy of *The Seasons* shortly afterwards, that he had written his first poem, and since then he had lived and composed in the open air:

> He is happier in the presence of Nature than elsewhere. He looks as anxiously on her face as if she were a living friend, whom he might lose; and hence he has learnt to notice every change in her countenance, and to delineate all the delicate varieties of her character. Most of his poems were composed under the immediate impression of this feeling, in the fields, or on the road-sides. He could not trust his memory, and therefore he wrote them down with a pencil on the spot, his hat serving him for a desk; and if it happened that he had no opportunity soon after of transcribing these imperfect memorials, he could seldom decypher them, or recover his first thoughts. From this course several of his poems are quite lost, and others exist only in fragments.

Clare, wrote Taylor, was 'most thoroughly the Poet as well as the Child of Nature', and having established the biographical background he proceeded to introduce the poetry. He gave particular attention to Clare's idiosyncratic use of language, hoping to forestall the misunderstandings of 'those who are critically nice in the construction of a sentence': 'from his ignorance of

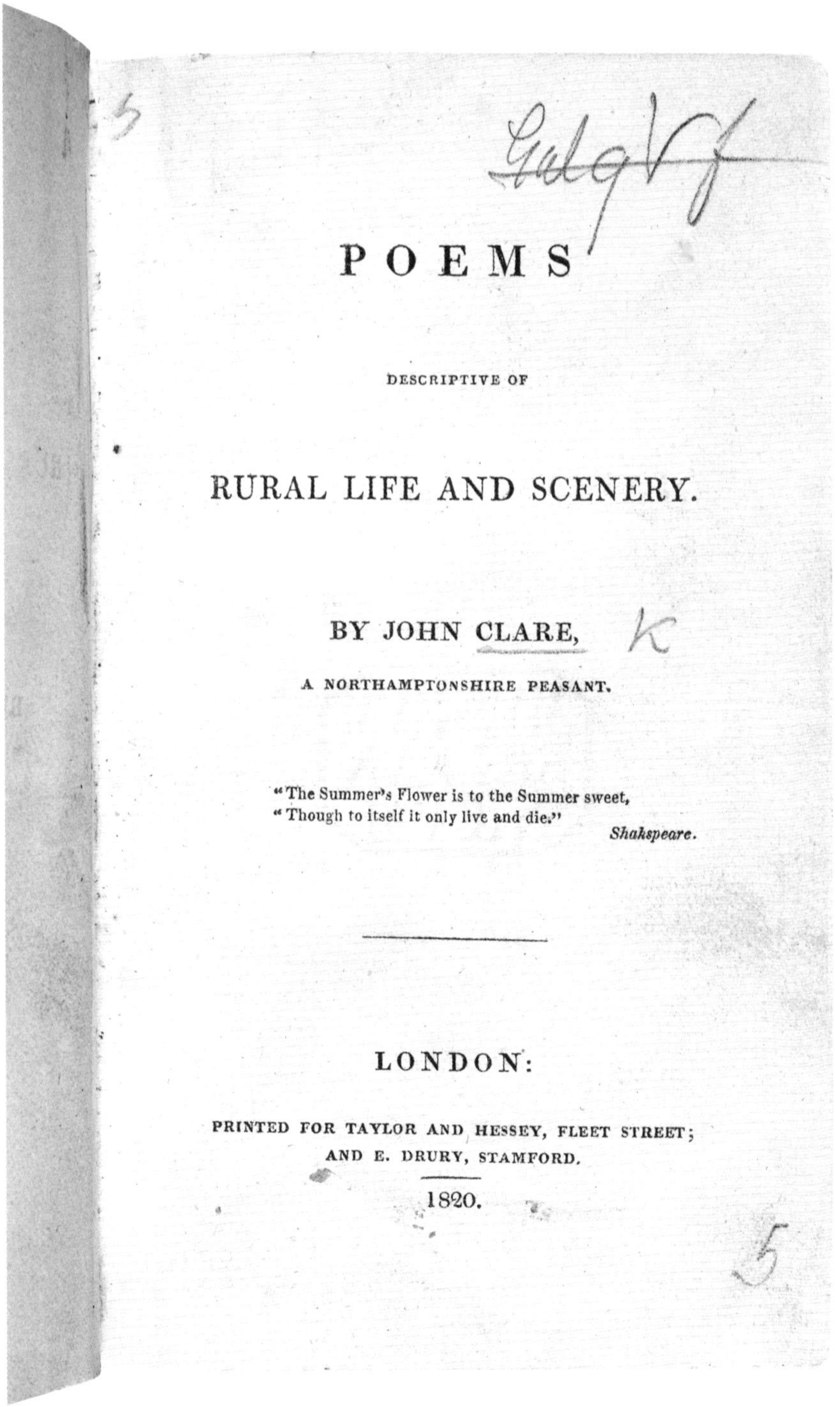

POEMS

DESCRIPTIVE OF

RURAL LIFE AND SCENERY.

BY JOHN CLARE,

A NORTHAMPTONSHIRE PEASANT.

"The Summer's Flower is to the Summer sweet,
"Though to itself it only live and die."
Shakspeare.

LONDON:

PRINTED FOR TAYLOR AND HESSEY, FLEET STREET;
AND E. DRURY, STAMFORD.

1820.

John Clare's first publication, *Poems Descriptive of Rural Life and Scenery*, 1820.

grammar, he seems to labour under great disadvantages. On the other hand, his want forces him to an extraordinary exertion of his native powers, in order to supply the deficiency.' Taylor also defended Clare's use of dialect and provincial expressions, claiming that they drew upon the oral, non-literary tradition of the countryside, 'the unwritten language of England'.

'The Author and his Poems are now before the public,' Taylor concluded, 'whatever be the result to either, this will at least be granted, that no Poet of our country has shewn greater ability, under circumstances so hostile to its development.' Gilchrist had caricatured Clare as a socially awkward, untutored genius. Taylor, more seriously, argued that a knowledge of Clare's circumstances aided and enriched one's appreciation of his poetry.

As a publisher, however, Taylor knew that the fortunes of *Poems Descriptive* depended on how successfully he exploited the current vogue for 'peasant poetry'. In recent years, picturesque tourists, poetry lovers and art enthusiasts had been admiring the peasantry of England for their aesthetic qualities. The idealised shepherd had become an integral part of the idealised landscape. On his visit to Grasmere in 1765 Thomas Gray had delighted in the 'happy poverty' of the inhabitants, which had seemed so in harmony with the paradisal scenery. In his *Excursion to the Lakes, in Westmoreland and Cumberland*, published in 1774, William Hutchinson had described a chance encounter, near Ullswater, with 'a female native full of youth, innocence and beauty'. His companion, 'in rapture', had attempted to sketch her, 'but the unaffected impatiency, and sweet confusion of the maid, overcame our wishes to detain her, and we let her pass reluctantly'. In February 1790 Mary Hartley told William Gilpin how, after a dose of the sublime, she liked to compose her imagination with 'a softer scene',

> where a little straw-roofed cottage shou'd peep out from behind an old hollow oak, with fantastical branches elbowing over it—a little blue smoke coming out from a small chimney, backed by the dark shade of a high & deep wood behind—a young woman at the door, with an innocent unaffected countenance the rose of health on her cheek, & an infant in her arms—on the steps of the door & round about it, 4 & 5 other children, playing with one another, in all the beautiful attitudes of infant sport—at a little distance the father of the family, returning from his work & stooping to embrace two little boys, who run to catch the first kiss—These are what I call Pastorals in painting ...

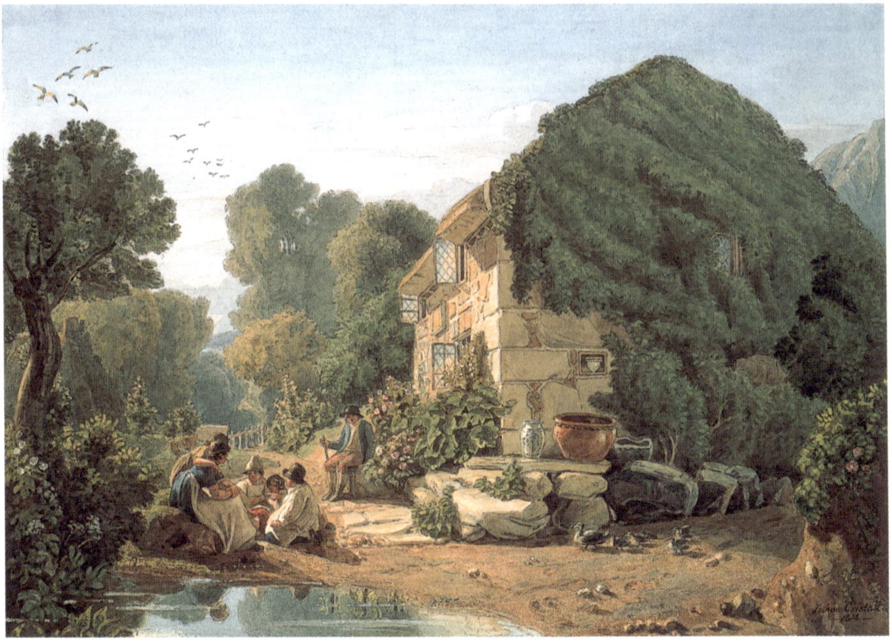

An idealised pastoral scene of a cottage at St Lawrence, Isle of Wight, by Joshua Cristall, 1814.

This idealised picture of rustic innocence and cheerful industry was part of a pastoral myth as old as Virgil's *Georgics*, and of which Thomson's *The Seasons*, first published in full in 1730, was the most popular recent example. Here, for instance, are some lines from his *Autumn*:

> Soon as the morning trembles o'er the sky,
> And unperceived unfolds the spreading day,
> Before the ripened field the reapers stand
> In fair array, each by the lass he loves,
> To bear the rougher part and mitigate
> by nameless gentle offices her toil.
> At once they stoop, and swell the lusty sheaves;
> While through their cheerful band the rural talk,
> The rural scandal, and the rural jest
> Fly harmless, to deceive the tedious time
> And steal unfelt the sultry hours away.
> Behind the master walks, builds up the shocks,
> And, conscious, glancing oft on every side
> His sated eye, feels his heart heave with joy.

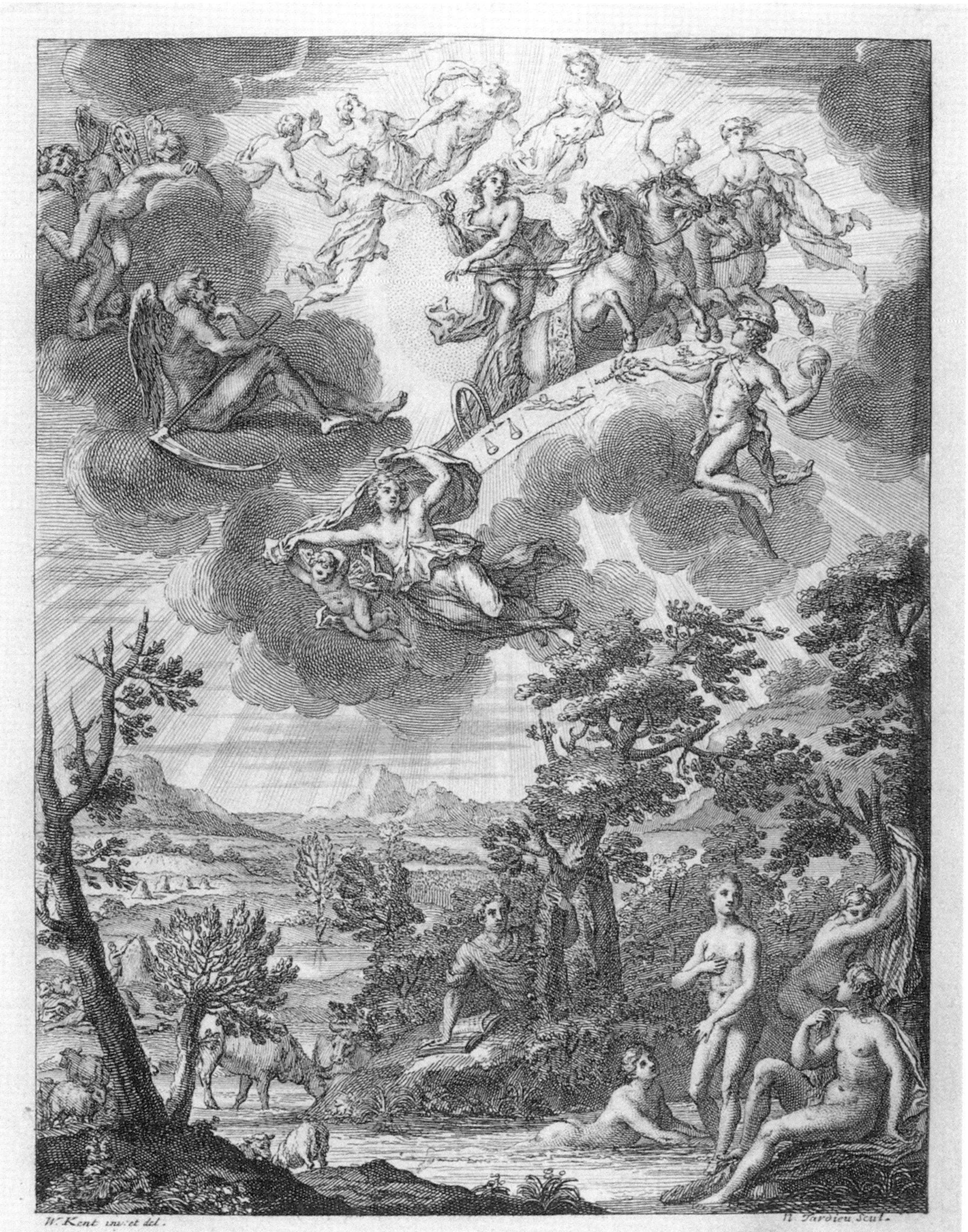

'Summer', an illustration by William Kent for Thomson's *Seasons*, 1730.

Huge numbers of readers were entranced by such idealised scenes, although there were dissenting voices. In 1783, for example, George Crabbe, a parish doctor and keen botanist, published *The Village*, a poem in heroic couplets which drew an unrelentingly grim portrait of rural life. His intention in doing so, he said, was to 'paint the cot / As Truth will paint it, and as Bards will not'. 'Can poets soothe you, when you pine for bread, / By winding myrtles round your ruin'd shed?' he demanded. Crabbe's landscape is not the sunlit fields of Thomson's *The Seasons*, but the bleak coastline of Suffolk where he lived; its wild sea, 'sterile soil' and 'frowning fields':

> Here joyless roam a wild amphibious race,
> With sullen woe display'd in every face;
> Who, far from civil arts and social fly,
> And scowl at strangers with suspicious eye.

'See them alternate suns and showers engage, / And hoard up aches and anguish for their age', continued Crabbe relentlessly, admonishing those 'gentle souls, who dream of rural ease, / Whom the smooth stream and smoother sonnet please'. He presents the reader with aged shepherds weeping under hillocks, labourers muttering angrily as they mend hedges in the wind and rain, village drunks and poachers, and a poorhouse full of orphans, the sick and the dying.

The Village established Crabbe's reputation as a poet. Samuel Johnson admired his work, and Byron called him 'Nature's sternest painter yet the best'. Others, however, saw his bleak realism, and regrettable tendency to moralise rather than sympathise, as essentially unpoetic. 'Poetry should be the handmaid of the imagination, and the foster-nurse of pleasure and beauty,' wrote William Hazlitt in *The Spirit of the Age*. 'Mr Crabbe's Muse is a determined enemy to the imagination, and a spy on nature.' On the one hand Thomson, argues Hazlitt, 'describes not so much the naked object as what he sees in his mind's eye, surrounded and glowing with the mild, bland, genial vapours of his brain'. Crabbe, on the other hand, is 'a repulsive writer … his morbid feelings droop and cling to the earth, grovel where they should soar, and throw a dead weight on every aspiration of the soul after the good or beautiful. … He sings the country; and he sings it in a pitiful tone. He chooses this subject only to take the charm out of it, and to dispel the illusion, the glory, and the dream, which had hovered over it in golden verse from Theocritus to Cowper. He sets out with professing to overturn the theory which had hallowed a shepherd's life, and made the names of grove and valley music to our ears, in order to give us truth in its stead.'

Clare agreed with Hazlitt. 'Crabbe writes about the peasantry as much like the Magistrate as the Poet,' he wrote to Taylor. 'He is determined to show you their worst side.' In a letter to Samuel Rogers of 29 September 1808, Wordsworth referred contemptuously to 'Crabbe's *verses*; for poetry in no sense can they be called. ... After all, if the Picture were true to nature, what claim would it have to be called Poetry?' He found Crabbe's work 'at the best ... the meanest kind of satire, except the purely personal. The sum of all is, that 19 out of 20 of Crabbe's Pictures are mere matters of fact; with which the Muses have just about as much to do as they have with a Collection of medical reports, or of Law Cases.'

Wordsworth himself neither idealised nor moralised. In the second edition of *Lyrical Ballads* (1800), he published two poems which he called 'pastorals': 'The Brothers' and 'Michael'. In the first, the main character, Leonard, returns after time at sea to the place of his birth, a Lake District village in remote Ennerdale. There, in conversation with the local vicar, who has not recognised him, he learns that his beloved brother James has died. He leaves without revealing his identity, still a stranger to his native landscape. 'Michael' tells of the lives of an old shepherd, his wife Isobel and only son Luke on their Grasmere farm. In order to retain his land Michael is forced to send Luke to London to earn money. He promises to finish building a sheepfold in his absence. Luke falls into dissolution and never returns; the sheepfold remains unfinished. Wordsworth described his intentions in writing these poems in a letter to the Whig politician Charles James Fox:

> In the two Poems ... I have attempted to draw a picture of the domestic affections as I know they exist amongst a class of men who are now almost confined to the North of England. They are small independent *proprietors* of land here called statesmen, men of respectable education who daily labour on their own little properties. The domestic affections will always be strong amongst men who live in a country not crowded with population, if these men are placed above poverty. But if they are proprietors of small estates, which have descended to them from their ancestors, the power which these affections will acquire amongst such men is inconceivable by those who have only had an opportunity of observing hired labourers, farmers, and the manufacturing Poor. Their little tract of land serves as a kind of permanent rallying point for their

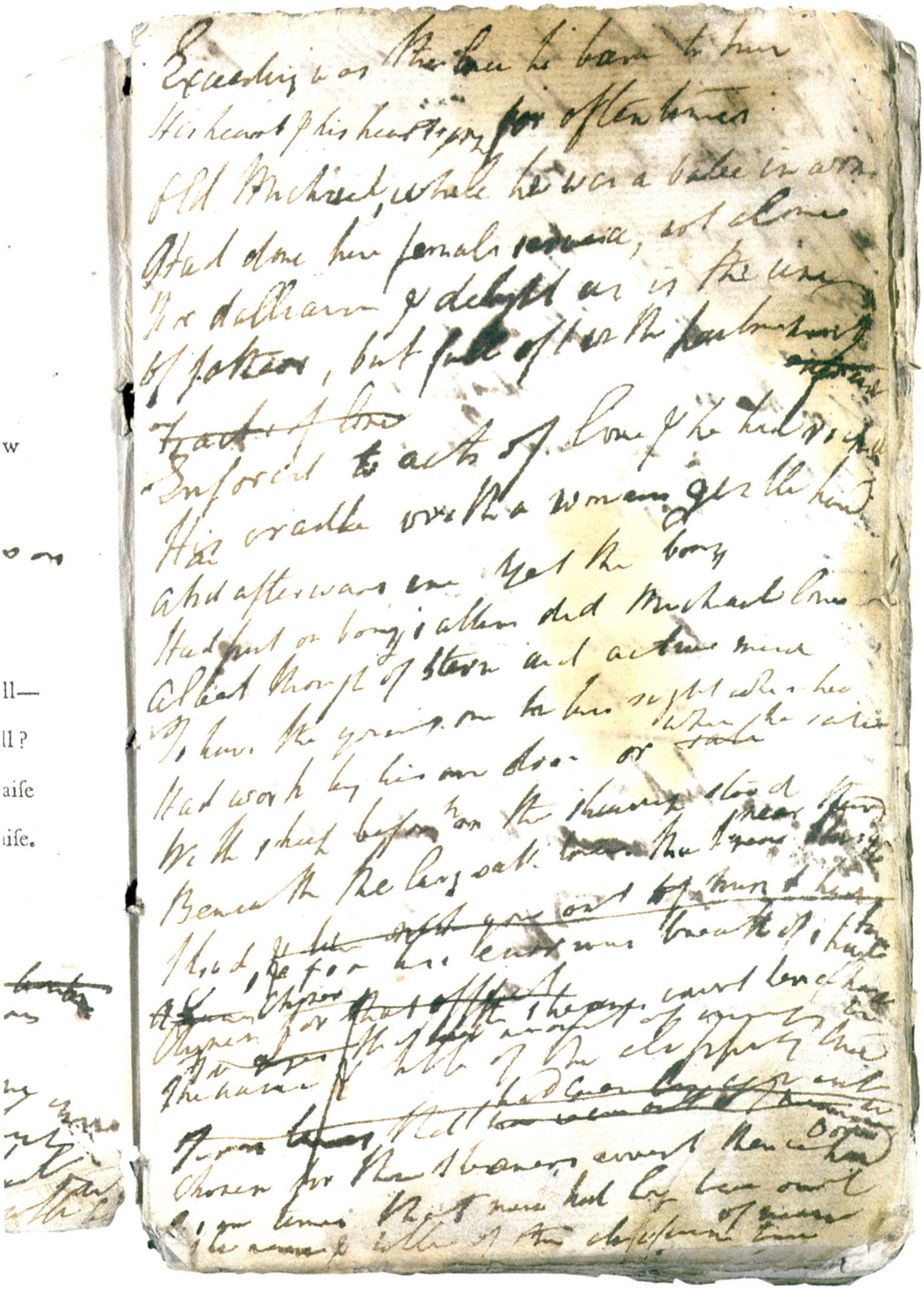

William Wordsworth, manuscript of 'Michael', 1802.

> domestic feelings, as a tablet upon which they are written which makes them objects of memory in a thousand instances when they would otherwise be forgotten. It is a fountain fitted to the nature of social man from which supplies of affection, as pure as his heart was intended for, are daily drawn. This class of men is rapidly disappearing.

Wordsworth told Fox that he had written 'Michael' and 'The Brothers' to show 'that men who do not wear fine cloaths can feel deeply'. The greatness of the poems lies in their ability to look beneath the individual circumstances of the characters and explore fundamental human passions:

> There is a comfort in the strength of love;
> 'Twill make a thing endurable which else
> Would break the heart: – Old Michael found it so.
> I have conversed with more than one who well
> Remember the Old Man, and what he was
> Years after he had heard this heavy news.
> His bodily frame had been from youth to age
> Of an unusual strength. Among the rocks
> He went, and still looked up upon the sun,
> And listened to the wind; and as before
> Performed all kinds of labour for his Sheep,
> And for the land his small inheritance.
> And to that hollow Dell from time to time
> Did he repair, to build the Fold of which
> His flock had need. 'Tis not forgotten yet
> The pity which was then in every heart
> For the Old Man – and 'tis believed by all
> That many and many a day he thither went,
> And never lifted up a single stone.

Wordsworth told his friend Henry Crabb Robinson, in 1837, that he wanted to be remembered only 'for the way in which his poems exhibit man in his essentially human character and relations – as child, parent, husband – the qualities which are common to all men, as opposed to those which distinguish one man from another'. In *Lyrical Ballads* he had chosen episodes from low and rustic life, not as a social statement, but, as he explained in the preface to the second edition of 1800, 'because in that situation the essential passions of the heart find a better soil in which they can attain their maturity, are less under restraint, and speak a plainer and more emphatic language; because in that situation our elementary feelings exist in a state of greater simplicity and consequently may be more accurately contemplated and more forcibly communicated; because the manners of rural life germinate from those elementary feelings; and from the necessary character of rural occupations are more easily comprehended; and are more durable; and lastly, because in that situation the passions of men are incorporated with the beautiful and permanent forms of nature.'

Some people found the idea that rustic characters could express universal human truths absurd. In his review of Crabbe's *Poems* (1807) in the April 1808 edition of the *Edinburgh Review*, Francis Jeffrey praised Crabbe's realistic characters and ridiculed Wordsworth's 'inventions':

> Mr Crabbe exhibits the common people of England pretty much as they are, and as they must appear to every one who will take the trouble of examining into their condition ... The gentlemen of the new school, on the other hand, scarcely ever condescend to take their subjects from any descriptions of persons that are at all known to the common inhabitants of the world; but invent for themselves certain whimsical and unheard of beings, to whom they impute some fantastical combination of feelings, and labour to excite our sympathy for them, either by placing them in incredible situations, or by some strained and exaggerated moralization of a vague and tragical description. ... Instead of men and women of ordinary humanity, we have certain moody and capricious personages, made after the poet's own heart and fancy, – acting upon principles, and speaking in a language of their own.

Coleridge, in later life, tended to agree. In *Biographia Literaria*, published in 1817, he observed that Wordsworth's characters 'are by no means taken "from low or rustic life" in the common acceptation of those words'. Not everyone benefited from their proximity to beautiful and permanent forms of nature, Coleridge argued; for those people to prosper, 'a certain vantage-ground is pre-requisite'. 'Education, or original sensibility, or both, must pre-exist, if the changes, forms, and incidents of nature are to prove a sufficient stimulant. And where these are not sufficient, the mind contracts and hardens by want of stimulants; and the man becomes selfish, sensual, gross, and hard-hearted.'

In a notebook entry he remarked that the countryside could just as easily deprave as benefit its inhabitants, 'Hence the violent vindictive passions—& the outrageous & dark & wild cruelties—of many country folks'.

William Hazlitt went further. 'However we may sympathise with Mr. Wordsworth in his attachments to groves and fields, we cannot extend the same admiration to their inhabitants, or to the manners of country life in general,' he wrote in his review of Wordsworth's *Excursion*, and then launched into an extraordinary attack on rural life. 'All country people hate each other,' he proclaimed. 'They have so little comfort that they envy their neighbours the smallest pleasures or advantage, and nearly grudge themselves the necessaries of life. ... You live out of the world. ... There is a perpetual round of mischief-making and backbiting for want of any better amusement. There are no shops, no taverns, no theatres, no opera, no concerts, no pictures, no public-buildings, no crowded streets, no noise of coaches, or of courts of law, – neither courtiers nor courtesans, no literary parties, no fashionable routs, no society, no books, or knowledge of books. Vanity and luxury are the civilisers of the world, and sweeteners of human life. Without objects either of pleasure or action, it grows harsh and crabbed: the mind becomes stagnant, the affections callous, and the eye dull. Man left to himself soon degenerates into a very disagreeable person. Ignorance is always bad enough; but rustic ignorance is intolerable.'

While the literary world argued about peasant life and its representation in poetry, Clare actually lived it. Uniquely among the poets of the period, he experienced its hardships, attachments and delights, and then wrote about them. In a number of unpublished prose fragments he traced the various stages by which he became a poet. First there were the carefree 'raptures' of his childhood (the quote is spaced to allow for Clare's lack of punctuation):

> I hunted curious flowers in raptures and mutterd thoughts in their praise I lovd the pasture with its rushes and thistles and sheep tracks I adord the wild marshy fen with its solitary hernshaw sweeing along in its mellan[c]holy sky I wandered the heath in raptures among the rabbit burrows and golden blossomd furze I dropt down on a thymy mole hill or mossy eminence to survey the summer landscape as full of raptures as now I markd the varied colors in flat

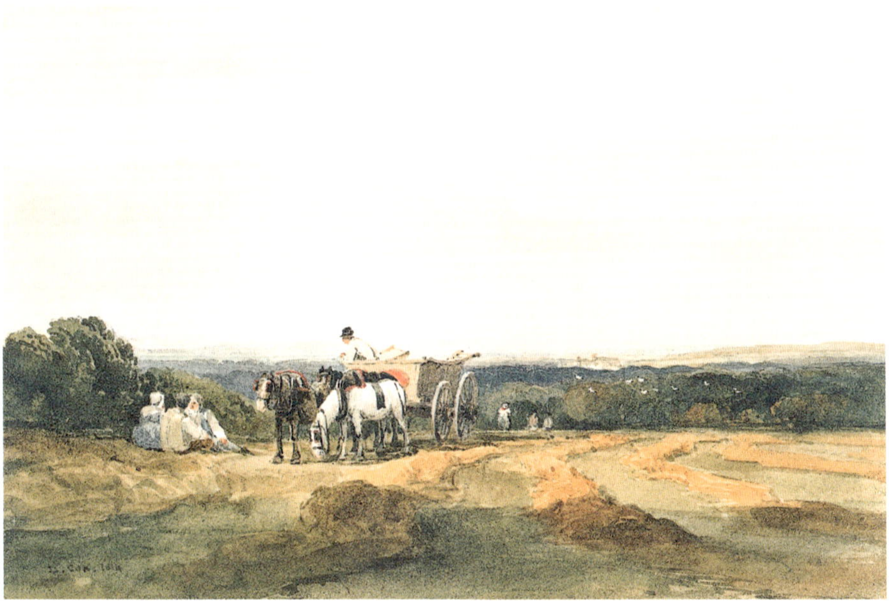

A harvesting scene, by David Cox, 1814.

spreading fields checkerd with closes of different tinted grain like the colors in a map the copper tinted colors of clover in blossom the sun tand green of the ripening hay the lighter hues of wheat and barley intermixd with the sunny glare of the yellow c[h]alock and the sunset imitation of the scarlet head aches with the blue corn bottles crowding their splendid colors in large sheets over the lands and 'troubling the corn fields' with destroying beauty the different greens of the woodland trees the dark oak the paler ash the mellow Lime the white poplar peeping above the rest like leafy steeples the grey willow shining chilly in the sun as if the morning mist still lingerd in its cool green I felt the beauty of these with eager delight the gad flyes noon day hum the fainter murmer of the bee flye 'spiring in the evening ray' the dragon flyes in their spangld coats darting like 'winged arrows down the stream' the swallow darting through its one arched brig the shepherd hiding from a thunder shower in an hollow dotterel the wild geese scudding along and making all the letters of the Alphabet as they flew the motley clouds the whispering wind that mutterd to the leaves and summer grass as it flutterd among them like things at play I observd all this with the same raptures as I have done since but I knew nothing of poetry it was felt and not utterd ...

It was a small, enclosed world, and whether he was working in the fields during the week, or walking through the woods on Sundays, Clare knew it with a deeply felt intimacy, every field, stream, path, hedge, stile and tree. A sense of belonging to Helpston and its few inhabitants rooted his intense and acutely sensitive nature, his spirits anchored by the spire of the village church that was hardly ever out of his sight.

Then, as Clare grew older, he developed a strong desire not just to feel the landscape, but to voice it, to put it into words, to become, as Taylor wrote in his introduction to *Poems Descriptive*, 'most thoroughly the Poet as well as the Child of Nature'. Clare's response to the landscape remained instinctive, but also became highly literary. Tellingly, his first poem was inspired not by the familiar landscape of Helpston, but by the artifice of Thomson's *The Seasons*, and the landscaped grounds of Burghley Park:

> the Scenery around me was uncommonly beautiful at that time of the year and what with reading the book and beholding the beautys of artful nature in the park I got into a strain of descriptive rhyming on my journey home this was 'the morning walk' the first thing I commited to paper ...

As a poet, he came to regard nature with a poet's, not a labourer's eye; 'to look at nature with a poetic feeling magnifyes the pleasure', he wrote. A description of a flower transformed it; poetry became the enriching medium through which he saw the landscape. 'The man of taste', he wrote,

> looks on the little Celandine in spring & mutters in his mind some favourite lines from Wordsworths address to that flower; he never sees the daisy without thinking of Burns; & who sees the taller buttercup carpeting the closes in golden fringe without a remembrance of Chatterton's beautiful ... 'The kingcup brasted with the morning dew' ... to look on nature with a poetic eye magnifies the pleasure, she herself being the very essence & soul of Poesy.

'I always feel delighted when an object in nature brings up in ones mind an image of poetry that describes it from some favourite author,' Clare said, 'a clown may say he loves the morning but a man of taste feels it in a higher degree by bringing up in his mind that beautiful line of Thomsons "The meek eyd morn appears mother of dews".'

The more Clare turned landscape into words, and the more he committed his previously unspoken thoughts and feelings onto paper, the more separated he became from his unconscious identification with that landscape and its inhabitants. As a child, even the ability to read and his love of books had set him apart:

> I began to wean off from my companions and sholl about the woods and fields on Sundays alone   conjectures filld the village about my future destinations on the stage of life, some fanc[y]ing it symptoms of lunacy and that my mothers prophecys would be verified to her sorrow and that my reading of books (they would jeeringly say) was for no other improvement then quallyfiing an idiot for a workhouse, for at this time my taste and pasion for reading began to be furious and I never sholld out on a Sabbath day but some scrap or other was pocketed for my amusment ...

In his childhood, Clare said, he had nursed a 'restless hope of being something better than a plough boy   my little ambitions kept burning about me every now and then to make a better figure in the world and I knew not what to be at'. And the more he thought of fame, the more he turned to what he called 'that lonly and solitary musing which ended in rhyme': 'poetry was a troublesome but pleasant companion anoying and cheering me at my toils   I coud not stop my thoughts and often faild to keep them till night so when I fancyd I had hit upon a good image or natural description I usd to steal into a corner of the garden and clap it down but the appearance of my employers often put my fancys to flight and made me loose the thought and the muse together for I always felt anx[i]ous to consceal my scribbling and woud as leave have confessd to be a roober as a rhymer.'

Clare's poetic ambitions took him from the secret world of Helpston into the public eye. In a remarkable prose passage he described the process by which, from their beginnings in a hidden nook of Helpston, his feelings became words, were written out, and then revealed to the 'gentle reader':

> Among these trifles are many keepsakes of my early days when I used to drop down under a bush and scribble the fresh thoughts on the crown of my hat—since the world has found me I feel it a presumption to hide my self and fancy I feel as I felt then—I have more knowledge—as I found nature then so I made her—if an old pond with its pendant

> sallows fringing its mossy sides happened to be in the pleasant nook where I sat concealed among the black thorns drawing its picture—I called it a pond and if it was a flood wash in the meadows I called it a lake or imagined it one or if I sat under the ragged sides of a stone pit I fancied my self under the shadows of a rock and so my feelings were stirred into praise and my promises were muttered in prose or rhyme as the mood might suit at the moment and then these moods often repeated grew unperceived into quantity on paper and then I indulged my vanity in thinking how they would look in print and then I selected what I thought best and hid the others out of shames way as laughing stocks for the crowd who think it a childs occupations to indulge in such feelings and inexcusable folly in a man but on flitting from my native place I hunted over my bundles of paper intending to save the trouble of carriage by destroying those I set least store bye and the bundle[s] from whence these were taken were among the first of my intentions but I read them and paused thinking of old days and old feelings and excuse my vanity gentle reader—if I did not think them worthy of your praise I felt I could not burn them ...

Clare made his first approach to the literary world in 1818. In 1814 he had purchased a blank notebook for his first poems from J.B. Henson, a bookseller and preacher in nearby Market Deeping. Four years later, Henson offered to publish a volume of Clare's poetry by subscription. At his request Clare wrote an address to the public. Fearful of their reaction, his tone was defensive and diffident. He asked his prospective readers to make allowances for the poems' imperfections:

> It is hoped that the humble situation which distinguishes their author will be some excuse in their favour, and serve to make an atonement for the many inaccuracies and imperfections that will be found in them. The least touch from the iron hand of *Criticism* is able to crush them to nothing, and sink them at once to utter oblivion. May they be allowed to live their little day, and give satisfaction to those who may choose to honour them with a perusal, they will gain the end for which they were designed, and their author's wishes will be gratified. Meeting with this encouragement, it will induce him to publish a similar collection, of which this is offered as a specimen.

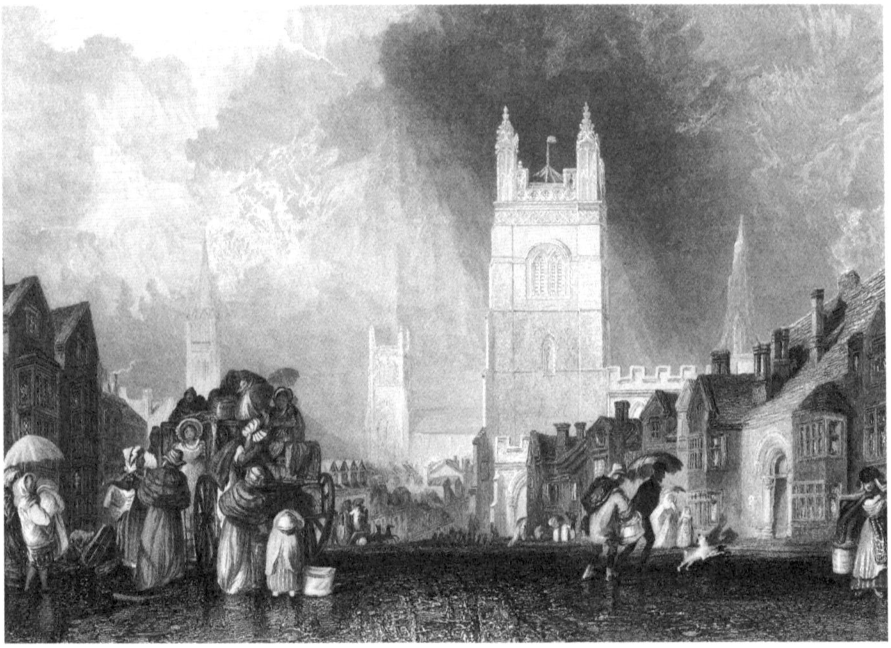

Stamford, where Clare met his future publishers, by W. Miller after J.M.W. Turner.

The prospectus was printed with Clare's sonnet 'The Setting Sun'. It was the first time Clare had seen his work in print: 'for the first time [I] saw a sonnet of mine in print and I scarcly knew it in its new dress and felt a prouder confidence then I had hither too done thinking it got merit by its dress'. Soon he was writing excitedly to Henson: 'I send you some of the principal subscribers which I have procured lately, the first of which is a Baronet!!! who speaks very highly of my "Sonnet" in the prospectus—good God, how great are my Expectations, what hopes do I cherish! as great as the unfortunate Chatterton on his first entrance into London which is now pictured in my Mind—& undoubtedly like him I may be building "Castles in the Air" but Time will prove it.'

But after this promising start, interest died away and Henson began to back away from their agreement. Clare was then taken up by Edward Drury, a rival bookseller from Stamford, who thought he had spotted a chance to make his mark on the literary world. Drury lent Clare money and books, and Clare, encouraged, worked towards a first collection, while continuing to earn his living as a lime burner and gardener. Drury then put the manuscript poems before his cousin, Keats's publisher John Taylor: 'They are written by

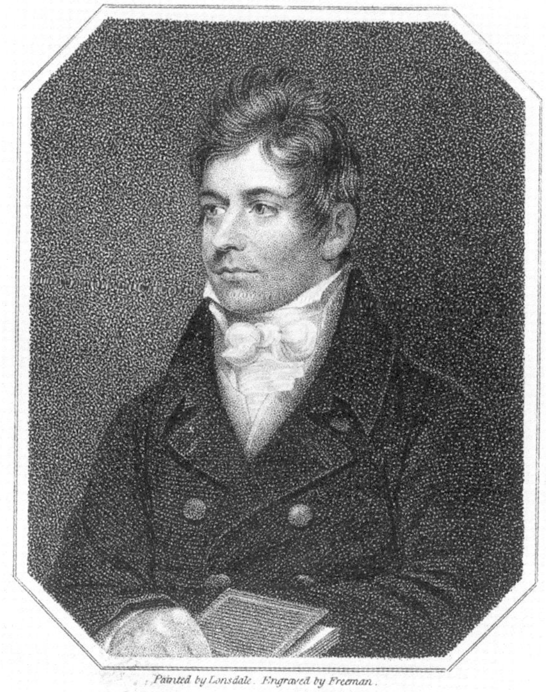

Octavius Gilchrist, by Freeman after J. Lonsdale, 1810.

a laboring man in this neighbourhood, who seems to have a strange taste for poetry, and if *his* compositions are poetry, there cannot be a stronger proof of the art being a *gift*, as it is called.' He asked Taylor's help with correcting and editing the manuscripts. Impressed with the poems, Taylor agreed, and with Clare's active participation worked towards publishing a collection. *Poems Descriptive* was duly published in January the following year. At the same time, Octavius Gilchrist's article on Clare was published in the *London Magazine*. By March all 1,000 copies of the first printing had been sold and a second printing of 2,000 copies was underway. By the end of May a third run had come off the press. Keats's final collection, by contrast, struggled to sell 500 copies in its first year.

Inevitably, Clare was compared with earlier 'peasant poets', chief among whom were Robert Burns and Robert Bloomfield. The former had made the most of his humble origins when he had published his first collection, *Poems, Chiefly in the Scottish Dialect*, in 1786. The son of a poor farmer, he had worked as a ploughman and a smallholder, and was emphatically not a member of the Edinburgh literary élite. But even so he was a skilful writer in both Scots

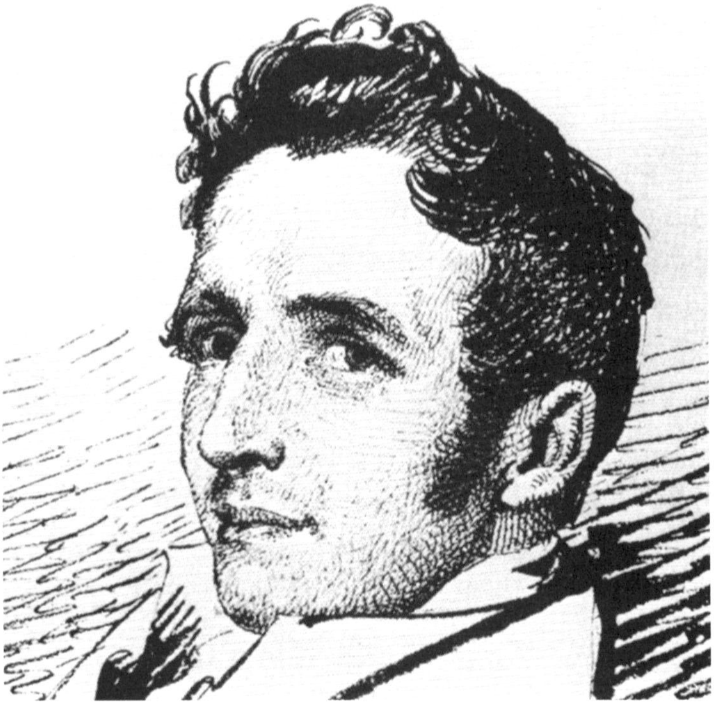

An undated portrait of John Taylor, by an unknown artist.

and English, he had a wide knowledge of English literature, and was not at all the ignorant rustic, the 'Heaven-taught ploughman', he put forward in his three-and-a-half-page introduction to the poems:

> The following trifles are not the production of the Poet, who, with all the advantages of learned art, and perhaps amid the elegancies and idlenesses of upper life, looks down for a rural theme, with an eye to Theocritus or Virgil. To the Author of this, these and other celebrated names their countymen are, in their original languages, 'A fountain shut up', and a 'book sealed.' Unacquainted with the necessary requisites for commencing Poet by rule, he sings the sentiments and manners, he felt and saw in himself and his rustic compeers around him, in his and their native language. Though a Rhymer from his earliest years, at least from the earliest impulses of the softer passions, it was not till very lately, that the applause, perhaps the partiality, of Friendship, wakened his vanity so far as to make him think any thing of his was worth showing; and none of the following works were ever composed with

a view to the press. To amuse himself with the little creations of his own fancy, amid the toil and fatigues of a laborious life; to transcribe the various feelings, the loves, the griefs, the hopes, the fears, in his own breast; to find some kind of counterpoise to the struggles of the world, always an alien scene, a task uncouth to the poetical mind; these were his motives for courting the Muses, and in these he found Poetry to be it's own reward.

Burns asked his readers, 'particularly the Learned and the Polite, who may honor him with a perusal', to 'make every allowance for Education and Circumstances of Life'. The *Edinburgh Magazine* obliged, pronouncing *Poems, Chiefly in the Scottish Dialect* 'a striking example of native genius bursting through the obscurity of poverty and the obstructions of labouring life'. A second edition was published the following year.

Robert Bloomfield was one of Clare's favourite poets, and the two men had much in common. Born in poverty in Suffolk, in 1766, Bloomfield had worked as a farmer's boy on his uncle's farm and then as a cobbler, while all the time educating himself and reading poetry. Among his favourite works were Thomson's *The Seasons* and Burns's *Poems*. At one point he made a living manufacturing Aeolian harps. Then, in May 1796, Bloomfield began composing the poem that would make his name. *The Farmer's Boy* was written in heroic couplets, and like Thomson's *The Seasons* was divided into four parts, one for each of the seasons. It described the fortunes of a young farm labourer called Giles, and his close relationship with the natural world. Bloomfield had originally intended the poem to be a present for his mother, but when it was published in 1800 it was a huge success: 26,000 copies were sold in under three years. Several years of celebrity followed, but each subsequent volume of poetry was less successful than the last, and in old age Bloomfield was beset by financial difficulties.

Bloomfield never met Clare, but he was impressed by his work and heartened by his success. He wrote to his 'Brother Bard, and fellow Labourer' in July 1820:

> ... nothing upon the great theatre of what is called the world (our English world) can give me half the pleasure I feel at seeing a man start up from the humble walks of life and show himself to be what I think you are,—What that is, ask a higher power, – for though learning is not to be contemn'd it did not give you this.

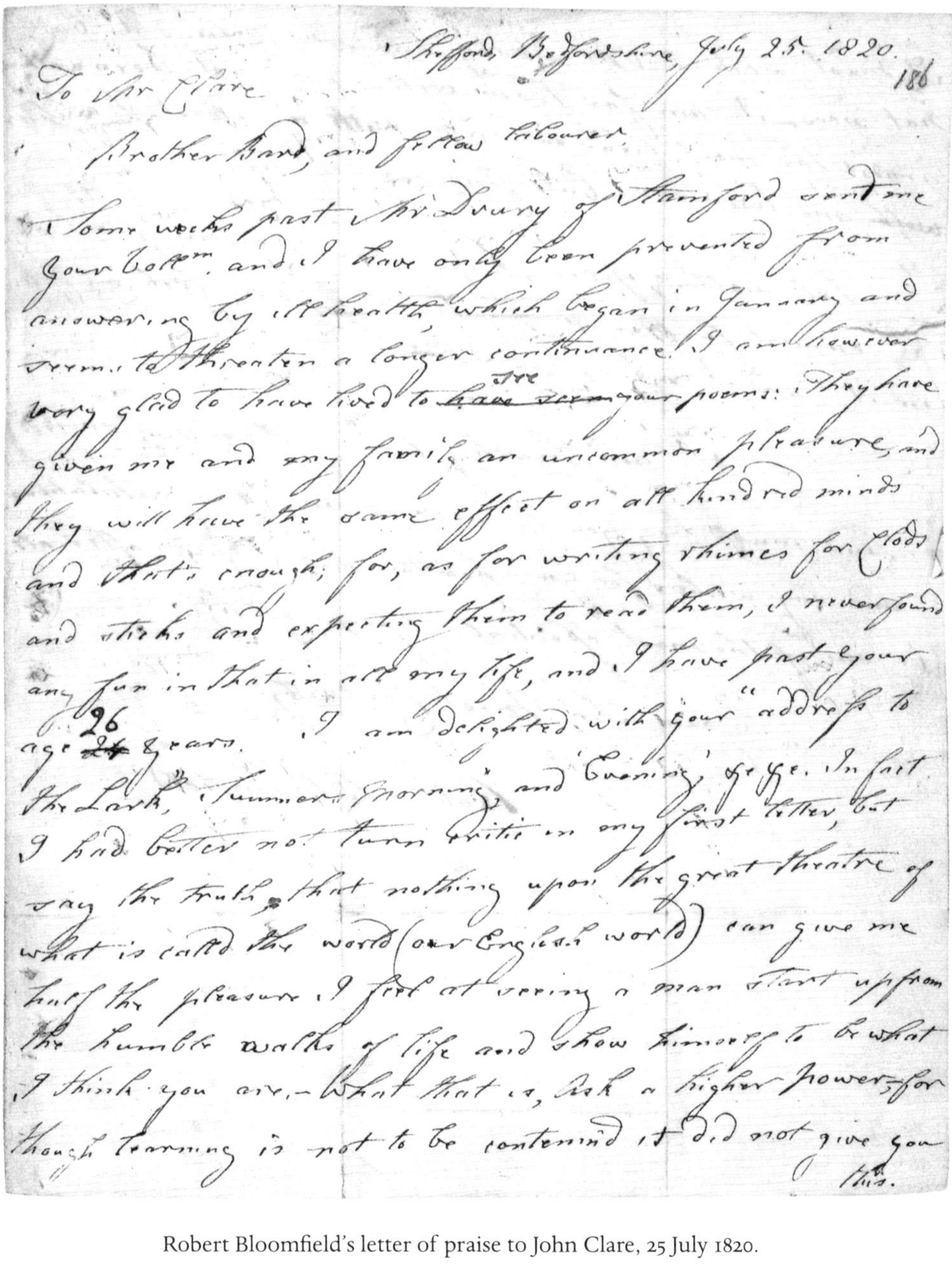
Shefford, Bedfordshire, July 25. 1820.

To Mr Clare 186

Brother Bard, and fellow labourer

Some weeks past Mr Drury of Stamford sent me your Volm. and I have only been prevented from answering by ill health, which began in January and seems to threaten a longer continuance. I am however very glad to have lived to ~~have seen~~ see your poems: They have given me and my family an uncommon pleasure, and they will have the same effect on all kindred minds and that's enough; for, as for writing rhimes for Clods and sticks and expecting them to read them, I never found any fun in that in all my life, and I have past your age ~~24~~ 26 years. I am delighted with your "address to the Lark," "Summer Morning" and 'Evening' &c &c. In fact I had better not turn critic in my first letter, but say the truth, that nothing upon the great theatre of what is called the world (our English world) can give me half the pleasure I feel at seeing a man start up from the humble walks of life and show himself to be what I think you are, - What that is, ask a higher Power, - for though learning is not to be contemned it did not give you this.

Robert Bloomfield's letter of praise to John Clare, 25 July 1820.

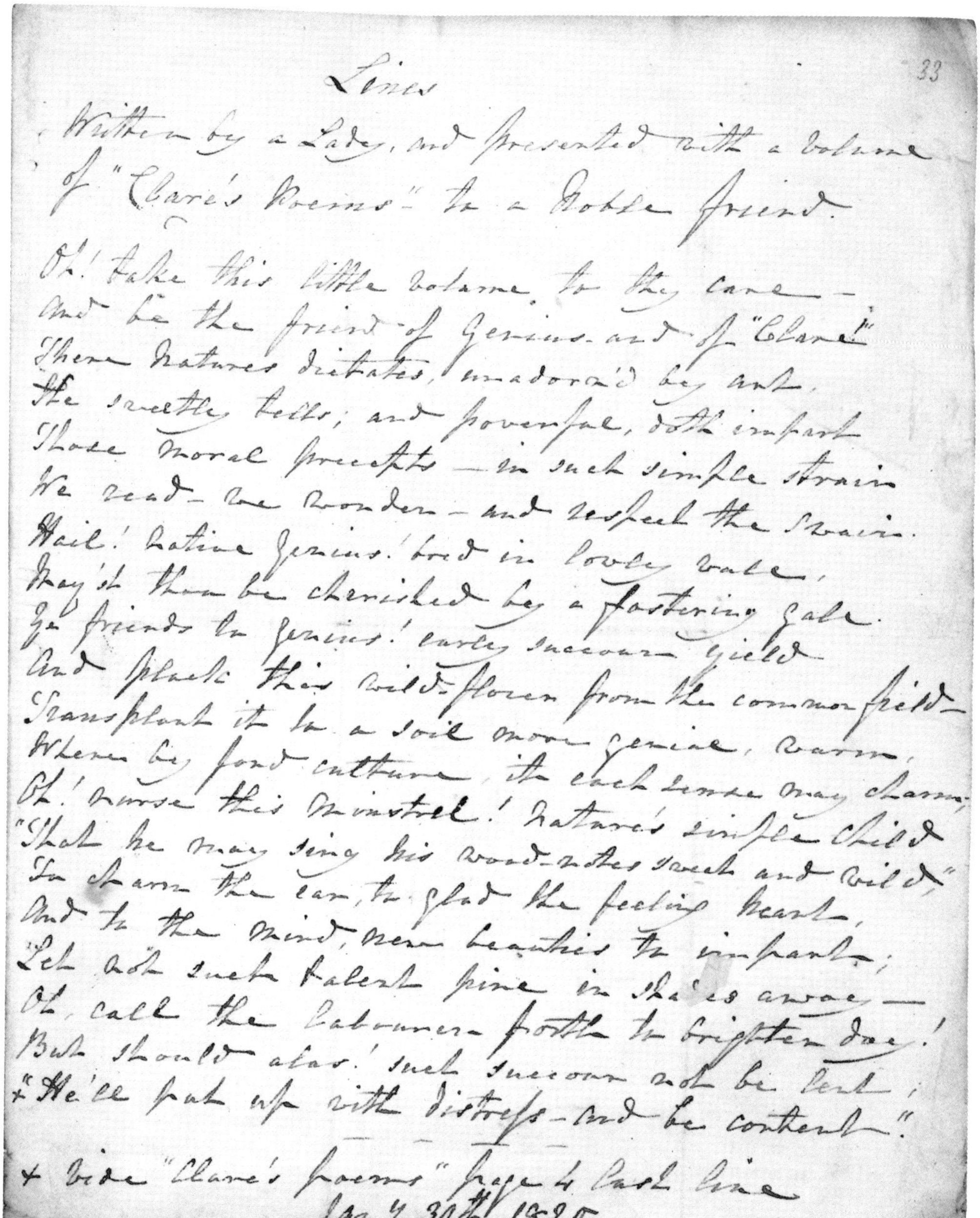

33

Lines

Written by a Lady, and presented with a Volume of "Clare's Poems" to a Noble friend.

Oh! take this little volume to thy care—
And be the friend of Genius and of "Clare"
There Natures dictates, unadorn'd by art,
He sweetly tells; and powerful, doth impart
Those moral precepts—in such simple strain
We read—we wonder—and respect the Swain.
Hail! Native Genius! bred in lowly vale,
May'st thou be cherished by a fostering gale.
Ye friends to genius! early succour yield
And pluck this wild-flower from the common field—
Transplant it to a soil more genial, warm,
Where by fond culture, its each sense may charm;
Oh! nurse this Minstrel! Nature's simple Child
"That he may sing his wood-notes sweet and wild,"
To charm the ear, to glad the feeling heart,
And to the mind, new beauties to impart;
Let not such talent pine in shades away—
Oh, call the labourer forth to brighter day!
But should alas! such succour not be lent;
+"He'll put up with distress—and be content."

+ vide "Clare's poems" page 4 last line

Jany 30th 1820

Eliza Emmerson's lines to John Clare, published in the *Morning Post*, February 1820.

Like Burns, and equally misleadingly, Bloomfield was praised for being a 'natural' poet, a rustic genius free from the chains of classical learning and cold artifice. And this was how Mrs Eliza Emmerson, one of Clare's most devoted, if histrionic, supporters saw their successor. Her enthusiastic poem greeting the publication of *Poems Descriptive* appeared in the *Morning Post* in February 1820:

Oh! take this little volume to thy care—
And be the friend of Genius—and of 'Clare!'
There Nature's dictates, unadorn'd by art,
She sweetly tells; and powerful, doth impart
Those moral precepts—in such simple strain
We read—we wonder—and respect the swain.
Hail! native genius! bred in lowly vale,
May'st thou be cherish'd by a fostering gale.
Ye friends to genius! early succour yield
And pluck this wild flower from the common field—
Transport it to a soil more genial, warm,
Where by fond culture it each sense may charm;
Oh! nurse this minstrel! Nature's simple child
'That he may sing his wood-notes sweet and wild,'
To charm the ear, to glad the feeling heart,
And to the mind, new beauties to impart;
Let not such talent pine in shades away—
Oh, call the labourer forth to brighter day!
But should alas! such succour not be lent
'He'll put up with distress—and be content'.

The reviewers were more cautious. On the one hand, Clare was indeed a child of nature 'unadorn'd by art', unspoiled by the cultural sophistication and artificial aesthetics of the picturesque, and thus closer to the real landscape. No one could doubt the humbleness of his background. But on the other hand, what relation did his work, with its preponderance of visual description and frequent use of dialect words, have to the classical artistry and the lofty philosophic strains of true poetry? 'The efforts of the uncultivated mind – the outpourings of genius unmoulded by scholastic system and unimbued with scholastic lore must ever be interesting to the lover of literature, and the observer of human nature,' commented the *New Times*:

> We have seldom an opportunity of learning the unmixed and unadulterated impression of the loveliness of nature on a man of vivid perception and strong feeling, equally unacquainted with the arts and reserve of the world, and with the riches, rules, and prejudices of literature. Such a man is Clare.

The *New Monthly Magazine* thought him 'strictly a descriptive poet', but nevertheless one whose 'daily occupation in the fields has given him a manifest advantage over those minstrels whose pastoral strains are inspired by the contemplation of the furze and stinted herbage of Hampstead Heath, or the sooty verdure of a London square'. 'This untaught Northamptonshire hind,' it said, 'is acquainted with a language less understood than Greek or Latin – the language of the human heart.' Regrettably, however, Clare sometimes employs 'mere vulgarisms' that 'may as well be excluded from the poetical lexicon, as they have long since been banished from the dictionary of polite conversation'.

The *Monthly Review*, though praising Clare for his 'representations of simple and natural feeling', as opposed to 'the effusions of a poet writing pastorals as he wanders through the fields to the north-east of London', wrote more critically:

> however extraordinary these poems may be as the productions of a very uneducated man, and estimable as faithful representations of rural life and scenery, it would be injustice to their author to compare them with the writings of those whose superior stores of mind have enabled them to embellish the strong efforts of native genius with the ornaments of learning and refinement. ... In mentioning a peasant-poet, we immediately remember Burns: but Clare must not be ranked with him whose talents would bear a comparison with the noblest intellects of modern times, and whose compositions, though perpetually enriched with illustrations from the beauties of nature, were filled with the deepest and truest sentiment, or lightened up with the most brilliant wit.

'Of all the manias in this mad age,' John Gibson Lockhart had written in 1818 in his ruthlessly dismissive review of Keats's *Endymion*, 'the most incurable, as well as the most common, seems to be no other than the *Metromanie*. The just celebrity of Robert Burns and Miss Baillie has had the melancholy effect of turning the heads of we know not how many farm-servants and unmarried ladies; our very footmen compose tragedies, and there is scarcely a superannuated governess in the island that does not leave a roll of lyrics behind her in her band-box.' He had advised Keats to return to medicine, and now he wrote impatiently of Clare's celebrity:

> ... one cannot help feeling some qualms concerning the late enormous puffing of the Northamptonshire peasant, John Clare. ... Clare has exhibited powers that not only justify but demand attention and kindness – but his generous and enlightened patrons ought to pause ere they advise him to become anything else than a peasant — for a respectable peasant is a much more comfortable man, and always will be so, than a mediocre poet.

The *British Critic* wrote in similar fashion in a review of Robert Millhouse's *Vicissitude: a Poem*:

> Nothing is more easy than for any person, of moderate talents, be his situation in life what it may, who can read and write, and is in possession of Thomson's Seasons and Beattie's Minstrel, and one or two other poems of that class, to cultivate a talent for making verses ... without perhaps one single good line of poetry being produced, we shall have geniuses starting up in every village, to the great detriment, we will venture to say, both of the happiness and morality, not only of these unhappy persons themselves, but of the little communities over which they will probably reside.

So spoke the 'iron hand of *Criticism*'. But this was only one of the new pressures confronting Clare, 'the Northamptonshire Peasant', as he entered literary society. There were, for instance, the demands of his numerous patrons, who were generous, well-meaning and sincere, but who could also be argumentative and censorious. Lord Exeter of Burghley House, near Stamford, was the son of the tenth Earl of Exeter and his second wife, a farmer's daughter known as the 'Cottage' or 'Peasant' Countess. Exeter warned Clare to be wary of booksellers like Drury, and after only their first meeting agreed to give him an annuity of fifteen guineas a year for life. In 1827 Clare dedicated *The Shepherd's Calendar* to him. *Poems Descriptive* was dedicated to Lord Milton, the only son of the second Earl Fitzwilliam of Milton Hall, near

Peterborough. Milton gave Clare a ten pound note on their first meeting, while the old Earl gave him a five pound note and 'bade me beware of booksellers and warnd me not to be fed with promises'. Clare would often have to manoeuvre diplomatically between these two rival grandees, one, Exeter, a Whig, and the other, Fitzwilliam, a Tory.

The most energetic of Clare's patrons was William Waldegrave, first Baron Radstock, who had been a distinguished admiral in the Royal Navy. Radstock introduced Clare to Eliza Emmerson, wrote him up in the press, and promoted him in the best literary and social circles in London. 'Lord Radstock at first sight appears to be of a stern and haughty character,' said Clare after their first meeting in London in March 1820, 'but the moment he speaks his countenance kindles up into a free good-hearted man.'

But Radstock was also an evangelical Christian, and he appointed himself Clare's protector and guide. He was not the first to worry about the poet's supposed vulnerability. Clare may have been a genius, but he was still seen as an innocent rustic, and therefore in need of protection. Both Gilchrist and Taylor had worried that sudden success might have a damaging effect on Clare's personality. 'It is greatly to be feared that the man will be afflicted with insanity if his talent continues to be forced as it has been these 4 months past,' Gilchrist had written to Taylor before the publication of *Poems Descriptive*, 'he has no other mode of easing the fever that oppresses him after a tremendous fit of rhyming except by getting tipsy.' 'The lower the condition of its possessor, the more unfavourably, generally, has been the effect of genius on his life,' Taylor had written in his introduction to *Poems Descriptive*. Clare must not be 'injured by prosperity', he warned, 'and that he may escape in future, it is hoped that those persons who intend to shew him kindness, will not do it suddenly or partially, but so as to yield him permanent benefit'.

Radstock went much further than Gilchrist or Taylor. He took responsibility for Clare's personal morality. For in his role as peasant poet, Clare was expected to show an example to others of his class. James Plumptre, for instance, playwright, Church of England clergyman, protector of public morals and editor of *The English Drama Purified* (1812), wrote to him in April 1820: 'You will probably write and publish much more, and I hope you will turn your thoughts towards some instructive popular Songs for the lower classes.' Burns's decline in popularity had in part been due to tales of his dissipated and promiscuous personal life, and there were aspects of Clare's character that did not fit in with the popular image of the industrious farm labourer: his fondness for drink, pretty women and bawdy language. Radstock fought

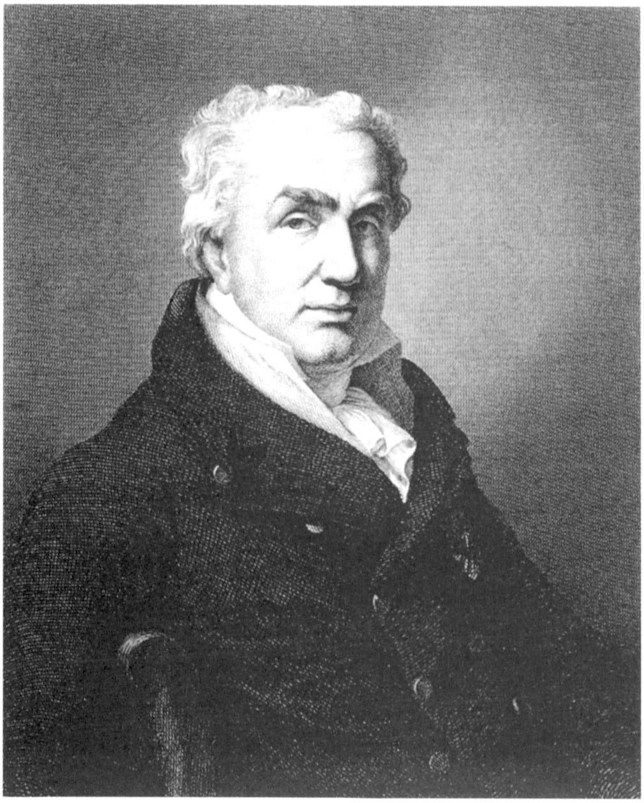

Lord Radstock, by T. Landseer after G. Hayter, 1820.

to have two bawdy poems dropped from the next edition of *Poems Descriptive* – 'My Mary' and 'Dolly's Mistake', both favourites of Clare.

Radstock also expected Clare to show proper respect for his social superiors, and strongly objected to certain lines in 'Helpston' in which the poet lamented the policy of enclosure, whereby common land was fenced and divided up for private ownership:

> Now all laid waste by desolation's hand
> Whose cursed weapon levels half the land
> Oh who could see my dear green willows fall
> What feeling heart but dropt a tear for all
> Accursed wealth o'er bounding human laws
> Of every evil thou remainst the cause
> Victims of want those wretches such as me
> Too truly lay their wretchedness to thee

> Thou art the bar that keeps from being fed
> And thine our loss of labour and of bread
> Thou art the cause that levels every tree
> And woods bow down to clear a way for thee.

Radstock considered this 'radical slang', and furthermore thought Clare was being extremely ungrateful to his land-owning patrons. In May 1820 he wrote to Eliza Emmerson requesting her to persuade Clare to drop the lines:

> If you are determined to serve poor Clare – you *must do your duty*! You must tell him to expunge certain highly objectionable passages in his 1st Volume before the 3rd Edition appears, passages, wherein, his then depressed state hurried him not only into error, but into the most flagrant acts of injustice; by accusing those of pride, cruelty, vices, and ill-directed passions – who are the very persons by whose truly generous and noble exertions he has been raised from misery and despondency. ... It has been my anxious desire of late, to establish our poet's character, as that of an honest and upright man – as a man feeling the strongest sense of gratitude for the encouragement he has received ... *he must expunge expunge*!

Mrs Emmerson dutifully wrote to Clare, assuring him that Radstock was both 'an ornament and blessing to mankind', and entreating him to *'expunge, expunge'*. Clare wrote immediately to Taylor:

> Being very bothered lately I must trouble you to leave out the 8 lines in 'Helpstone' beginning 'Accursed wealth' and two under 'When ease and plenty' – and one in 'Dawnings of Genius' 'That necessary tool' leave it out and put ——— to fill up the blank this will let em see I do it as negligent as possible   D—n that canting way of being forced to please I say – I cant abide it and one day or other I will show my Independence more strongly than ever   you know who's the promoter of the scheme I dare say –

Taylor, who had no liking for the old system of publishing by patronage, grew increasingly exasperated by Radstock's demands. 'Lord Radstock still exterts his utmost Interest to sell the Book,' Taylor wrote to Clare in February 1820, 'and did I not hate Patronage for its *selfishness* (for such it is too frequently), I could not but admire the pains he takes.' 'After being *required* to feel grateful,' he was writing more angrily in December, 'and being told that you never can make an adequate Return, this Consciousness of having nobody but God to thank, is a thousand fold sweeter than ever. L.R.'s voracious Appetite is satisfied, you will feel independent, but I fear he will not be content till he is acknowledged your supreme Friend, & pre-eminent Patron.' Taylor finally gave in, and omitted the offending lines in the next edition of *Poems Descriptive*: 'let them be expunged and welcome ... When the Follies of the Day are passed with all the Fears they have engendered we can restore the Poems according to the Earlier Editions.'

Taylor was the single most important figure in Clare's professional life. A liberal, unconventional, and deeply religious man, he developed unusually close personal and financial links with many of his writers. 'Damn them who could act in so cruel a way to a young man of undoubted genius,' he confided to Clare on the damning reviews of Keats's poetry. 'I hate that Irish Mode of pummelling a poor Fellow when he is down, and Poets especially who never seek to hurt others.' It is entirely consistent with Taylor's character that he should have advanced Keats money, and then organised his voyage to Italy. Clare would often disagree with his publisher, but he recognised him as a sympathetic friend and, what is more, the most important link between the worlds of rural Helpston and literary London. 'He is a kind of screne between me and the world,' said Clare, 'a sort of hiding place for me in the hour of danger.'

Taylor's tasks as Clare's publisher were unusually heavy. Clare wrote compulsively; manuscripts arrived from Helpston in enormous profusion, and in all states – some quite finished, others barely legible. Taylor was required to decipher, edit, revise, consider the dialect elements, and punctuate. His appointed role was to translate Clare's rough, spontaneous manuscripts into a form that could be put before literary society. 'I have been trying songs,' Clare wrote to Taylor in May 1820 when a second collection was being considered, '& want your judgment only either to stop me or to set me off at full gallop which your disaproval or applause has as much power to effect as if spoken by a magician the rod of criticism in your hand has as much power over your poor sinful rhymer as the rod of Aaron in the Land of Egypt.' It was a challenge, and one Taylor enjoyed, but it was also exhausting; 'if I could have found any one who would [have] taken the Editing off my Hands, so as to have done it to my Mind, I would gladly have given them 100£', he wrote on one occasion.

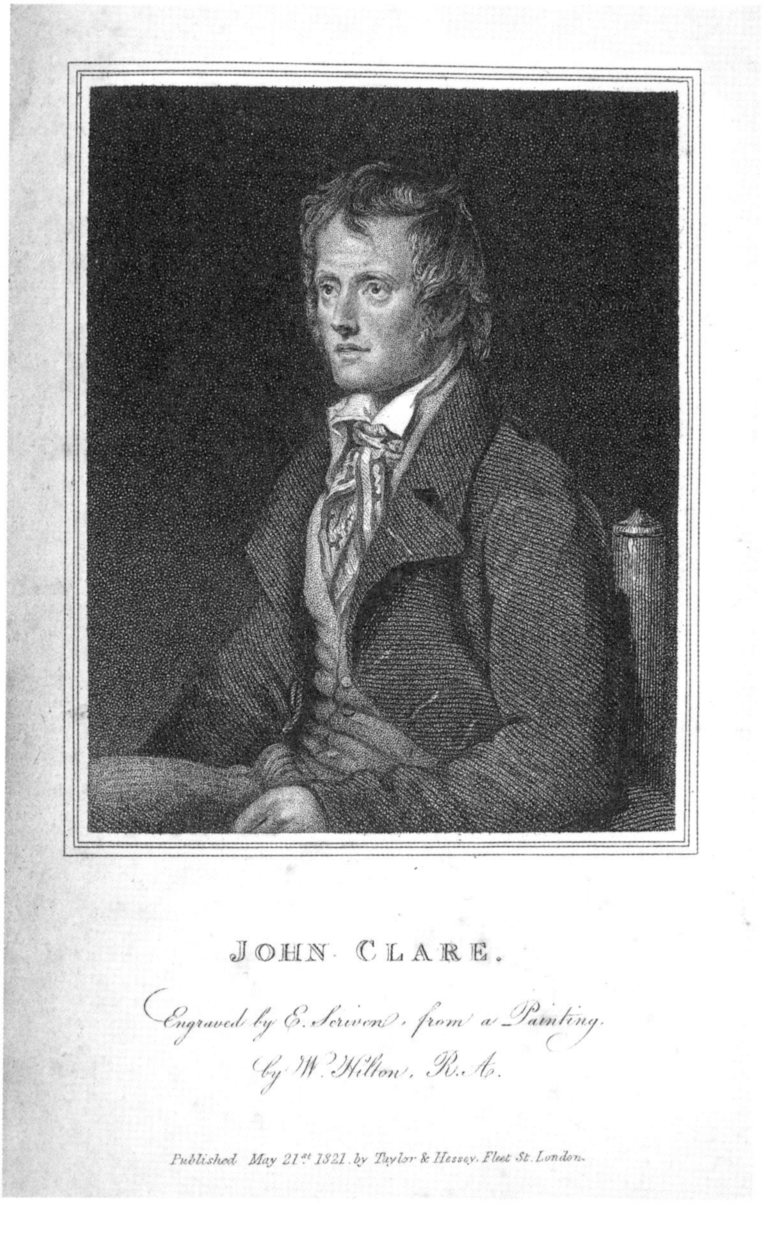

The frontispiece to John Clare's *The Village Minstrel*, 1821.

A fourth edition of *Poems Descriptive* appeared in 1821, and later that year Clare's second collection, *The Village Minstrel and other Poems*, was published. It sold reasonably, but nothing like as well as the first book. 'I rather feel hipt at the Village Minstrels success,' Clare wrote to Taylor in February 1822, 'the Old Vol: had gone thro 2 editions ere this and I think a notice in the London [*London Magazine*] agen of a New Vol of Poems preparing is necessary as a stimulant to revive the flatness of these for I am jealous of their ill success at least I feel something that tells me they don't go off like the others and I prevent that feeling as much as ever I can from damping my further exertions but I cannot help it doing so at some times.'

The frontispiece to *The Village Minstrel* carried a likeness of Clare, based on a portrait painted by William Hilton during the poet's first visit to London in 1820. 'And look!' wrote T.G. Wainewright on the engraving. 'Did you ever see a thing copied so accurately, and with so much feeling, as this brilliant little print by Scriven, after Hilton's natural and characteristic portrait of Clare? What life in the eyes! What ardent thirst for excellence, and what flexibility and susceptibility to outward impression in the quivering lips! Observe the thigh caught up unconsciously by the hand! It does Hilton's penetration credit to have arrested that most unsophisticated and speaking action.'

Clare made further trips to London in May and June 1822, and then from May to August 1824. He attended the dinners held by Taylor for his *London Magazine* and met many of the most prominent literary figures of the day, including Coleridge, Lamb, Hazlitt, De Quincey, John Hamilton Reynolds, and the Dante translator Henry Cary. Among the artists Clare befriended were E.V. Rippingille and Peter De Wint. He enjoyed the literary life of the capital, but Hilton's portrait conveys something of the discomfort he felt in polite society. On his way to London he had watched his fellow labourers from the coach: 'when I turnd to the reccolections of the past by seeing people at my old occupations of ploughing and ditching in the fields by the road side while I was lolling in a coach the novelty created such strange feelings that I coud almost fancy that my identity as well as my occupations had changd that I was not the same John Clare but that some stranger soul had jumpd into my skin.'

Clare started to feel increasingly dislocated between the two worlds of John Clare the peasant, and John Clare the celebrated poet. He suffered frequent bouts of illness and depression. 'I wish I livd nearer you at least I wish London woud creep within 20 miles of Helpstone,' he wrote to Taylor in

February 1822. 'I don't wish Helpstone to shift its station I live here among the ignorant like a lost man in fact like one whom the rest seems careless of having anything to do with – they hardly dare talk in my company for fear I shoud mention them in my writings & I find more pleasure in wandering the fields then in mixing among my silent neighbours who are insensible of everything but toiling & talking of it & that to no purpose.'

Clare even felt this sense of alienation in his own cottage. For, with success, came celebrity, and the other villagers looked on as innumerable poetry readers, nature lovers and gossiping gentry arrived in Helpston to see him. Some simply drew up outside to gawp at the famous peasant poet, but others invited themselves inside to talk about literature and fine landscapes. '[T]he first publication of my poems brought many visitors to my house out of a mere curosity to expect to know wether I realy was the son of a thresher and a laboring rustic as had been stated,' he later wrote, 'and when the[y] found it realy was so they lookd at each other as a matter of satisfied supprise askd some gossiping questions and on finding me a vulgar fellow that mimicd at no pretentions but spoke in the rough ways of a th[o]rough bred clown they soon turnd to the door and dropping their heads in a good morning attitude they departed.' Clare was annoyed by such visits, and avoided them whenever he could. The tempers of his wife and mother were not improved when uninvited guests caught them with an untidy house. '3 days scarcely pass but somebody calls,' he told Taylor, 'some rather entertaining people & some d–d knowing fools – surely the vanity would have kill'd me 4 years ago if I had known then how I should have been hunted up – & extolld by personal flattery – but let me wait another year or two & the peep show will be over – & my vanity if I have any will end in its proper mortification to know that obscurity is happiness & that John Clare the thresher in the onset & neglected rhymer in the end are the only two comfortable periods of his life.'

Literary tastes, however, were changing, and Clare's popularity began to decline. Fashionable readers were moving away from poetry towards annuals and miscellanies, or what the journalist Cyrus Redding, reflecting in 1842 on Clare's fortunes, dismissed as 'the puling, wordy, pseudo-sentimental effusions of boarding-school misses'. From 1823 Clare worked on a third collection, *The Shepherd's Calendar, with Village Stories, and other poems*. The title poem was an ambitious attempt to paint the life of a shepherd through the changing seasons, but Taylor delayed publication, making extensive revisions and trying to persuade Clare to write in a different way, and elevate his matter-of-fact descriptions into something more philosophical:

> What you ought to do is to elevate your Views, and write with the Power that belongs to you under the Influence of true Poetic Excitement – never in a low or familiar Manner, unless at the Time some strong Sensibility is awakened by the Situation of the Writer or those he writes about. For this Reason I cannot quite admire your Imitation of Wordsworth, though it is very clever – to him it is out of the Way to write on the familiar Topics of humble Life – his education has made a retired, a proud philosophic Poet of him, and when he chuses a Simple Theme, it is interesting to see how such a Man will treat it. But it has a Poetry also then, from various Singular Associations which are unexpectedly conjoined with it, which it cannot have when actually written in Simple Life – it seems then too *real* to be very poetical – You should write as you suppose he would think, to be even with him when he writes as he imagines you would think – Try by way of Experiment some little piece of the Kind I allude to – Don't make it artificial but avoid what you know & feel to be vulgar. – Between affectation on the one hand, & the common plain homely language of every Day Life on the other, there is a vast Field for your Genius to roll over in, & frolic, & kick about like a young Colt in a Pasture.

Taylor's partner James Hessey, facing the same commercial pressures, wrote to Clare reinforcing these opinions, and entreating the poet to give some thought to his reading public:

> In each of the poems now sent there are many beauties, but they have evidently been written in too much haste and without the fear of the Public before your eyes. The great fault of the whole of them is that they abound too much in mere description & are deficient in Sentiment and Feeling and human Interest. You have already described in admirable colours the Morning & the Noon & the Evening, & the Summer & the Winter, & the Sheep & Cattle & Poultry & Pigs & Milking Maids & foddering Boys – but the world will now expect something more than these – let them come in incidentally – let them occupy their places in the picture, but they must be subordinate to higher objects. A man who has travelled & mixed in Society, and read, and reflected, as you have, should give us some fruits of his experience & the result [of] his refl[ection]s. You may still be a descriptive poet if [you] please, but, when you describe Nature to those who see but little of her or to

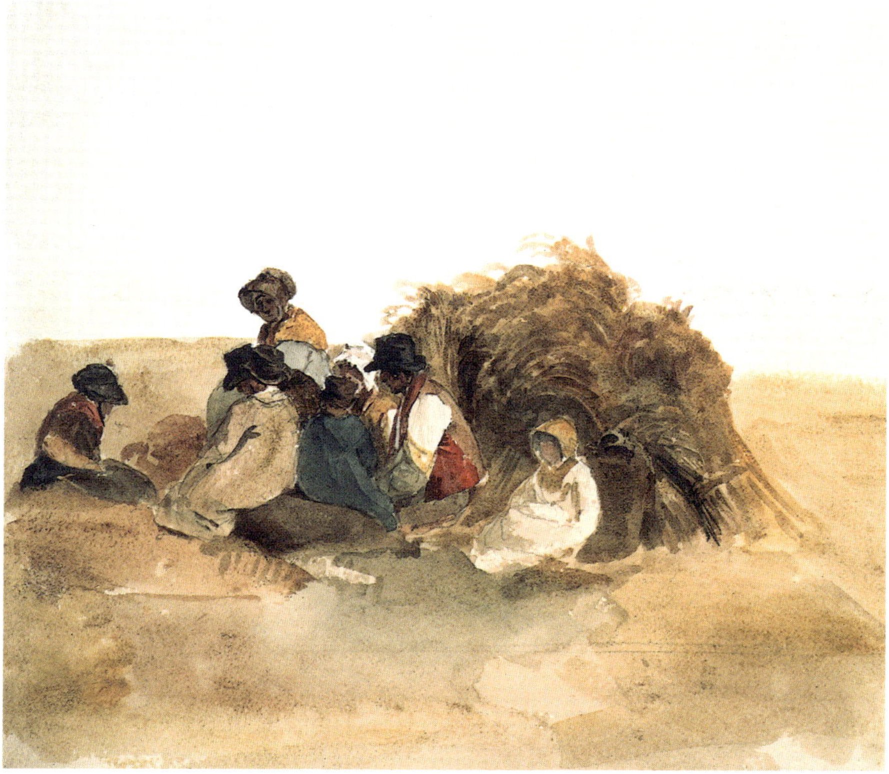

Harvesters resting, by Peter De Wint, Clare's favourite landscape artist.

> those who daily live with her, shew her as she appears to the Poet & the Man of Mind. Your colouring and your sketching are excellent but your Landscapes want Life and human Feelings.

Clare refused to follow their advice, and by the time *The Shepherd's Calendar* was finally published in 1827 (with a dedication to the Marquis of Exeter) his relations with his publishers had become very strained. '[M]y hopes of success are as warm as ever,' Clare wrote in the preface. 'I hope my low station in life will not be set off as a foil against my verses, and I am sure I do not wish to bring it forward as an excuse for any imperfections that may be found in them.' But only 400 copies were sold in the first year.

And yet, as Clare cast off the demands of being the public's 'peasant poet', he began to thrive creatively. '[A]ll I wish now is to stand on my own bottom as a poet without any apology as to want of education or anything else,' he

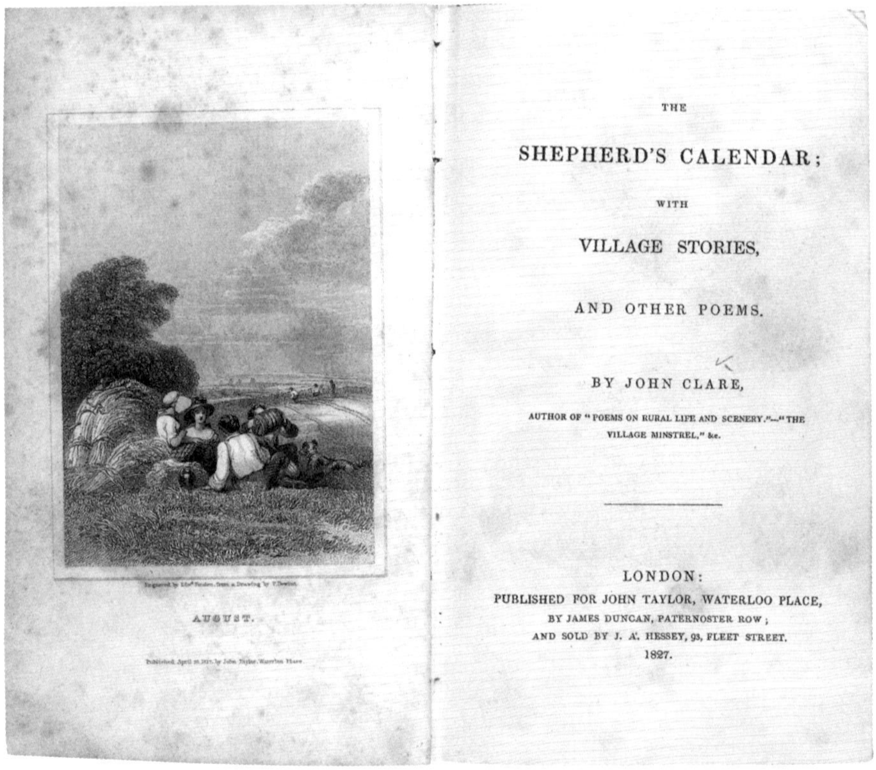

John Clare, *The Shepherd's Calendar*, 1827, with a frontispiece by Peter De Wint.

wrote to Eliza Emmerson in November 1832, '& I say it not in the feeling of either ambition or vanity but in the spirit of common sense.' As celebrity faded away, his confidence grew, and his writing became more assured. 'I shoud imagine that my low origin in life will not be a mote in the eye of literature to bear against me and I will not urge it as an excuse for what I have written,' he wrote. His early poems, though popular, had been derivative. 'Helpston', for example, was an obvious imitation of Goldsmith's *Deserted Village*, and his vocabulary and end-stopped couplets owed much to eighteenth-century pastoral literature. But now, back in the secret nooks of Helpston, Clare found his own unique poetic voice, and wrote with originality, skill and power. After *The Shepherd's Calendar* he gathered material together for a new volume, which he called 'The Midsummer Cushion'. It is here that his best work is to be found. The writing is still descriptive and matter-of-fact, but it has a weight and an immediacy that command attention:

I love to see the old heath's withered brake
Mingle its crimpled leaves with furze and ling
While the old heron from the lonely lake
Starts slow and flaps his melancholy wing
And oddling crow in idle motions swing
On the half-rotten ash tree's topmost twig
Beside whose trunk the gypsy makes his bed –
Up flies the bouncing woodcock from the brig
Where a black quagmire quakes beneath the tread;
The fieldfare chatters in the whistling thorn
And for the 'awe round fields and closen rove,
And coy bumbarrels twenty in a drove
Flit down the hedgerows in the frozen plain
And hang on little twigs and start again.

The hushed, intimate discoveries of the later poems, as he comes across birds' nests and praises nature's shyest, humblest creatures, are infused with moods and feelings that come straight from his own, unspoken experiences: the utopian vision of pre-enclosure Helpston, the vanishing landscape which he remembered so vividly; his childhood love for Mary Joyce who acted as his muse; and the humming tensions of his own nervous sensibility. Here is his poem 'The Sand Martin':

Thou hermit haunter of the lonely glen
And common wild and heath – the desolate face
Of rude waste landscapes far away from men
Where frequent quarries give thee dwelling place,
With strangest taste and labour undeterred
Drilling small holes along the quarry's side,
More like the haunts of vermin than a bird
And seldom by the nesting boy descried –
I've seen thee far away from all thy tribe
Flirting about the unfrequented sky
And felt a feeling that I can't describe
Of lone seclusion and a hermit joy
To see thee circle round nor go beyond
That lone heath and its melancholy pond.

In the end, however, the various pressures proved too much for Clare. 'The Midsummer Cushion' was endlessly delayed, and he went through periods of deep depression. In 1832 he and his family moved from Helpston to Northborough, which, though only a few miles away, seemed like an alien world. Three years later *The Rural Muse* was published, a small selection by Eliza Emmerson of poems taken from 'The Midsummer Cushion', and Clare's last published work.

Gradually Clare descended into insanity, and in 1837 he was taken to an asylum at Epping Forest in Essex. In 1841 he escaped and walked the eighty miles back to Northborough, eating grass and sleeping rough:

> a cart met me with a man and a woman and a boy in it when nearing me the woman jumped out and caught fast hold of my hands and wished me to get into the cart but I refused and thought her either drunk or mad but when I was told it was my second wife Patty I got in and was soon at Northborough but Mary was not there neither could I get any information about her further then the old story of her being dead six years ago which might be taken from a bran new old Newspaper printed a dozen years ago but I took no notice of the blarney having seen her myself about a twelvemonth ago alive and well and as young as ever – so here I am homeless at home and half gratified to feel I can be happy any where ...

Later that year he was committed to Northampton Asylum, where he spent the rest of his life. 'I felt uncomfortable very often,' he had written in his unpublished autobiography, 'but my heart burnt over the pleasures of solitude and the restless revels of rhyme that was eternaly sapping my memorys like the summer sun over the tinkling brook till it one day should leave them dry and unconsous of the thrilling joys brin[g]ing anxiety and restless cares which it had created and the praises and censures which I shall leave behind me I knew nothing of the poets experience then or I shoud have remaind a labourer on and not livd to envy the ignorance of my old companions and fellow clowns I wish I had never known any other.'

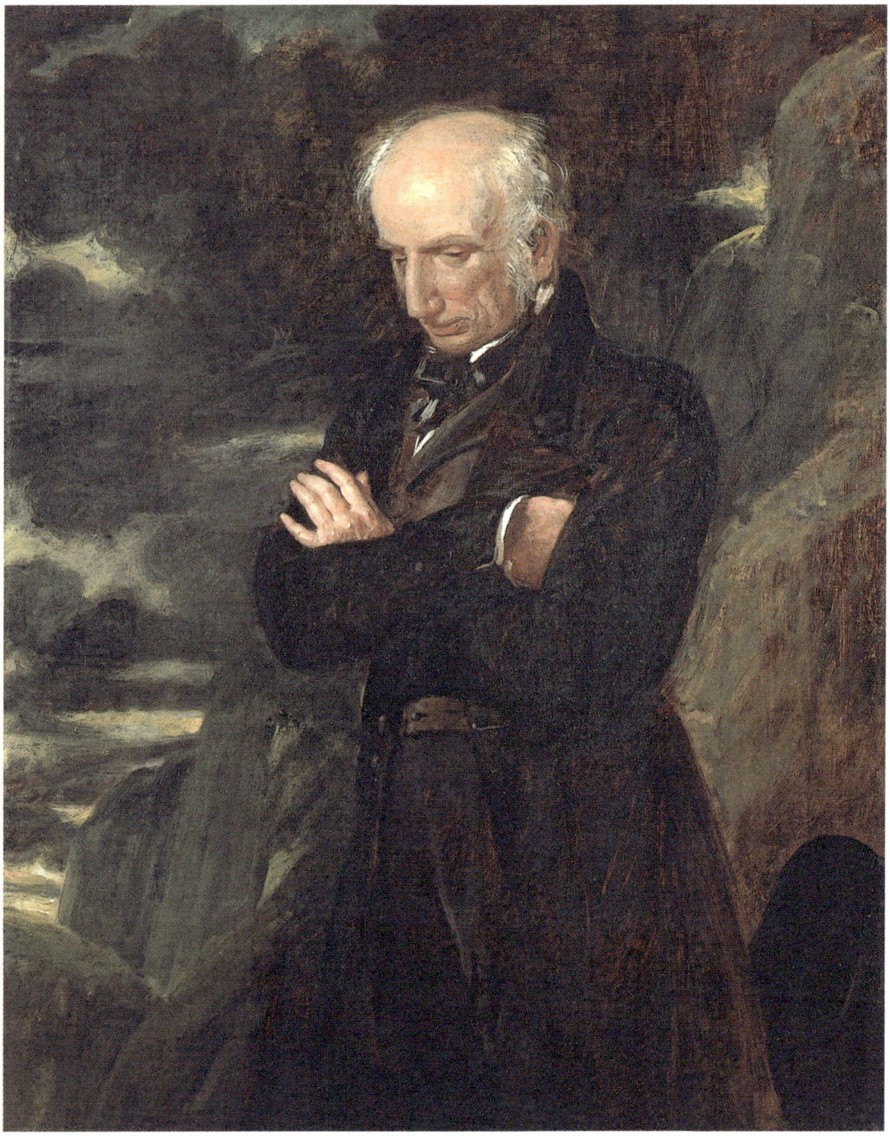

Wordsworth musing on Helvellyn, by Benjamin Robert Haydon, 1842.

'THESE TOURISTS, HEAVEN PRESERVE US!'

Wordsworth and the Lakes, 1810–1850

In 1844 the Kendal and Windermere Railway Company announced plans to build a branch line from Oxenholme, on the main Lancaster to Carlisle route, to Low Wood on the eastern shore of Lake Windermere. It was hoped that, at a later stage, it would cut right through the central Lake District and join up with the Keswick-to-Cockermouth line in the north. Wordsworth, then seventy-four and living at Rydal Mount, was passionately opposed to this scheme. On 12 October he composed a sonnet, 'On the Projected Kendal and Windermere Railway':

Is then no nook of English ground secure
From rash assault? Schemes of retirement sown
In youth, and mid the busy world kept pure
As when their earliest flowers of hope were blown,
Must perish;—how can they this blight endure?
And must he too the ruthless change bemoan
Who scorns a false utilitarian lure
Mid his paternal fields at random thrown?
Baffle the threat, bright Scene, from Orrest-head
Given to the pausing traveller's rapturous glance:
Plead for thy peace, thou beautiful romance
Of nature; and, if human hearts be dead,
Speak, passing winds; ye torrents, with your strong
And constant voice, protest against the wrong.

'We are this neighbourhood all in consternation, that is, every man of taste and feeling,' he wrote to William Gladstone, then President of the Board of Trade. 'The project if carried into effect will destroy the *staple* of the Country which is its beauty.' The next morning his sonnet was published in the *Morning Post*. 'The degree and kind of attachment which many of the yeomanry feel to their small inheritances can scarcely be over-rated,' he wrote in a footnote. 'Near the house of one of them stands a magnificent tree, which a neighbour of the owner advised him to fell for profit's sake. "Fell it," exclaimed the yeoman, "I had rather fall on my knees and worship it." It happens, I believe, that the intended railway would pass through this little property, and I hope that an apology for the answer will not be thought necessary by one who enters into the strength of the feeling.'

It was almost forty-five years since Wordsworth had retired to Grasmere to work on 'The Recluse'. He had spent eight years at Dove Cottage, and there had written his masterpeice, *The Prelude*, a long autobiographical poem which, because of its personal nature, was not published until after his death. In 1808 he had moved his growing family to Allan Bank, a large, new house on the other side of Grasmere lake. There he was joined by Coleridge, who since his return from Malta in 1806 had been lodging in London at the offices of the *Courier* newspaper. But Coleridge's return to Grasmere was brief and upsetting. His old delight in the landscape had gone, and he spent most of his time in his room, where, fortifying himself with opium and brandy, he worked almost single-handedly on a journal, *The Friend*. 'Coleridge (it may be thought) could not sequester himself so profoundly as at the *Courier* Office within his own shell,' wrote Thomas De Quincey, a fellow guest at Allan Bank, 'or shut himself out so completely from that large dominion of ear and eye amongst the hills, the fields, and the woods, which once he had exercised so pleasantly to himself, and with a participation so immortal, through his exquisite poem.' De Quincey, himself an opium addict, blamed Coleridge's behaviour on 'that accursed drug', which 'poisoned all natural pleasure at its sources'. The former fell-walker now 'burrowed continually deeper into scholastic subtleties and metaphysical abstraction, and ... lived chiefly by candlelight'. In 1810, Coleridge quarrelled with Wordsworth and returned to London. A serious and long-running rift followed, and Coleridge made only one further, brief, visit to the Lakes, in 1812.

In 1813 Wordsworth moved to Rydal Mount, a roomy house in the neighbouring valley, and his home for the rest of his life. There he completed a long poem he had begun at Allan Bank, *The Excursion*. It was published the following year, and under the title were the words 'Being a Portion of The Recluse, a Poem'. Wordsworth explained in a preface:

> It may be proper to state whence the Poem, of which The Excursion is a part, derives its title of THE RECLUSE.—Several years ago, when the Author retired to his native Mountains, with the hope of being enabled to construct a literary work that might live, it was a reasonable

> thing that he should take a review of his own Mind, and examine how far Nature and Education had qualified him for such employment. As subsidiary to this preparation, he undertook to record, in Verse, the origin and progress of his own powers, as far as he was acquainted with them. That Work, addressed to a dear Friend, most distinguished for his knowledge and genius, and to whom the Author's Intellect is deeply indebted, has been long finished; and the result of the investigation which gave rise to it was a determination to compose a philosophical Poem, containing views of Man, Nature, and Society; and to be entitled, The Recluse; as having for its principal subject the sensations and opinions of a Poet living in retirement.

It was Wordsworth's first public reference to the great philosophical work conceived in the Quantocks, and the reason, and justification, for his decision to retire to the Lake District.

The critics were unimpressed. 'This will never do,' wrote Francis Jeffrey, the editor of the *Edinburgh Review* and Wordsworth's great literary enemy. Jeffrey had put Wordsworth at the head of 'a *sect* of poets', '*dissenters* from the established systems in poetry and criticism', and saw his residence in the Lake District as proof of anti-social principles. To his annoyance, Wordsworth had found himself grouped with Coleridge, Lamb and Southey into a fictional 'Lakes School'. 'This author is known to belong to a certain brotherhood of poets, who have haunted for some years about the Lakes of Cumberland,' Jeffrey had written in his 1807 review of *Poems in Two Volumes*. 'As to the School about which so much noise (I am told) has been made,' an irritated Wordsworth wrote to Thelwall in January 1804, 'I do not know what is meant by it nor of whom it consists. The only names I ever heard of were Coleridge, Southey, Lamb and myself. Now as far as relates to opinions and judgements in Poetry, and also to the style and subjects of our several compositions, *if accurately examined*, it is scarcely possible that a greater difference should exist between these four men with the exception of Coleridge and myself, who though I believe not differing in essentials in judgement, do very materially so, strikingly so, in composition.'

Jeffrey saw *The Excursion* as further evidence of Wordsworth's egotistical isolation. It was not the business of poets to withdraw into the country and commune with nature. They were sociable men who participated in urban cultural life and mingled with their peers. 'Long habits of seclusion, and an excessive ambition of originality, can alone account for the disproportion

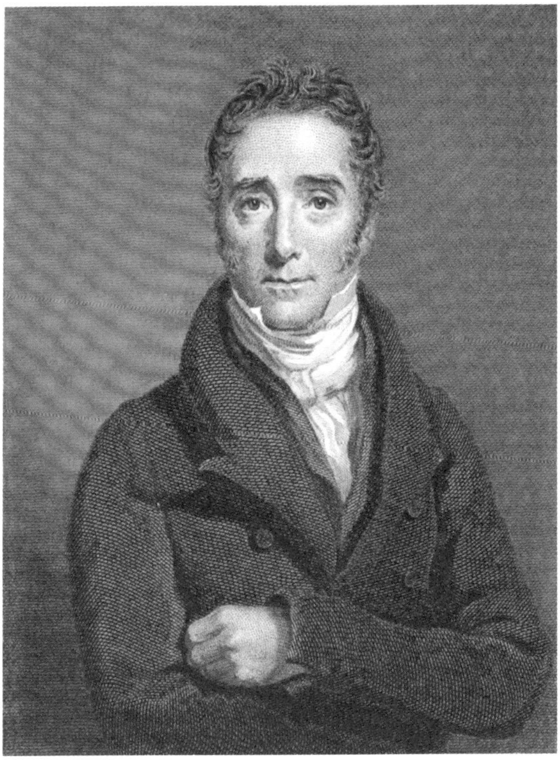

Francis Jeffrey, by Robert Bell after Colvin Smith.

which seems to exist between this author's taste and his genius,' Jeffrey wrote in his review of *The Excursion*, 'or for the devotion with which he has sacrificed so many precious gifts at the shrine of those paltry idols which he has set up for himself among his lakes and his mountains. Solitary musings, amidst such scenes, might no doubt be expected to nurse up the mind to the majesty of poetical conception, – (though it is remarkable, that all the greater poets lived, or had lived, in the full current of society): – But the collision of equal minds, – the admonition of prevailing impressions – seems necessary to reduce its redundancies, and repress that tendency to extravagance or puerility, into which the self-indulgence and self-admiration of genius is so apt to be betrayed, when it is allowed to wanton, without awe or restraint, in the triumph and delight of its own intoxication.' Instead of associating with dalesmen, cottagers, cronies and little children, Jeffrey wrote, Wordsworth should have 'lived or mixed familiarly with men of literature and ordinary judgment in poetry'. Byron, that most convivial and cosmopolitan of poets, said as much when he wrote in *Don Juan*:

And Wordsworth, in a rather long 'Excursion,'
(I think the Quarto holds five hundred pages),
Has given a sample from the vasty version
Of this new system to perplex the sages;
'Tis poetry – at least by his assertion,
And may appear so when the dog-star rages –
And he who understands it would be able
To add a story to the Tower of Babel.

You – Gentlemen! By dint of long seclusion
From better company, have kept your own
At Keswick, and, through still continued fusion
Of one another's minds, at last have grown
To deem as a most logical conclusion,
That Poesy has wreaths for you alone:
There is a narrowness in such a notion,
Which makes me wish you'd change your lakes for Ocean.

Paradoxically, however, the rural seclusion that Wordsworth sought, and Jeffrey condemned, had been slowly disappearing from the Lakes. Wordsworth had first known the area as a boy at Hawkshead Grammar School from 1779 to 1787. Situated in the vale of Esthwaite between Windermere and Coniston, Hawkshead was quiet and little-visited. De Quincey later wrote wistfully of a tourist-free, pre-lapsarian paradise:

> Esthwaite, therefore, being no object for itself, and the sublime head of Coniston being accessible by a road which evades Hawkshead, few tourists ever trouble the repose of this little village town. And in the days of which I am speaking, (1778–1787,) tourists were as yet few and infrequent to any parts of the country. Mrs Radcliffe had not begun to cultivate the sense of the picturesque in her popular romances; guide books, with the sole exception of 'Gray's Posthumous Letters,' had not arisen to direct public attention to this domestic Calabria; roads were rude, and, in many instances, not wide enough to admit post-chaises; but, above all, the whole system of travelling accommodations was barbarous and antediluvian for the requisitions of the pampered south. As yet the land had rest; and annual fever did not shake the very hills; and (which was the happiest immunity of the whole) false taste,

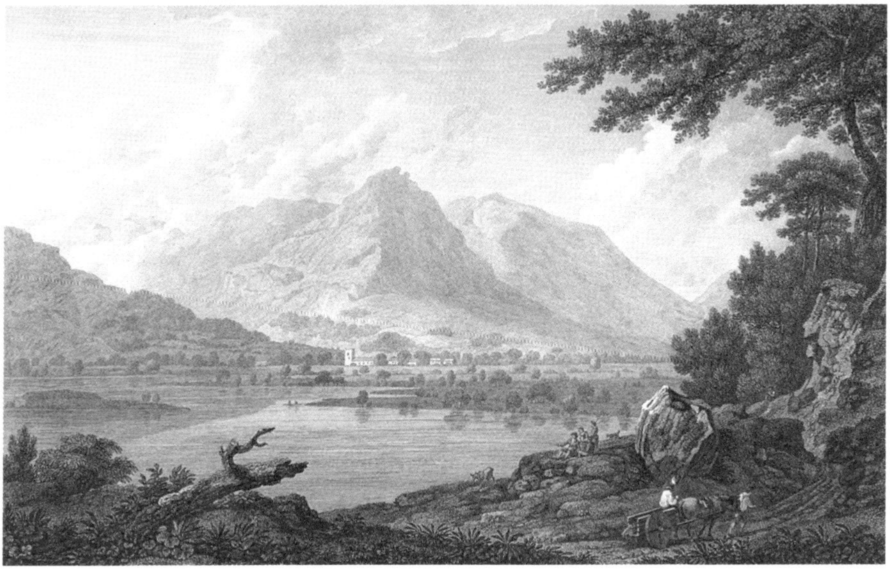

The first published view of Grasmere, by B.T. Pouncey after Joseph Farington, 1789.

> the pseudo-romantic rage, had not violated the most awful solitudes amongst the ancient hills by opera-house decorations. Wordsworth, therefore, enjoyed this labyrinth of valleys in a perfection that no one can have experienced since the opening of the present century. The whole was one paradise of virgin beauty …

When Wordsworth returned to the Lake District in 1799, the situation had changed. Since the publication of Thomas Gray's tour in 1770, and the first engravings of the Lakes by Joseph Farington some years later (with accompanying prose descriptions by Wordsworth's uncle, William Cookson), the area had become increasingly celebrated. 'I have taken a house in the Vale of *Grasmere*,' Wordsworth wrote to Anne Taylor in April 1801, 'a very beautiful spot of which almost every body has heard.' He and Dorothy were sometimes stared at admiringly by well-to-do travellers. One morning in June 1800, for example, after working in the garden, they were sitting on a wall by the road. 'A coronetted Landau went by,' recorded Dorothy in her journal. 'The ladies (evidently Tourists) turned an eye of interest upon our little garden & cottage.' Coleridge looked with contempt upon those who were so attached to the fashionable depictions of nature in guidebooks and engravings that they barely noticed the landscape itself. 'Ladies reading Gilpin's &c while passing by the very places instead of looking at the places', he remarked in his notebook during a stay at Dove Cottage. 'Of the fashionable travellers, who pass through Grasmere in the summer months, I have observed no small number asleep,' he later wrote in the *Morning Post*. 'A much greater number are reading descriptions of the place, or lost in admiration of the landscape in aqua-tinta. Still, however, I hope, and trust, that a majority will remain of those, who have kept their eyes open, and their hearts awake.'

Tourists brought an incongruous air of leisure to places of hard work and frugality. Wordsworth's poem 'The Brothers', written at Dove Cottage, opens with the industrious priest of remote Ennerdale spinning and carding wool on his doorstep one July evening, and looking baffled at someone, surely a tourist, who had been meditating in the churchyard for hours:

> These Tourists, Heaven preserve us! Needs must live
> A profitable life: some glance along,
> Rapid and gay, as if the earth were air,
> And they were butterflies to wheel about
> Long as their summer lasted; some, as wise,
> Upon the forehead of a jutting crag
> Sit perched with book and pencil on their knee,
> And look and scribble, scribble on and look,
> Until a man might travel twelve stout miles,
> To reap an acre of his neighbour's corn.

With popularity came the guidebooks. In 1778 Thomas West published, in both London and Kendal, *A Guide to the Lakes: dedicated to the Lovers of Landscape Studies, and to all who have visited, or intend to visit the Lakes in Cumberland, Westmorland, and Lancashire*. Born in Scotland, West was a Jesuit priest, and had worked for some years on the continent before being appointed to Dalton in Furness in Lancashire in 1765. In 1774 he published the *Antiquities of Furness*, which was primarily concerned with the history of Furness Abbey. His *Guide to the Lakes* was the first comprehensive guidebook to the area, but drew extensively upon earlier literature, particularly Thomas Gray. West recommended particular viewing points, or 'stations': 'The design of the following sheets, is to encourage the taste of visiting the lakes, by furnishing the traveller with a Guide; and for that purpose are here collected and laid before him, all the select stations, and points of view noticed by those authors who have made the tour of the lakes.' Sometimes he would disagree with Gray. Grasmere, for instance, he said, was best seen not from Dunmail

Raise, but from the south. West recommended a tour of the Lake District to people who wished 'to unbend the mind from anxious cares, or fatiguing studies', for they 'will meet with agreeable dissipation and useful relaxation'. 'The contemplative traveller,' he adds, 'will be charmed with the sight of the sweet retreats, that he will observe in these enchanting regions of calm repose.'

West's guide was immediately popular. In 1780 a second edition was published, edited and considerably enlarged by William Cockin, a Kendal schoolmaster, and by 1821 it had reached its eleventh edition. Also widely read, but very different to West, was William Gilpin's *Observations, Relative Chiefly to Picturesque Beauty*, first published in 1786, and based on a tour made in 1772, two years after his visit to the Wye Valley. Like West, Gilpin brought tourists to the lakes with preconceived ideas of what constituted a beautiful landscape, and created a vogue that encouraged travellers and connoisseurs to publish their own accounts. At least thirty such books were published in the thirty years following the first appearance of West's *Guide*.

It was while he was living at Allan Bank that Wordsworth first began to think about writing his own description of the Lake District. In 1809, a clergyman from the north east of England, the Reverend Joseph Wilkinson, asked him if he would contribute an introduction to a book of engravings made after his own watercolours. Wordsworth hesitated at first, as he had a decidedly low opinion of Wilkinson's drawings, but the essay that he eventually wrote was published, anonymously, the following year, as the introduction to Wilkinson's *Select Views in Cumberland, Westmoreland, and Lancashire*

Over the course of the next twenty-five years Wordsworth developed this relatively short description, in a private publication, into the most popular guidebook to the Lakes. It first appeared under his name in 1820, as the 'annex' to *The River Duddon, A Series of Sonnets*. 'This Essay,' ran the explanatory advertisement, 'which was first published several years ago as an Introduction to some Views of the Lakes, by the Rev. Joseph Wilkinson, (an expensive work, and necessarily of limited circulation,) is now, with emendations and additions, attached to these volumes; from a consciousness of its having been written in the same spirit which dictated several of the poems, and from a belief that it will tend materially to illustrate them.'

Two years later, the essay was published separately as *A Description of the Lakes in the North of England*, with a fold-out map and an added section at the end entitled 'Directions and Information to the Tourist'. The first edition of five hundred copies quickly sold out, and a second edition, of 1,000 copies,

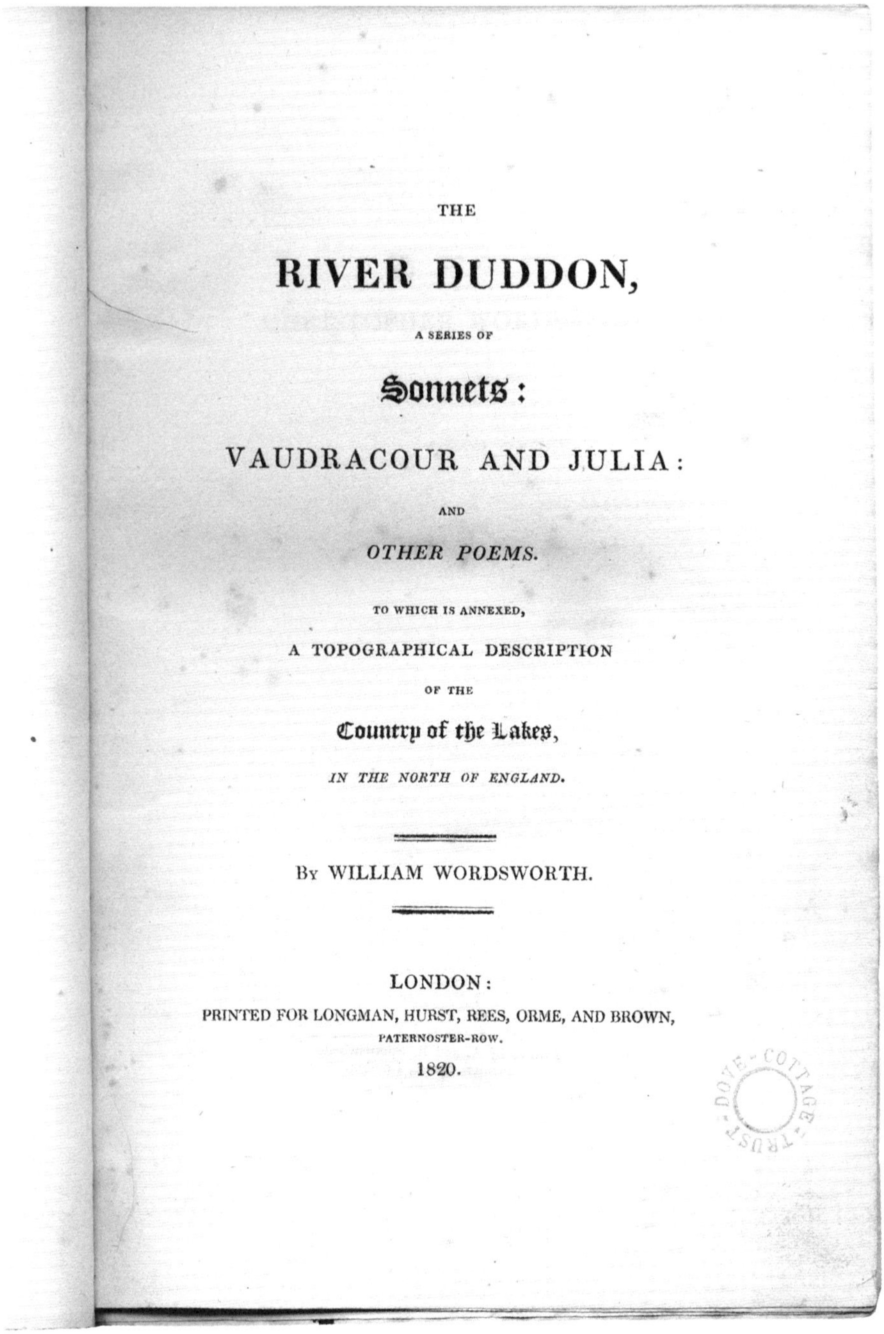

THE

RIVER DUDDON,

A SERIES OF

Sonnets:

VAUDRACOUR AND JULIA:

AND

OTHER POEMS.

TO WHICH IS ANNEXED,

A TOPOGRAPHICAL DESCRIPTION

OF THE

Country of the Lakes,

IN THE NORTH OF ENGLAND.

By WILLIAM WORDSWORTH.

LONDON:

PRINTED FOR LONGMAN, HURST, REES, ORME, AND BROWN,

PATERNOSTER-ROW.

1820.

The first widely available version of Wordsworth's guide
to the Lake District, published with *The River Duddon*, 1820.

was printed with some revisions the following year. A third edition was published in 1835 with the title *A Guide Through the District of the Lakes in the North of England, with a Description of the Scenery, etc. For the Use of Tourists and Residents*. For this edition, the 'Directions and Information for the Tourist' was moved to the front of the book, and an itinerary was given at the back, 'for the use of tourists'. In 1842, *A Complete Guide to the Lakes, Comprising Minute Directions for the Tourist* was printed in Kendal and published both there and in London, complete with engravings of Windermere, Derwentwater, Rydal and Ullswater. Added to *Mr Wordsworth's Description of the Country, etc.* were *Three Letters on the Geology of the Lake District, by the Rev. Professor Sedgwick*. This version, the last to be prepared in Wordsworth's lifetime, went through five editions in seventeen years.

Introducing the 1835 edition of the *Guide*, Wordsworth wrote that his 'principal wish' was 'to furnish a Guide or Companion for the *Minds* of Persons of taste, and feeling for landscape, who might be inclined to explore the District of the Lakes with that degree of attention to which its beauty may fairly lay claim'. Throughout the *Guide* Wordsworth emphasises the interaction between the mind and the landscape, between the observer and observed. He believed that by furnishing the minds of visitors with a better knowledge of the Lake District, he would enable them to appreciate it more fully. This, in turn, would lead to the proper care and preservation of that landscape. Wordsworth wished to train the eye of the visitor; supplying them with directions and practical information was, by contrast, a 'humble and tedious task'.

The main part of the *Guide* had remained essentially unchanged since 1810. It was divided into three sections: 'View of the country as formed by nature'; 'Aspect of the country, as affected by its inhabitants'; and 'Changes, and rules of taste for preventing their bad effects'. Wordsworth begins the first section with a general outline of the area:

> The delineation, if tolerably executed, will, in some instances, communicate to the traveller, who has already seen the objects, new information; and will assist in giving to his recollections a more orderly arrangement than his own opportunities of observing may have permitted him to make; while it will be still more useful to the future traveller, by directing his attention at once to distinctions in things which, without such previous aid, a length of time only could enable him to discover.

Thomas West, in his *Guide to the Lakes*, had carefully selected a series of low-level viewing stations which emphasised the artistic qualities of the lakes and fells. Wordsworth, however, adopted a high, imaginary station midway between Great Gavel and Scafell: 'we shall see stretched at our feet a number of valleys, not fewer than eight, diverging from the point, on which we are supposed to stand, like spokes from the nave of a wheel.' The unique quality of the area, he writes, is the variety of effects of light and shadow, and the different effects they have upon the heights and gradations of the fells:

> For example, in the vale of Winandermere, if the spectator looks for gentle and lovely scenes, his eye is turned towards the south; if for the grand, towards the north: in the vale of Keswick, which (as hath been said) lies almost due north of this, it is directly the reverse. Hence, when the sun is setting in summer far to the north-west, it is seen, by the spectator from the shores or breast of Winandermere, resting among the summits of the loftiest mountains, some of which will perhaps be half or wholly hidden by clouds, or by the blaze of light which the orb diffuses around it; and the surface of the lake will reflect before the eye correspondent colours through every variety of beauty, and through all degrees of splendour. In the vale of Keswick, at the same period, the sun sets over the humbler regions of the landscape, and showers down upon *them* the radiance which at once veils and glorifies,—sending forth, meanwhile, broad streams of rosy, crimson, purple, or golden light, towards the grand mountains in the south and south-east, which, thus illuminated, with all their projections and cavities, and with an intermixture of solemn shadows, are seen distinctly through a cool and clear atmosphere. Of course, there is as marked a difference between the *noontide* appearance of these two opposite vales. The bedimming haze that overspreads the south, and the clear atmosphere and determined shadows of the clouds in the north, at the same time of the day, are each seen in these several vales, with a contrast as striking. The reader will easily conceive in what degree the intermediate vales partake of a kindred variety.
>
> I do not indeed know any tract of country in which, within so narrow a compass, may be found an equal variety in the influences of light and shadow upon the sublime or beautiful features of landscape; and it is owing to the combined circumstances to which the reader's attention has been directed.

Wordsworth proceeds to give a detailed survey of the mountains, vales, lakes, tarns, islands and woods. Everything is carefully delineated, described and compared, from the general shape of the mountains to the 'minute beauties' of mosses and lichens: the effects of water; the intermixture of colour; the texture and shape of fern, turf and leaf; the behaviour of water fowl; the geological forms of the rocks; the changing appearances of the fells according to the seasons; the effects of mist and haze which 'in a country of this character, is like that of magic'.

Wordsworth brings an intuitive eye to the landscape, tracing the profound effect its forms have upon the feelings and the mind:

> The form of the lake is most perfect when, like Derwent-water, and some of the smaller lakes, it least resembles that of a river;—I mean, when being looked at from any given point where the whole may be seen at once, the width of it bears such proportion to the length, that, however the outline may be diversified by far-receding bays, it never assumes the shape of a river, and is contemplated with that placid and quiet feeling which belongs peculiarly to the lake—as a body of still water under the influence of no current; reflecting therefore the clouds, the light, and all the imagery of the sky and surrounding hills; expressing also and making visible the changes of the atmosphere, and motions of the lightest breeze, and subject to agitation only from the winds—
>
> ————The visible scene
> Would enter unawares into his mind
> With all its solemn imagery, its rocks,
> Its woods, and that uncertain heaven received
> Into the bosom of the *steady* lake!

Wordsworth is writing within a literary tradition, and he employs the fashionable terminology of eighteenth-century aesthetics used by 'persons of taste', but there is an excitement and engagement about the writing that comes from a deeper identification with the landscape than previously found in Lake District guidebooks. A new, holistic attitude is evident in the detail, with the inclusion of less dramatic features like small, remote mountain tarns. Here was the unifying 'one intellectual breeze' of Coleridge's 'Eolian Harp', the pantheistic spirit that made Wordsworth, as he wrote in 'Tintern Abbey', 'a worshipper of Nature'.

Having described the physical landscape of the Lake District, Wordsworth then considers 'in what manner it is indebted to the hand of man'. He does this by describing the lives and occupations of the the area's inhabitants, past and present. This was a new subject for guides to the Lakes. Thomas West had briefly mentioned the 'purely pastoral' life of the inhabitants of Buttermere, where 'the women spin woolen yarn, and drink tea', and had praised 'mountain virtue', which 'constitutes a pleasing difference betwixt travelling here and on the continent, where every innholder is an extortioner'. Otherwise he barely mentions the people of the Lake District; his interest was exclusively in the aesthetic qualities of the landscape.

The most celebrated native of the Lake District at the beginning of the nineteenth century was probably Mary Robinson, of Buttermere. In 1792, Joseph Budworth had published *A Fortnight's Ramble to the Lakes in Westmoreland, Lancashire and Cumberland*, which included an account of his visit to the remote village of Buttermere among the western fells, and its 'fourteen families'. At the local inn he was served by a young girl called Mary. Budworth extravagantly praised her in his book (though incorrectly calling her Sally), and recommended that travellers should not fail to see her, rather as one should not miss a particularly good view:

> Her mother and she were spinning woolen yarn in the back kitchen; on our going into it, the girl flew away as swift as a mountain sheep, and it was not until our return from Scale Force, that we could say we first saw her; she brought in part of our dinner, and seemed to be about fifteen. Her hair was thick and long, of a dark brown, and though unadorned with ringlets, did not seem to want them; her face was a fine contour, with full eyes, and lips as red as vermillion; her cheeks had more of the lily than the rose; and although she had never been out of the village, (and, I hope, will have no ambition to wish it) she had a manner about her which seemed better calculated to set off dress, than dress her. She was a very Lavinia,
>
> 'Seeming when unadorn'd, adorn'd the most.'
>
> When we first saw her at her distaff, after she had got the better of her first fears, she looked an angel, and I doubt not but she is the *reigning lily* of the valley.
>
> Ye travellers of the Lakes, if you visit this obscure place, such you will find the fair SALLY OF BUTTERMERE.

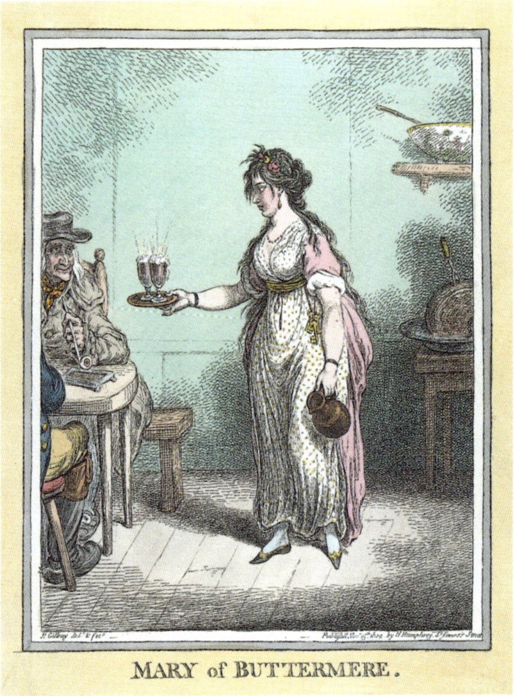

An engraving of Mary of Buttermere, after Gillray.

It was a picture of sequestered rural innocence. But Mary was later to be the victim of a famous scandal. She was seduced by a stranger, an imposter called James Hatfield who pretended to be the Honourable Augustus Hope, Member of Parliament for Linlithgowshire, and the brother of the Earl of Hoptoun. Hatfield and Mary married, but when his real identity was revealed it was discovered that he already had a wife. Hatfield escaped, but was later caught, tried and hanged. This cautionary tale was put before the public by Coleridge, in a series of articles in the *Morning Post* in 1801 and 1802, and entered into the popular imagination. It owed its power not just to the dramatic nature of the story, but to its symbolic significance: an innocent beauty, in a remote, beautiful valley, is seduced and ruined by an outsider, an invader. In 1810, in the third edition of his *Ramble*, Budworth added an extra note on Mary, regretting that he had ever brought her to the public's notice:

> The young person who was a few years ago deceived by a person under the assumed character of a man of rank; as specious an imposter as ever practised treachery; and during the consequently arduous period,

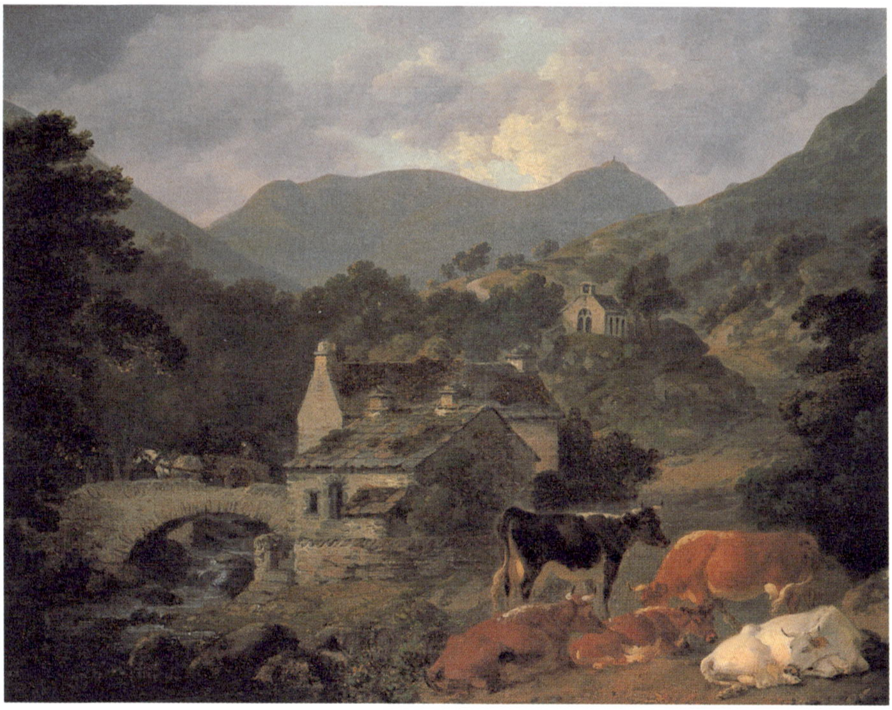

Buttermere, by Julius Caesar Ibbetson, 1814.

her conduct was regulated by such good sense and becoming manners as to arrest universal interest and commiseration. We have heard that she is greatly altered in appearance; a careworn countenance depicting the agonies she had laboured under; such cannot fail impressing the candid as sincerely in her favour as when a Rambler first saw her in 1792, an industrious comely looking girl of fifteen, at her spinning-wheel.

Cleared from human entanglement, a general respect towards her grew out of her sufferings; having borne them with humility, she judiciously re-settled in her native valley, and is married to a young man from the neighbourhood of Carlisle, who has taken an extensive farm at Buttermere; they have an interesting little Mary, and are, we hope, crowned with blessings.

Having brought her into notice, as the reigning Lily of the Valley, when her days were few; and in a re-visit to Buttermere witnessed her unassuming and correct behaviour, under the gaiety of rural festivity; a Rambler will always retain his cordial good wishes; at the same time, takes this opportunity of deploring that he ever

> wrote in commendation of any young living creature, as vanity, alas, is the most intoxicating of human plants! And too apt to spread, when unfortunately introduced to public approval. Indeed, few minds are proof against it; and happy would it be for many a flower, were they
> 'Born to blush unseen.'

Idealised engravings of Mary were published, and her story became a subject for increasingly bad poems, novels and melodramas. On 9 July 1803, shortly before Hatfield's trial, Charles and Mary Lamb and Robert Southey saw a play, 'Mary of Buttermere', performed at Sadler's Wells theatre in London. Mary Lamb wrote:

> We went last week with Southey and Rickman and his sister to Sadler's Wells, the lowest and most London-like of all our London amusements – the entertainments were Goody Two Shoes, Jack the Giant Killer, and Mary of Buttermere! Poor Mary was very happily married at the end of the piece, to a sailor her former sweetheart. We had a prodigious fine view of her father's house in the vale of Buttermere – mountains very like large haycocks, and a lake like nothing at all. If you had been with us, would you have laughed the whole time like Charles and Miss Rickman or gone to sleep as Southey and Rickman did?

Wordsworth, by contrast, felt a kinship with Mary, who he had visited, with Coleridge, when walking through Buttermere. In Book VII of *The Prelude* he noted that they had both been born on the banks of the river Derwent, she at Buttermere and he at Cockermouth, and contrasted her story with his own life as a stranger in London:

> thy image rose again,
> Mary of Buttermere! She lives in peace
> Upon the spot where she was born and reared;
> Without contamination does she live
> In quietness, without anxiety:
> Beside the mountain-Chapel sleeps in earth
> Her new-born Infant, fearless as a lamb
> That thither comes, from some unsheltered place,
> To rest beneath the little rock-like Pile
> When storms are blowing. Happy are they both
> Mother and Child!

In his *Guide to the Lakes*, Wordsworth showed how much the landscape owed its appearance to the actions of its inhabitants. It is their native rootedness, their dwelling in the landscape, that gives the region its distinctive character. Wordsworth pays considerable attention to their dwellings, and the way they blended modestly and fittingly into their surroundings:

> The dwelling-houses, and contiguous outhouses, are, in many instances, of the colour of the native rock, out of which they have been built; but, frequently the Dwelling or Fire-house, as it is ordinarily called, has been distinguished from the barn or byer by rough-cast and white wash, which, as the inhabitants are not hasty in renewing it, in a few years acquires, by the influence of weather, a tint at once sober and variegated. As these houses have been, from father to son, inhabited by persons engaged in the same occupations, yet necessarily with changes in their circumstances, they have received without incongruity additions and accommodations adapted to the needs of each successive occupant, who, being for the most part proprietor, was at liberty to follow his own fancy: so that these humble dwellings remind the contemplative spectator of a production of nature, and may (using a strong expression) rather be said to have grown than to have been erected;—to have risen, by an instinct of their own, out of the native rock—so little is there in them of formality, such is their wildness and beauty.

Wordsworth describes how plants willingly attach themselves to the walls of these buildings, such is their rough-hewn native fittingness:

> Hence buildings, which in their very form call to mind the processes of nature, do thus, clothed in part with a vegetable garb, appear to be received into the bosom of the living principle of things, as it acts and exists among the woods and fields; and, by their colour and their shape, affectingly direct the thoughts to that tranquil course of nature and simplicity, along which the humble-minded inhabitants have, through so many generations, been led. Add the little garden with its shed for bee-hives, its small bed of pot-herbs, and its borders and patches of flowers for Sunday posies, with sometimes a choice few too much prized to be plucked; an orchard of proportioned size; a cheese-press, often supported by some tree near the door; a cluster of embowering sycamores for summer shade; with a tall fir, through which the winds sing when

> other trees are leafless; the little rill or household spout murmuring in all seasons; combine these incidents and images together, and you have the representative idea of a mountain-cottage in this country so beautifully formed in itself, and so richly adorned by the hand of nature.

Concluding the second section of the *Guide*, Wordsworth describes the Lake District community as a natural republic, created by habits and traditions that had remained essentially unaltered for hundreds of years:

> Towards the head of these Dales was found a perfect Republic of Shepherds and Agriculturists, among whom the plough of each man was confined to the maintenance of his own family, or to the occasional accommodation of his neighbour. Two or three cows furnished each family with milk and cheese. The chapel was the only edifice that presided over these dwellings, the supreme head of this pure Commonwealth; the members of which existed in the midst of a powerful empire, like an ideal society or an organized community, whose constitution had been imposed and regulated by the mountains which protected it. Neither high-born nobleman, knight, nor esquire, was here; but many of these humble sons of the hills had a consciousness that the land, which they walked over and tilled, had for more than five hundred years been possessed by men of their name and blood; and venerable was the transition, when a curious traveller, descending from the heart of the mountains, had come to some ancient manorial residence in the more open parts of the Vales, which, through the rights attached to its proprietor, connected the almost visionary mountain republic he had been contemplating with the substantial frame of society as existing in the laws and constitution of a mighty empire.

It is into this perfect republic that the outsider (the tourist, the incomer, the builder) comes, and it is with this threat that Wordsworth deals in the final section of his *Guide*, 'Changes, and rules of taste for preventing their bad effects'. Quoting Gray's well-known description of Grasmere as a 'little unsuspected paradise', he writes that it is as well that Gray is no longer alive, and so able to see the changes that have been wrought on the landscape by the addition of ostentatious and inappropriate new houses that imposed their foreign forms on to the landscape:

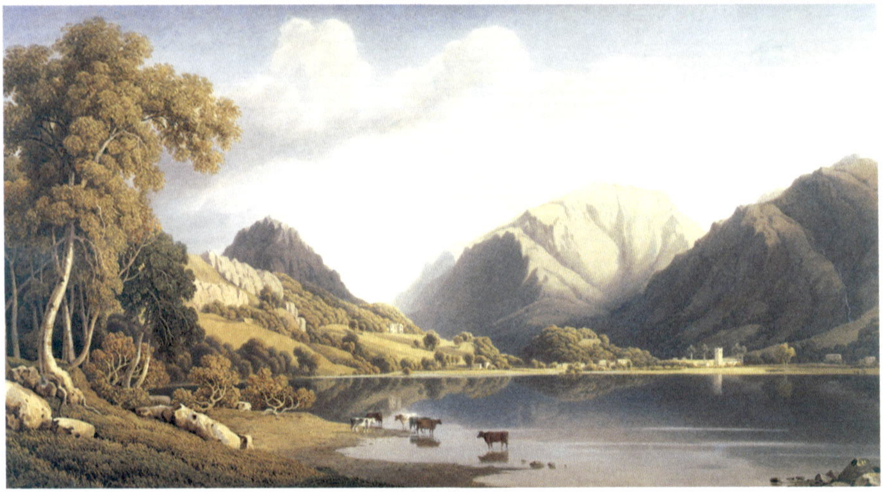

Grasmere, by George Fennel Robson, showing Allan Bank, centre.

> It was well for the undisturbed pleasure of the Poet that he had no forebodings of the change which was soon to take place; and it might have been hoped that these words, indicating how much the charm of what *was*, depended upon what was *not*, would of themselves have preserved the ancient franchises of this and other kindred mountain retirements from trespass; or (shall I dare to say?) would have secured scenes so consecrated from profanation. The lakes had now become celebrated; visitors flocked hither from all parts of England; the fancies of some were smitten so deeply, that they became settlers; and the Islands of Derwentwater and Winandermere, as they offered the strongest temptation, were the first places seized upon, and were instantly defaced by the intrusion.

Allan Bank, Wordsworth's home in Grasmere between 1808 and 1810, was one such example. As a piece of architecture it could not have been more different from his former modest cottage, and he despised it. In 1805 he had watched with horror as it was being built for a Liverpool lawyer, 'a wretched creature ... of the name of Crump', and had written to a friend in dismay: 'When you next enter the sweet Paradise of Grasmere you will see staring you in the face, upon that beautiful ridge that elbows out into the vale (behind the church and towering far above its steeple) a temple of abomination ... this House will stare you in the face from every part of the Vale, and entirely destroy its character of simplicity and seclusion.'

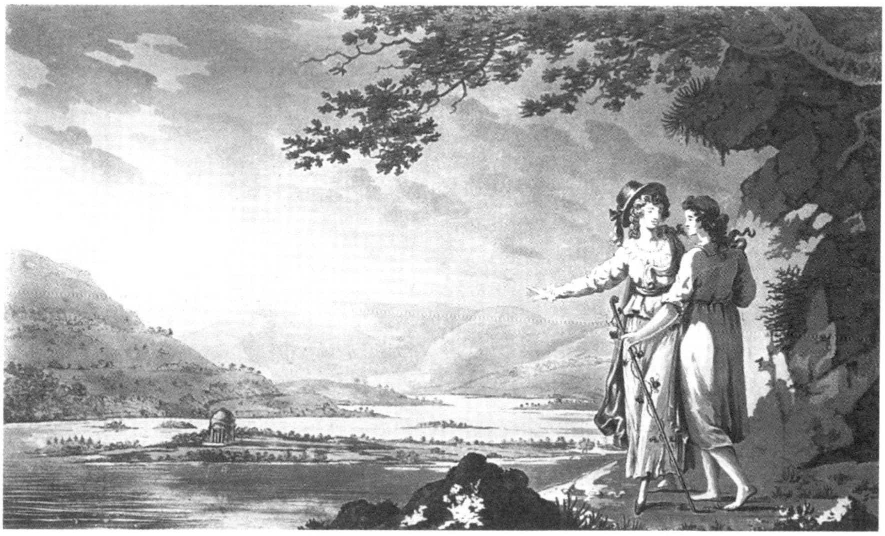

Frontispiece to John Plaw's *Rural Residences*, showing Belle Isle.

In the *Guide*, Wordsworth singles out another example of offensive architecture, Vicar's Island on Lake Windermere. This was the site of the first of the explicitly classical villas built to adorn the landscape of Windermere: the circular house on Belle Island, Windermere, designed by John Plaw in 1775 for Thomas English. Before he began to build his house, he set about altering the grounds with Chinese bridges, nectarine and peach trees, and a walled vegetable garden. This, in itself, was considered by some to be an insensitive intrusion on the unspoilt, paradisal beauty of the area. William Hutchinson complained about its 'square plan', condemning it as a 'Dutch Burgomaster's palace'. 'The sweet secreted cottage is no more,' wrote Thomas West, 'and the sycamore grove is fled. The present owner has modernised a fine slope in the bosom of the island into a formal garden. An unpleasing contrast to the natural simplicity and insular beauty of the place.'

Evidently, however, the owners (first Thomas English, and then after he became bankrupt the Christian/Curwens) felt that the house, with its round classical tower in emulation of landscapes by Claude Lorrain, was more in keeping with their paradisal perception of the Lake District. Plaw's designs were exhibited by him as a 'fantasia' for Lake Windermere at the Royal Academy in 1775. For the frontispiece to his book, *Rural Architecture,* 1794, Plaw takes Barret's landscape of Windermere, figures by 'Mr Deare, sculptor at Rome' and explains that: 'The Subject is Taste, accompanying Rural Simplicity, and pointing to one of the Most beautiful Scenes this County can boast of, viz. The lake of Winandermere: or the largest Island in which is built a circular Villa after A Design of the Author's.' The house was strongly disliked by Dorothy Wordsworth when she crossed by the ferry in June 1802. Her hope was that the trees would hide the house as soon as possible:

> From the High Ray the view is very delightful, rich & festive, water & wood houses groves hedgerows green fields & mountains—white Houses large & small—We passed 2 or 3 nice looking statesmen's houses. Mr Curwen's shrubberies looked pitiful enough under the native Trees. We put up our horses, ate our dinner by the water-side & walked up to the Station. Then we went to the Island, walked round it, & crossed the lake with our horse in the Ferry. The shrubs have been cut away in some parts of the island. I observed to the Boatman that I did not think it improved—he replied—'We think it is for one could hardly see the house before.' It seems to me to be, however, no better than it was. They have made no natural glades, it is merely a lawn with a few miserable young trees standing as if they were half starved. There are no sheep no cattle upon these lawns. It is neither one thing nor another—neither *natural* nor wholly cultivated & artificial which it was before, & that great house! Mercy upon us! If it *could* be concealed it would be well for all who are not pained to see the pleasantest of earthly spots deformed by man. But it *cannot* be covered. Even the tallest of our old oak trees would not reach the top of it.

In Dorothy's journal we see her trying to arrange a view which avoided the new architecture. 'Came home by Clappersgate,' she wrote on 14 May 1800. 'The valley very green, many sweet views up to Rydale head when I could juggle away the fine houses, but they disturbed me even more than when I have been happier—one beautiful view of the Bridge, without Sir Michaels.'

Wordsworth, with his preference for traditional farmhouses that did not dramatically impose themselves onto the landscape, wrote in the *Guide* of Belle Isle:

> What could be more unfortunate than the taste that suggested the paring of the shores, and surrounding with an embankment this spot of ground, the natural shape of which was so beautiful! An artificial appearance has thus been given to the whole, while infinite varieties of minute beauty have been destroyed. Could not the margin of this

noble island be given back to nature? Winds and waves work with a careless and graceful hand: and, should they in some places carry away a portion of the soil, the trifling loss would be amply compensated by the additional spirit, dignity, and loveliness, which these agents and the other powers of nature would soon communicate to what was left behind. As to the larch-plantations upon the main shore,—they who remember the original appearance of the rocky steeps, scattered over with native hollies and ash-trees, will be prepared to agree with what I shall have to say hereafter upon plantations in general.

But there were, increasingly, other examples of such houses. For the rich merchants from Manchester and Liverpool, building a villa in the Lakes was a way to enjoy a 'prospect' and a measure of 'rural retirement' in comfort and safety; 'in truth', wrote Wordsworth in the *Guide*, 'no one can now travel through the more frequented tracts, without being offended, at almost every turn, by an introduction of discordant objects, disturbing that peaceful harmony of form and colour, which had been through a long lapse of ages most happily preserved.' Croft Lodge, for example, was built by one James Brancker, a wealthy sugar merchant from Liverpool. In 1828 he had demolished the earlier Croft Lodge, with its admired gardens. This 'neat white seat on the shores of Windermere' became, in Hartley Coleridge's phrase, a building in 'a style which neither Vitruvius, Palladio, Inigo Jones, Piranesi nor Sir Jeffrey Wyatville ever dream'd of, even in a nightmare, or under the influence of opium'.

One of the earliest, and certainly the most outrageous, of these architectural intruders was Joseph Pocklington, the son of a banker from Newark in Nottinghamshire, and an eccentric bachelor. In 1778 Pocklington had purchased Vicar's Island on Derwentwater, and, like the lord of a domain, renamed it Pocklington's Island. He built a classical villa in the centre of the island, and, around the shore, a series of ornamental buildings: a boathouse in the shape of a church, a small fort and a mock circle of druid stones.

This stage set was perhaps developed with Peter Crosthwaite, the local cartographer and museum keeper in Keswick, who styled himself as 'Admiral of keswick Lake & guide & Companion to Tourers & Lakers'. A former naval officer in the East Indies, Crosthwaite worked out the mock battles held around Pocklington's Island that were part of the Keswick regattas from 1781. In his keenness to increase the popularity of the Lake District with tourists, he also made a number of maps of the Lake District giving the location

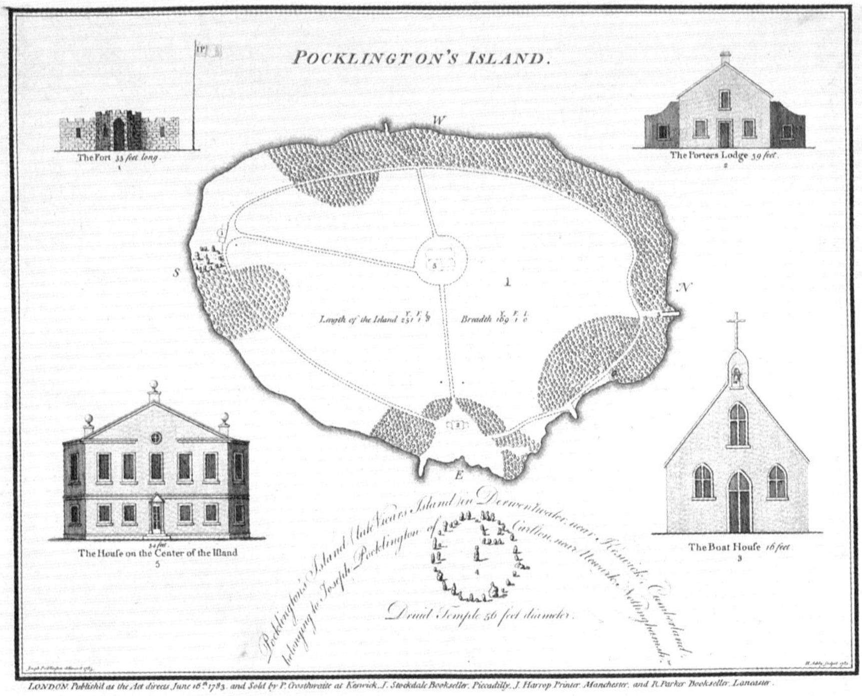

A plan of Pocklington's Island, by Peter Crosthwaite.

for each of West's viewing stations. Wordsworth wrote disparagingly in the *Guide* of Pocklington's Island:

> At the bidding of an alien improver, the Hind's Cottage, upon Vicar's island, in the same lake, with its embowering sycamores and cattle-shed, disappeared from the corner where they stood; and right in the middle, and upon the precise point of the island's highest elevation, rose a tall square habitation, with four sides exposed, like an astronomer's observatory, or a warren-house reared upon an eminence for the detection of depredators, or, like the temple of Œolus, where all the winds pay him obeisance. Round this novel structure, but at a respectful distance, platoons of firs were stationed, as if to protect their commander when weather and time should somewhat have shattered his strength. Within the narrow limits of this island were typified also the state and strength of a kingdom, and its religion as it had been, and was,—for neither was the druidical circle uncreated, nor the church of the present establishment; nor the stately pier, emblem of commerce

> and navigation; nor the fort to deal out thunder upon the approaching invader. The taste of a succeeding proprietor rectified the mistakes as far as was practicable, and has ridded the spot of its puerilities. The church, after having been docked of its steeple, is applied, both ostensibly and really, to the purpose for which the body of the pile was actually erected, namely, a boat-house; the fort is demolished; and, without indignation on the part of the spirits of the ancient Druids who officiated at the circle upon the opposite hill, the mimic arrangement of stones, with its *sanctum sanctorum,* has been swept away.

The inappropriateness of these buildings, Wordsworth argued, was due to the lack of knowledge of the builders, who brought a different mentality to the landscape, an ostentation and regularity that attempted to impose itself on the surroundings:

> The disfigurement which this country has undergone, has not, however, proceeded wholly from the common feelings of human nature which have been referred to as the primary sources of bad taste in rural imagery; another cause must be added, that has chiefly shown itself in its effect upon buildings. I mean a warping of the natural mind occasioned by a consciousness that, this country being an object of general admiration, every new house would be looked at and commented upon either for approbation or censure. Hence all the deformity and ungracefulness that ever pursue the steps of constraint or affectation. Persons, who in Leicestershire or Northamptonshire would probably have built a modest dwelling like those of their sensible neighbours, have been turned out of their course; and, acting a part, no wonder if, having had little experience, they act it ill. The craving for prospect, also, which is immoderate, particularly in new settlers, has rendered it impossible that buildings, whatever might have been their architecture, should in most instances be ornamental to the landscape; rising as they do from tile summits of naked hills in staring contrast to the snugness and privacy of the ancient houses.

Houses should be designed, Wordsworth wrote, with 'the invisible hand of art ... Far-winding vallies difficult of access, and the feelings of simplicity habitually connected with mountain retirements, prompt us to turn from ostentation as a thing there eminently unnatural and out of place.'

Wordsworth's insistence that tourists to the Lake District required an educated taste in order to appreciate the landscape attracted hostility after the publication of his sonnet on the proposed Windermere railway. On 30 November, for example, Keats's biographer Richard Monckton Milnes published a sonnet in the *Whitehaven Herald* entitled 'Projected Railways in Westmoreland. In Answer to Mr. Wordsworth's Late Sonnet', and containing the following lines:

> And Thou, the Patriarch of these pleasant ways,
> Cans't hardly grudge that crowded streets send out
> In Sabbath glee the sons of care and doubt,
> To read these scenes by light of thine own lays.

Wordsworth could hardly deny the landscape to those, less wealthy than him, who had the misfortune to live in polluted cities, and who, for the most part, were attracted to the Lake District by his own writings. A few days before the publication of Milnes's sonnet, Lady Richardson had visited Wordsworth at Rydal Mount, and later recollected Wordsworth's response to his critics:

> He spoke of his own pleasure in returning to [the Lakes], and of the effect of the first view from 'Orrest Head,' the point mentioned in his 'unfortunate sonnet which has,' he said, 'you are aware, exposed me to the most unlooked for accusations. They actually accuse me of desiring to interfere with the innocent enjoyments of the poor, by preventing this district becoming accessible to them by a railway. Now I deny that it is to that class that this kind of scenery is either the most improving or the most attractive. For the very poor the great God of Nature has mercifully spread out His Bible everywhere; the common sunshine, green fields, the blue sky, the shining river, are everywhere to be met with in this country; and it is only an individual here and there among the uneducated classes who feels very deeply the poetry of lakes and mountains; and such persons would rather wander about where they like, than rush through the country in a railway.'

These were the arguments that Wordsworth put forward in two long letters to the *Morning Post*, printed on 11 December and 20 December 1844, and later published as a separate pamphlet. The essential quality of the Lake District, he wrote, is 'its beauty and its character of seclusion and retirement;

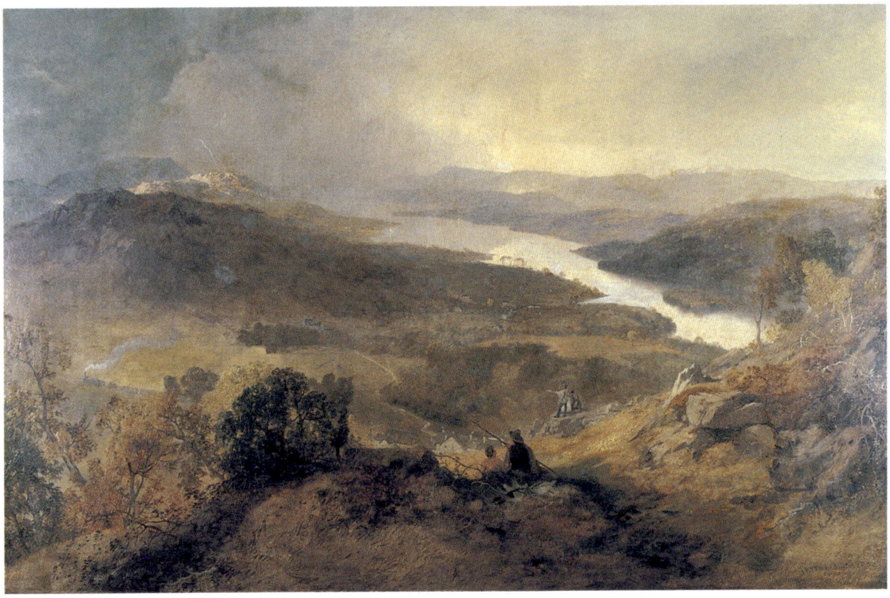

Windermere from Orrest Head, showing the new railway, by J.B. Pyne, 1849.

and to these topics and to others connected with them my remarks shall be confined'. The taste for 'natural *scenery*,' he argued, as opposed to ornamental parks and gardens, was a modern one; before Thomas Gray, travellers in the Alps had said nothing about their natural beauty: 'there is not, I believe, a single English traveller whose published writings would disprove the assertion, that, where precipitous rocks and mountains are mentioned at all, they are spoken of as objects of dislike and fear, and not of admiration'. Wordsworth recalled that the picturesque fashion for 'prospects' had been unknown among the Lake District fells in earlier days:

> In my youth, I lived sometime in the vale of Keswick, under the roof of a shrewd and sensible woman, who more than once exclaimed in my hearing, 'Bless me! folk are always talking about prospects: when I was young there was never sic a thing neamed.'

Early settlers chose practical, sheltered spots for their homes, regardless of the views or surrounding beauties. The new mansions around Windermere and Derwentwater were modern aberrations, and the reason for this was not so much their inherent lack of taste, but their inappropriateness. Mountainous scenery was not inherently beautiful, and so had to be cultivated slowly:

> a vivid perception of romantic scenery is neither inherent in mankind, nor a necessary consequence of even a comprehensive education. It is benignly ordained that green fields, clear blue skies, running streams of pure water, rich groves and woods, orchards, and all the ordinary varieties of human nature, should find an easy way to the affections of all men, and more or less so from early childhood till the senses are impaired by old age and the sources of mere earthly enjoyment have in a great measure failed. But a taste beyond this, however desirable it may be that every one should possess it, is not to be implanted at once; it must be gradually developed both in nations and individuals. Rocks and mountains, torrents and widespread waters, and all those features of nature which go to the composition of such scenes as this part of England is distinguished for, cannot, in their finer relations to the human mind, be comprehended, or even very imperfectly conceived, without processes of culture or opportunities of observation in some degree habitual.

Wordsworth admitted that the ability to appreciate this scenery was growing, but, he asked, 'what means are most likely to be beneficial in extending its operation?' He suggests that instead of being immediately transplanted to the fells, labouring men from the towns should, with their families, be first introduced to the milder scenery of green fields, where they can stroll on Sunday, 'after having attended divine worship'. What is more, the introduction of a railway, and the resulting hordes of people, would spoil the very things, quiet and seclusion, they had come in search of:

> What can, in truth, be more absurd, than that either rich or poor should be spared the trouble of travelling by the high roads over so short a space, according to their respective means, if the unavoidable consequence must be a great disturbance of the retirement, and in many places a destruction of the beauty of the country, which the parties are come in search of? Would not this be pretty much like the child's cutting up his drum to learn where the sound came from?

Popularity in the form of thousands arriving on works outings, Wordsworth concludes, would spoil the landscape: 'We should have the whole of Lancashire, and no small part of Yorkshire, pouring in upon us to meet the men of Durham, and the borderers from Cumberland and Northumberland.'

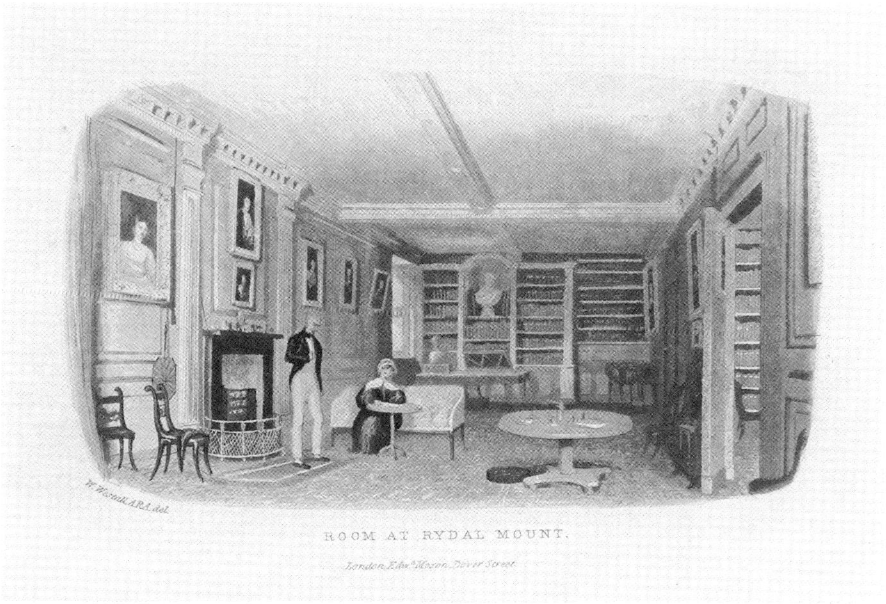

Wordsworth depicted in *Room at Rydal Mount*, by William Westall, 1840.

And it was not only the older inhabitants who felt this, but 'a gentry whose love of retirement has been a blessing to these vales'.

The letters provoked 'a torrent of abuse'. Among the charges was Wordsworth's claim that he was living in 'retirement'. In 1818, Keats had written that the poet, 'instead of being in retirement, has himself and his house full in the thick of fashionable visitors quite convenient to be pointed at all summer long'. Now people asked how such a well-known, successful poet, shown in a stately drawing room at Rydal Mount by William Westall, could call himself a recluse. 'If he had confined himself to *the Sonnets* on this subject of the Railway it would have been all within his vocation,' wrote Barron Field, 'but still I should have objected to the falseness & puerility of such Sonnets. How can the man who had been constantly publishing poetry for the last 40 years, and has at last made that poetry part of the food of the public mind, call himself a man of "retirement", if he means to include himself? and if not, how can he complain that he has at last, by his Lake and Mountain poetry, created a desire for realizing some of those beautiful descriptions of scenery and elements, in the inhabitants of Liverpool & Manchester, which may possibly bring them in crowds by Railway to Windermere?'

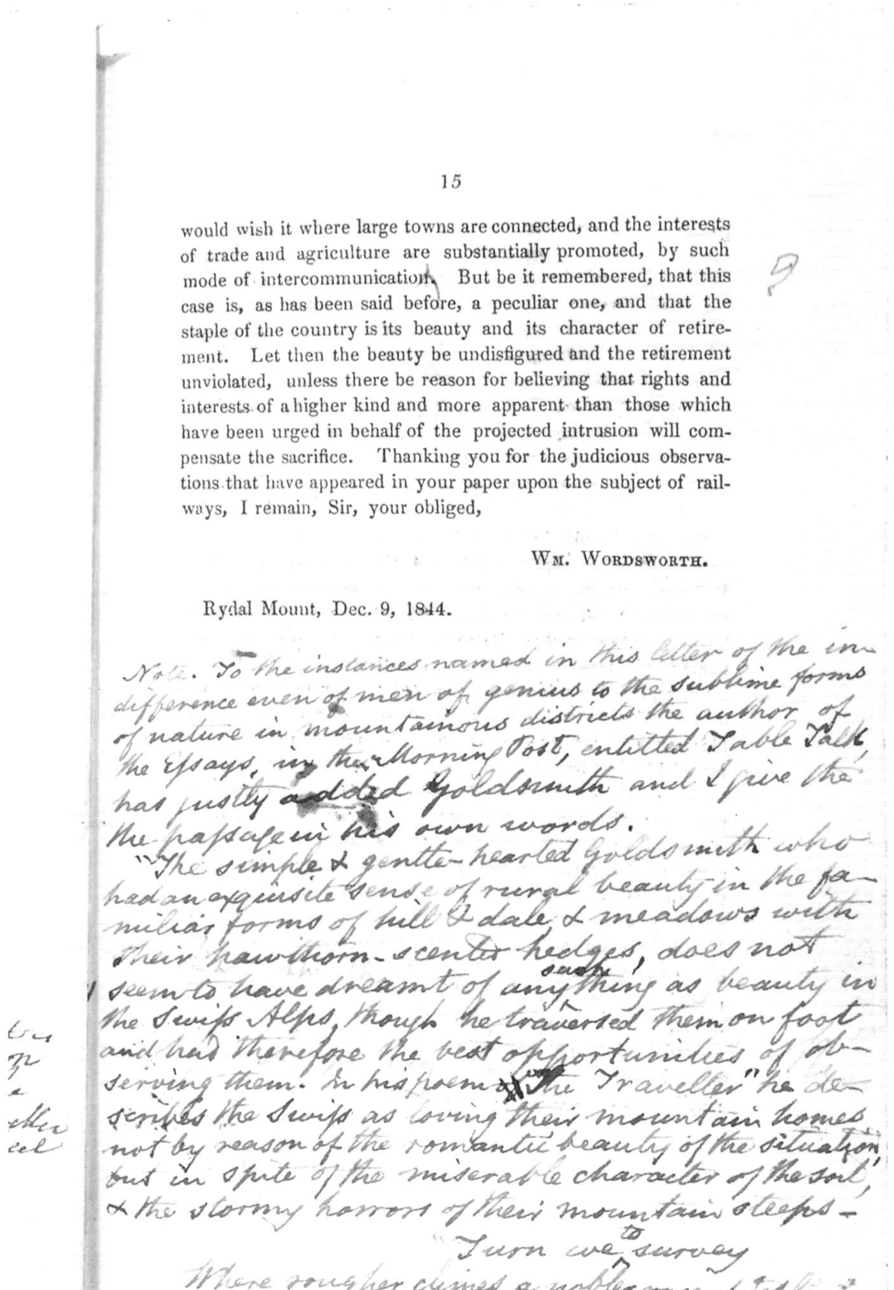

15

would wish it where large towns are connected, and the interests of trade and agriculture are substantially promoted, by such mode of intercommunication. But be it remembered, that this case is, as has been said before, a peculiar one, and that the staple of the country is its beauty and its character of retirement. Let then the beauty be undisfigured and the retirement unviolated, unless there be reason for believing that rights and interests of a higher kind and more apparent than those which have been urged in behalf of the projected intrusion will compensate the sacrifice. Thanking you for the judicious observations that have appeared in your paper upon the subject of railways, I remain, Sir, your obliged,

Wm. Wordsworth.

Rydal Mount, Dec. 9, 1844.

Note. To the instances named in this letter of the indifference even of men of genius to the sublime forms of nature in mountainous districts the author of the Essays, in the Morning Post, entitled Table Talk, has justly added Goldsmith and I give the passage in his own words.
"The simple & gentle-hearted Goldsmith who had an exquisite sense of rural beauty in the familiar forms of hill & dale & meadows with their hawthorn-scented hedges, does not seem to have dreamt of any such thing as beauty in the Swiss Alps, though he traversed them on foot and had therefore the best opportunities of observing them. In his poem "The Traveller" he describes the Swiss as loving their mountain homes not by reason of the romantic beauty of the situation but in spite of the miserable character of the soil & the stormy horrors of their mountain steeps –
"Turn we to survey
Where rougher climes a nobler race display,"

Wordsworth's letters to the *Morning Post* on the Kendal and Windermere railway were later published separately. This copy contains Wordsworth's revisions for the second edition.

Wordsworth's attempts to prevent the railway from extending into the Lake District were unsuccessful. The line from Oxenholme to Kendal was opened on 22 September 1846, and on 21 April 1847 it was extended to its present terminus just above Bowness. Three years later Wordsworth was dead. His extraordinary imaginative hold over the Lake District landscape, however, only increased after his death and, what is more, led to the kinds of conservation that he had first articulated in his *Guide to the Lakes*.

John Ruskin, who for much of his later life lived at Brantwood, by Coniston Water, first came to the Lake District as a young boy. In his autobiography, *Praeterita*, he looked back on those early days amongst nature in a manner which recalls Wordsworth's lines on his childhood in 'Tintern Abbey', where the 'sounding cataract ... haunted' him 'like a passion', or the 'Immortality Ode', where his first impressions 'fade into the light of common day'. Ruskin writes of

> ... an instinctive awe, mixed with delight; an indefinable thrill, such as we sometimes imagine to indicate the presence of a disembodied spirit. I could only feel this perfectly when I was alone; and then it would often make me shiver from head to foot with the joy and fear of it, when after being some time away from the hills, I first got to the shore of a mountain river, where the brown water circled among the pebbles, or when I saw the first swell of distant land against the sunset, or the first low broken wall, covered with mountain moss. ... These feelings remained in their full intensity till I was eighteen or twenty, and then, as the reflective and practical power increased, and the 'cares of this world' gained upon me, faded gradually away, in the manner described by Wordsworth in his *Intimations of Immortality*.

In 1843, Ruskin described Wordsworth's *Excursion* as a poem of 'magnificent comprehension and faultless majesty'. That same year he published the first volume of his great work *Modern Painters*, and compared J.M.W. Turner to Wordsworth: 'hear how Wordsworth, the keenest-eyed of all modern poets for what is deep and essential in nature, illustrates Turner here, as we shall find him doing in all other points'. Forty years later he sent a letter to the newly formed Wordsworth Society saying that its 'grand function' was 'to preserve as far as possible in England the conditions of rural life which made Wordsworth himself possible: and which if destroyed would leave his verse vainer than the Hymns of Orpheus'.

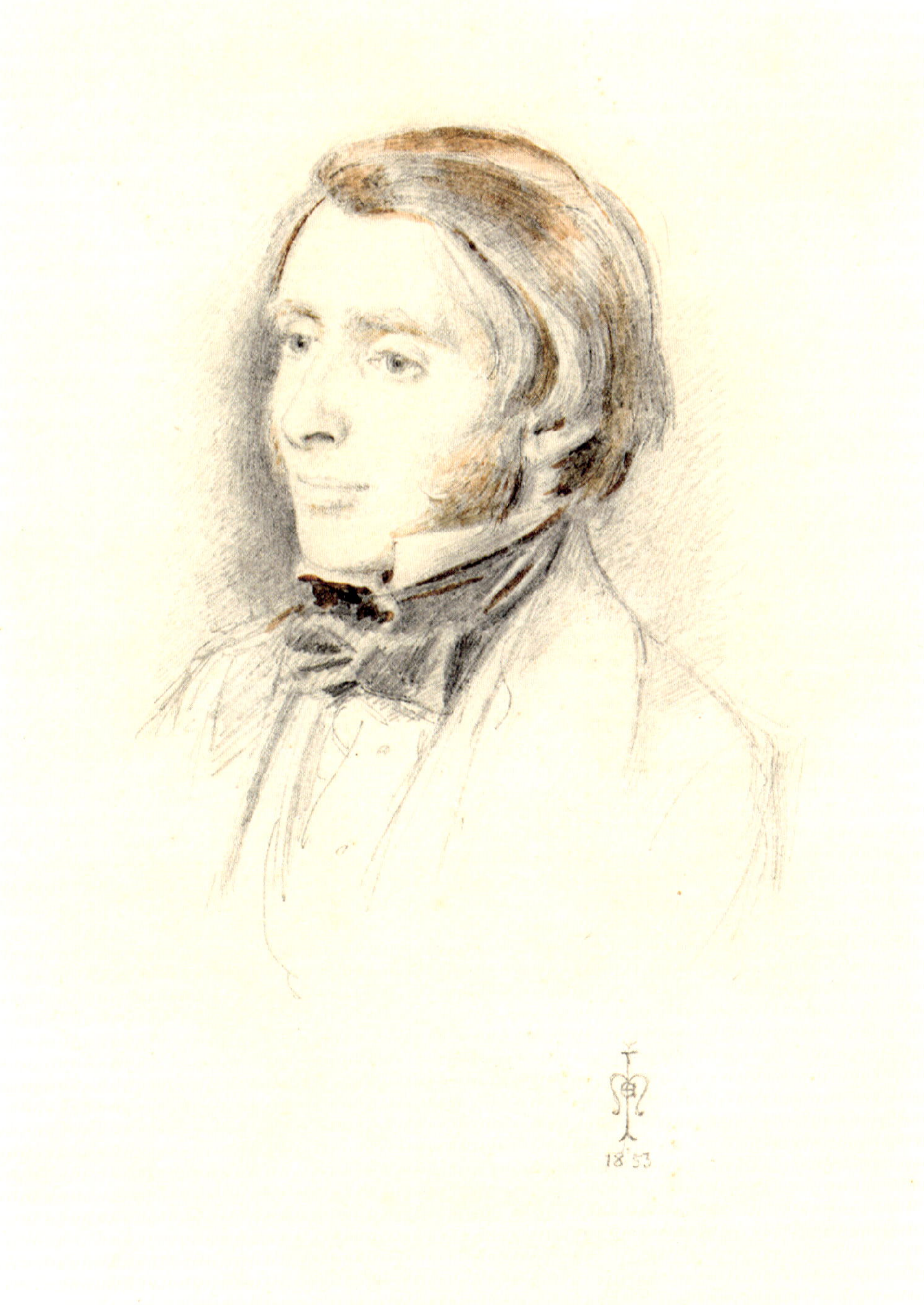

John Ruskin, by John Everett Millais, 1853.

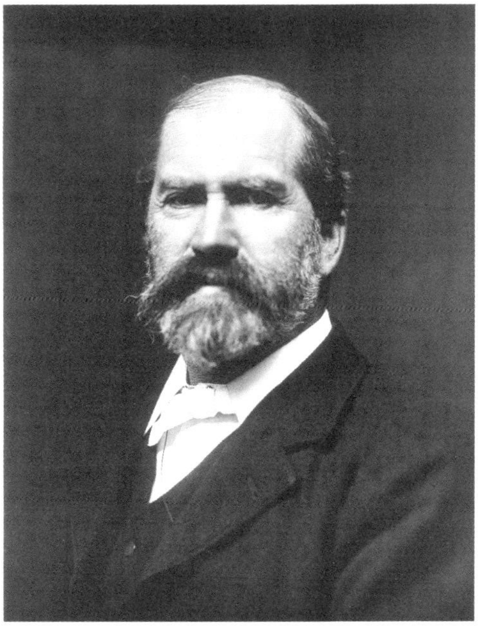

Hardwicke Rawnsley, by an unknown photographer.

Other Victorian admirers sought to memorialise and preserve the very places Wordsworth had made so famous: Grasmere, Rydal, Greenhead Ghyll, Silver How, Helm Crag. Their love of Wordsworth was inseparable from their love of the Lake District. In the early 1880s Hardwicke Drummond Rawnsley, the vicar of Low Wray on Windermere, erected a memorial at a point near Grisedale Tarn, high above Grasmere, where in 1800 Wordsworth and Dorothy said goodbye to their brother John, who was to die at sea five years later. Then, in 1877, it was proposed to flood Thirlmere and so bring millions of gallons of extra water to Manchester and its cotton mills. There was widespread opposition to the scheme, and Wordsworthians were painfully aware that it would involve the destruction of the so-called 'Rock of Names' by the side of the road that ran along Thirlmere's eastern shore. Over the months in which they were passing to and fro between Dove Cottage and Greta Hall, Wordsworth and Coleridge had carved their initials into this rock, along with those of Dorothy, John Wordsworth, Wordsworth's future wife Mary Hutchinson, and Mary's sister Sara. 'We parted from Coleridge at Sara's crag, after having looked at the letters whch C. carved in the morning. I kissed them all. William deepened the T. with C's pen-knife.' It was a sacred

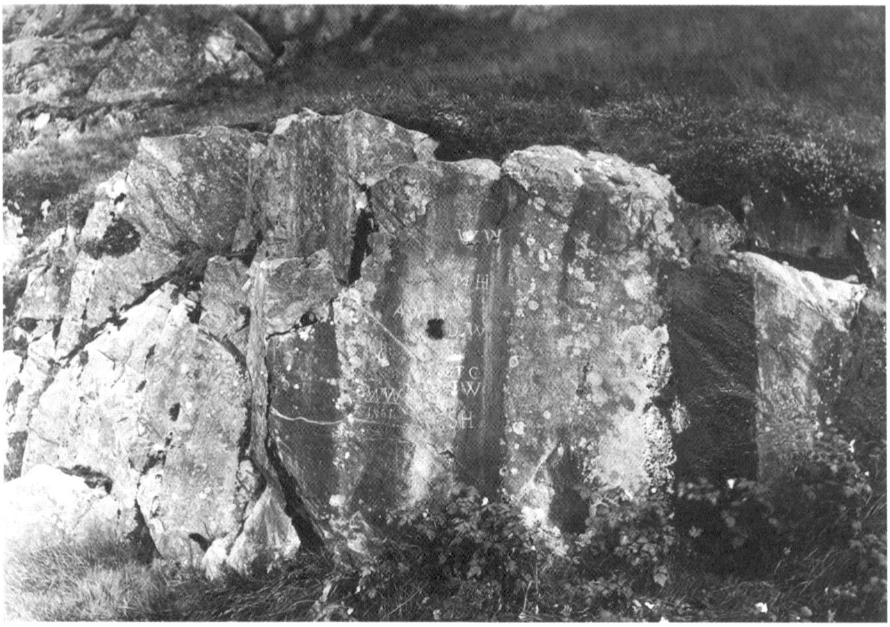

The Rock of Names in its original location near Thirlmere, by an unknown photographer.

memorial to a magical time. In his book *The English Lake District As Interpreted in the Poems of Wordsworth* (1878), William Knight traced those places that were 'undergoing change, and becoming more difficult to identify every year. Such a memorial, for example, as "the Rock of Names," on the shore of Thirlmere, is threatened with immersion fathoms deep below the waters of a Manchester reservoir.' The appeal was unsuccessful, and work went ahead, but Canon Rawnsley gathered the fragments of the Rock of Names together and they have now been reassembled behind Dove Cottage.

It was at a meeting of the Wordsworth Society at the end of the nineteenth century that William Knight proposed that Dove Cottage itself should be purchased for the nation. To this end, the Reverend Stopford Brooke, a Victorian man of letters with a deep love of Wordsworth, Grasmere and the Lake District, issued a fundraising booklet in which he made the proposition: 'Why should we not try and secure it, as Shakespeare's birthplace is secured, for the eternal possession of those who love English poetry all over the world?' He made visits to Dove Cottage and its garden, which he particularly loved, and there is a wonderful series of photographs recording the occasion. He wrote in his diary:

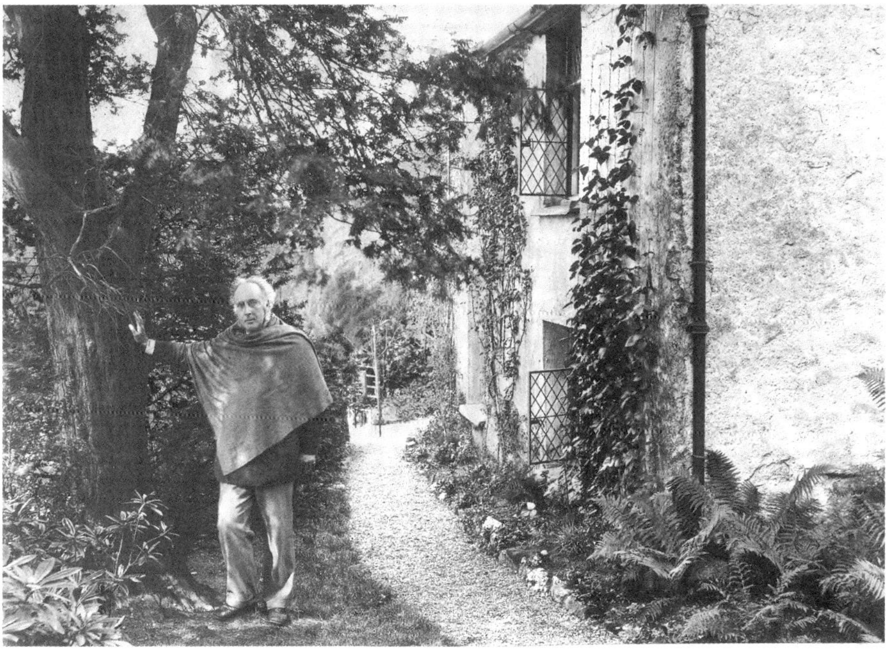

Stopford Brooke outside Dove Cottage, which he proposed should be purchased for 'those who love English poetry all over the world'.

> I went to see Dove Cottage this morning with Mr. New, & took over his drawings of the place. The garden looked charming. All the rhododendrons are in full flower, & make the grass & grey walls bright with lovely colour. The Osmunda Fern by the rock-pool is stately. It may well be called Regalis. The trees in the orchard are thick with apple-knobs. As to the grass, it is smooth, softer than sleep, of a lovely green.

After a public appeal, Wordsworth's best-loved home, so much a part of the landscape of Grasmere, was purchased, as Stopford Brooke wrote, 'for the pleasure and good of the English race'.

Most notably, Wordsworth was the inspiration behind Rawnsley's proposal for a Permanent Lake District Defence Society, which led in turn to the creation, in 1895, of the National Trust for Places of Historic Interest or Natural Beauty. 'At least the vales of Cumberland and Westmorland,' said Rawnsley, 'charged with the spirit of Wordsworth, must be left … as Nature's own English university in the age of great cities.' His belief was that the Lake District was 'not only pleasure grounds but thinking grounds, & capable only of enriching the nation with high thoughts & so are part of the nation's wealth'. Wordsworth had gone to the Lakes to live in retirement and seclusion, but in the *Guide to the Lakes* he first articulated the idea that the area should be preserved for the public. Even today he is remembered, inaccurately and not always fondly, as the man who blocked the railway and who was an enemy of tourists. But, in fact, his *Guide* was the first considered attempt to describe the native beauty of the lakes from the viewpoint of an inhabitant and to have ecological concerns for its sustainability; to suggest that visitors, in ever-increasing numbers, should have the knowledge to treat it with respect:

> ... it is probable, that in a few years the country on the margin of the Lakes will fall almost entirely into the possession of gentry, either strangers or natives. It is then much to be wished, that a better taste should prevail among these new proprietors; and, as they cannot be expected to leave things to themselves, that skill and knowledge should prevent unnecessary deviations from that path of simplicity and beauty along which, without design and unconsciously, their humble predecessors have moved. In this wish the author will be joined by persons of pure taste throughout the whole island, who, by their visits (often repeated) to the Lakes in the North of England, testify that they deem the district a sort of national property, in which every man has a right and interest who has an eye to perceive and a heart to enjoy.

BIBLIOGRAPHY

Precise references to all quotations can be found at www.stephenhebron.co.uk.

PRIMARY SOURCES

Quotations from Wordsworth, Coleridge, Keats and Clare have been taken from the following editions (retaining original spelling and punctuation):

Poetry

"I Am": The Selected Poetry of John Clare, ed. Jonathan Bate, New York, 2003
The Oxford Authors: Samuel Taylor Coleridge, ed. H.J. Jackson, Oxford, 1985
The Oxford Authors: John Keats, ed. Elizabeth Cook, Oxford, 1990
The Oxford Authors: William Wordsworth, ed. Stephen Gill, Oxford, 1984

Prose

John Clare by Himself, ed. Eric Robinson and David Powell, Ashington and Manchester, 1996
Biographia Literaria, ed. James Engell and W. Jackson Bate, in *The Collected Works of Samuel Taylor Coleridge*, VII, 2 vols., Princeton, 1983
The Prose Works of William Wordsworth, ed. W.J.B. Owen and Jane Worthington Smyser, 3 vols., Oxford, 1974
The Prose of William Wordsworth, ed. Alexander B. Grosart, 3 vols., London, 1876
The Fenwick Notes of William Wordsworth, ed. Jared Curtis, London, 1993

Letters and Journals

The Letters of John Clare, ed. Mark Storey, Oxford, 1985
Collected Letters of Samuel Taylor Coleridge, ed. Earl Leslie Griggs, 6 vols., Oxford, 1956–72
The Notebooks of Samuel Taylor Coleridge, 8 vols., ed. Kathleen Coburn, London, 1957–90
The Letters of John Keats, ed. Hyder E. Rollins, 2 vols., Cambridge, Mass., 1958
The Letters of William and Dorothy Wordsworth, ed. Ernest de Selincourt, 6 vols., Oxford 1935–9; rev. Alan G. Hill, 8 vols., Oxford, 1967–93

Contemporary reviews of and critical comments on Wordsworth, Coleridge, Keats and Clare have been taken from volumes in the *Critical Heritage* series:

Clare: The Critical Heritage, ed. Mark Storey, London, 1973
Coleridge: The Critical Heritage, ed. J.R. de J. Jackson, London, 1970
Keats: The Critical Heritage, ed. G.M. Matthews, London, 1971
Wordsworth: The Critical Heritage 1793–1820, ed. Robert Woof, London, 2001

GENERAL

Malcolm Andrews, *The Search for the Picturesque: Landscape, Aesthetics and Tourism in Britain, 1760–1800*, Aldershot, 1989

Jonathan Bate, *Romantic Ecology: Wordsworth and the Environmental Tradition*, London, 1991

— *The Song of the Earth*, London, 2000

Esther Moir, *The Discovery of Britain: The English Tourists, 1540–1840*

Ian Ousby, *The Englishman's England: Taste, Travel and the Rise of Tourism*, Cambridge, 1990

H.W. Piper, *The Active Universe: Pantheism and the Concept of Imagination in the English Romantic Poets*, London, 1962

William St Clair, *The Reading Nation in the Romantic Period*, Cambridge. 2004

Jonathan Wordsworth, Michael C. Jaye and Robert Woof, *William Wordsworth and the Age of English Romanticism*, New Brunswick and London, 1987

CHAPTER ONE: 'INTO THE LIFE OF THINGS'

Works quoted:

John Byng, *The Torrington Diaries: Containing the Tours through England and Wales of the Hon. John Byng (Later Fifth Viscount Torrington) between the Years 1781 and 1794*, ed. C. Bruyn Andrews, 4 vols., London, 1934–8

William Coxe, *An Historical Tour of Monmouthshire*, 2 vols., London, 1801

Sneyd Davis, 'A Voyage to *Tintern Abbey* in *Monmouthshire*', quoted by Andrews, *The Search for the Picturesque*

William Gilpin, *Observations on the River Wye, and Several Parts of South Wales, &c. Relative Chiefly to Picturesque Beauty; Made in the Summer of the Year 1770*, London, 1783

— letters to William Mason, quoted by Carl Paul Barbier, Oxford, 1963

Richard Gough, *Anecdotes of British Topography*, London, 1768

Charles Heath, *Descriptive Account of Tintern Abbey, Monmouthshire*, Monmouth, 1793

Samuel Ireland, *Picturesque Views of the River Wye*, London, 1797

Hannah More, letter September 1789, quote by Andrews, op. cit.

Leitch Ritchie, *The Wye and its Associations: A Picturesque Ramble*, London, 1838

John Thelwall, article in the *New Monthly Magazine*, May 1798

Richard Warner, *A Walk through Wales, in August 1797*, Bath, 1798

Henry Penruddocke Wyndham, *A Gentleman's Tour through Monmouthshire and Wales in the Months of June and July 1774*, London, 1775

Arthur Young, *Six Weeks Tour through the Southern Counties of England and Wales*, London, 1768

Suggested further reading:

Stephen Gill, *William Wordsworth: A Life*, Oxford, 1989

Jeremy Knight, *Tintern and the Romantic Movement*, London, 1977

Robert Woof and Stephen Hebron, *Towards Tintern Abbey*, Grasmere, 1998

CHAPTER TWO: 'A QUIET, SPIRIT-HEALING NOOK'

Works quoted:

Joseph Budworth, *A Fortnight's Ramble to the Lakes in Westmoreland, Lancashire, and Cumberland. By a Rambler*, London, 1792

William Cowper, 'Retirement', *Poems*, 2 vols., London, 1800

Thomas De Quincey, *Recollections of the Lakes and the Lake Poets*, ed. David Wright, London, 1970

Thomas Gray, *The Poems of Mr. Gray, to which are prefixed Memoirs of his Life and Writings*, ed. W. Mason, London, 1775

William Hazlitt, 'My First Acquaintance with Poets', *The Liberal*, London, 1823

William Hutchinson, *An Excursion to the Lakes in Westmoreland and Cumberland ... in the Years 1773 and 1774*, London, 1776

Charles Lamb, 'The Londoner', letter in the *Morning Post*, 1 February 1802

— *The Letters of Charles and Mary Lamb*, 3 vols., ed. Edwin J. Marrs, Jr., Ithaca and London, 1975

Mrs Henry Sandford, *Thomas Poole and his Friends*, 2 vols., London, 1888

John Thelwall, *Poems Chiefly Written in Retirement*, Hereford, 1801

Richard Warner, *Literary Recollections*, London, 1830

Dorothy Wordsworth, *The Grasmere and Alfoxden Journals*, ed. Pamela Woof, Oxford, 2002

— *Recollections of a Tour made in Scotland*, ed. Carol Kyros Walker, London and New Haven, 1997

Suggested further reading:

Richard Holmes, *Coleridge: Early Visions*, London, 1989

H.W. Howe (revised Robert Woof), *Greta Hall: Home of Coleridge and Southey*, Stoke Ferry, 1977

Molly Lefebure, *Samuel Taylor Coleridge: The Bondage of Opium*, London, 1977

Seamus Perry, *Coleridge's Notebooks: A Selection*, Oxford, 2002

— *Samuel Taylor Coleridge*, British Library *Writers' Lives*, London, 2003

Rebecca Solnit, *Wanderlust: A History of Walking*, London, 2002

Carol Kyros Walker, *Breaking Away: Coleridge in Scotland*, New Haven and London, 2002

Anne D. Wallace, *Walking, Literature, and English Culture: The origins and uses of peripatetic in the nineteenth century*, Oxford, 1993

CHAPTER THREE: 'THROUGH THE CLOUDS'

Works quoted:

Charles Armitage Brown, *Life of John Keats*, ed. Dorothy Hyde Bodurtha and Willard Bissell Pope, London, 1937

— *The Letters of Charles Armitage Brown*, ed. Jack Stillinger, Cambridge, Mass., 1966

Thomas De Quincey, *Recollections of the Lakes and the Lake Poets*, ed. David Wright, London, 1970

Edward Gibbon, *Decline and Fall of the Roman Empire*, 3 vols., ed. David Womersley, London, 1994
Collected Letters of Oliver Goldsmith, ed. Katharine C. Balderston, Cambridge, 1928
John Hamilton Reynolds, letter to William Wordsworth, MS The Wordsworth Trust
Hyder Edward Rollins (ed.), *The Keats Circle: Letters and Papers 1816–1878*, 2 vols., Cambridge, Mass., 1948
The Letters of Percy Bysshe Shelley, ed. Frederick L. Jones, 2 vols., Oxford, 1964
John Stoddart, *Remarks on Local Scenery and Manners in Scotland during the Years 1799 and 1800*, 2 vols., London, 1801
James Storer and John Greig, *Views in North Britain Illustrative of the Works of Robert Burns*, London, 1811

Suggested further reading:

Walter Jackson Bate, *John Keats*, Massachusetts and London, 1964
Nelson Bushnell, *A Walk after John Keats*, New York, 1936
Robert Gittings, *John Keats*, London, 1968
Carol Kyros Walker, *Walking North with Keats*, New Haven and London, 1992
Aileen Ward, *John Keats: The Making of a Poet*, New York, 1963 (revised, 1986)
Robert Woof and Stephen Hebron, *John Keats*, exhibition catalogue, Grasmere, 1995

CHAPTER FOUR: 'THE NORTHAMPTONSHIRE PEASANT'

Works quoted:

Robert Burns, *Poems, Chiefly in the Scottish Dialect*, Kilmarnock, 1786
Correspondence of John Clare (letters to Clare): British Library Egerton Manuscripts
George Crabbe, *The Village*, London, 1783
Thomas De Quincey, *Recollections of the Lakes and the Lake Poets*, ed. David Wright, London, 1970
Mary Hartley to William Gilpin, quoted by Carl Paul Barbier, Oxford, 1963
William Hazlitt, *The Spirit of the Age*, London, 1825
Markham L. Peacock (ed.), *The Critical Opinions of William Wordsworth*, Baltimore, 1950
James Thomson, *The Seasons and the Castle of Indolence*, ed. James Sambrook, Oxford, 1972
Richard Walker, *Regency Portraits*, 2 vols., London, 1985

Suggested further reading:

The Oxford Clare, 5 vols., ed. Eric Robinson, David Powell, Margaret Grainger and P.M.S. Dawson, Oxford, 1989–2003
The Oxford Authors: John Clare, ed. Eric Robinson and David Powell, Oxford, 1984
John Barrell, *The Idea of Landscape and the Sense of Place 1730–1840: An Approach to the Poetry of John Clare*, Cambridge, 1972
Jonathan Bate, 'John Clare: Prologue to a New Life', *Romantic Biography*, ed. Arthur Bradley and Alan Rawes, Aldershot, 2003
— *John Clare: A Biography*, London, 2003

Robert Bloomfield, *Selected Poems*, ed. John Goodridge and John Lucas, Nottingham, 1998
Timothy Brownlow, *John Clare and Picturesque Landscape*, Oxford, 1983
Tim Chilcott, *A Publisher and his Circle: The Life and Work of John Taylor, Keats's Publisher*, London and Boston, 1972
John Clare in Context, ed. Hugh Haughton, Adam Phillips and Geoffrey Summerfield, Cambridge, 1994

CHAPTER FIVE: 'THESE TOURISTS, HEAVEN PRESERVE US!'

Works quoted:

Stopford Brooke, Diary, MS The Wordsworth Trust
— *Dove Cottage: Wordsworth's Home from 1800–1808*, London, 1890
Joseph Budworth, *A Fortnight's Ramble to the Lakes in Westmoreland, Lancashire and Cumberland*, third edition, London, 1810
The Oxford Authors: Byron, ed. Jerome J. McGann, Oxford, 1986
Thomas De Quincey, *Recollections of the Lakes and the Lake Poets,* ed. David Wright, London, 1970
William Gilpin, *Observations Relative Chiefly to Picturesque Beauty, Made in the Year 1772, on Several Parts of England; particularly the Mountains, and Lakes of Cumberland, and Westmoreland*, London, 1786
The Letters of Charles and Mary Lamb, 3 vols., ed. Edwin J. Marrs, Jr., Ithaca and London, 1975
John Ruskin, *Praeterita*, 3 vols., Orpington, 1885–1900
Thomas West, *A Guide to the Lakes*, London and Kendal, 1778
Dorothy Wordsworth, *The Grasmere and Alfoxden Journals*, ed. Pamela Woof, Oxford, 2002

Suggested further reading:

Peter Bicknell and Robert Woof, *The Lake District Discovered 1810–1850: The Artists, Tourists and Wordsworth*, exhibition catalogue, Grasmere, 1983
Stephen Gill, *Wordsworth and the Victorians*, Oxford, 1998
David McCracken, *Wordsworth and the English Lake District*, Oxford, 1984
Hardwicke Rawnsley, *Literary Associations of the English Lakes*, 2 vols., Glasgow, 1894
— *Ruskin and the English Lakes*, Glasgow, 1901
David Thomason and Robert Woof, *Derwentwater: The Vale of Elysium*, exhibition catalogue, Grasmere, 1986
Robert Woof, 'The Matter of Fact Paradise', *The Lake District: A Sort of National Property*, ed. John Murdoch, London, 1986
— *A Perfect Republic of Shepherds*, exhibition catalogue, Grasmere, 1997
— *Treasures of the Wordsworth Trust*, Grasmere, 2005
William Wordsworth, *Guide to the Lakes*, ed. Ernest de Selincourt, London, 2004

Picture Credits

The British Library Board, pp. 2, 11, 25, 26, 40, 52, 60, 73, 74, 84, 89, 99, 102, 117, 118, 126, 131, 138.
© Copyright The Trustees of the British Museum, pp. 5, 12, 63, 79, 101.
© Fitzwilliam Museum, University of Cambridge / Bridgeman Art Library, p.130.
The Houghton Library, Harvard University, pp. 83, 94.
Keats House, Hampstead / London Metropolitan Archives, 115.
Llyfrgell Genedlaethol Cymru National Library of Wales, p. 8.
© Leeds Museums and Galleries (City Art Gallery) / Bridgeman Art Library, pp. 70, 93.
© National Maritime Museum, London, p. 123.
National Portrait Gallery, London, pp. 20, 58, 96, 114, 134.
Private Collections, pp. ii, 86.
Ruskin Library, University of Lancaster, p. 165.
V&A Picture Library, p. 55.
Whitworth Art Gallery, University of Manchester, p. 4.
The Wordsworth Trust, pp. x, 15, 16, 27, 29, 33, 34, 36, 37, 39, 42, 47, 51, 56, 67, 68, 77, 105, 109, 113, 140, 143, 148, 149, 153, 154, 157, 160, 162, 163, 166, 167, 168.

Acknowledgements

I would like to thank Lara Speicher and Charlotte Lochhead, my editors at the British Library, and Kate Hampson for the picture research. I am very grateful to Seamus Perry for reading through the manuscript and making many valuable suggestions, and to Sally Hebron for providing such a wonderful place to work on this book. Most of what I know about the Romantics and the landscape has come from working with Robert Woof at the Wordsworth Trust in Grasmere.

INDEX

Page numbers in italics refer to illustrations and information in their captions.